Teschner · Learn Chess in 40 Hours!

DATE DUE

ProgressinChess

Volume 11 of the ongoing series

2004
EDITION OLMS

Rudolf Teschner

Learn Chess in 40 Hours!

A Self-Tutor for Beginners and Advanced Players

Translated by Stephanie Salomo
Edited by Ken Neat

2004
EDITION OLMS

Bibliographic Information published by
Die Deutsche Bibliothek

Die Deutsche Bibliothek lists this publication in the
Deutsche Nationalbibliografie; detailed bibliographic
data is available in the internet at http://dnb.ddb.de.

Printed in Germany

Translated by Stephanie Salomo

Editor: Ken Neat

Typeset: Arno Nickel · Edition Marco, D-10551 Berlin

Printed by: Druckerei Friedr. Schmücker GmbH, D-49624 Löningen
Cover: Prof. Paul König, D-31137 Hildesheim

ISBN 3-283-00403-X

Contents

Chess Tactics

'This game is the touchstone of the brain'
J.W.Goethe (Adelheid in *Götz von Berlichingen*)

Preface

As a way of indulging the compulsion to play and at the same time practise creative thinking, the 'royal game' has long been popular – from the Middle Ages until the 18th century, especially with the nobility and the church. Only the Asian game of encirclement, Go, is comparable in its intellectual depth to chess, which also originates in the Far East.

Nearly 200 nations are currently registered as members of FIDE (Fédération International des Échecs, International Chess Federation) – forty years ago, there were only 64. Every two years the Chess Olympiad takes place, most recently in 2002 in Bled (Slovenia) with 134 men's and 67 women's national teams, which consisted of a great number of international grandmasters and masters. For almost half a century the Russians dominated this event, but Hungary and the United Kingdom were dangerous rivals. The German Chess Federation is one of the strongest members of FIDE with about 100,000 players. In the private sphere, according to unofficial estimates in Germany alone, chess is the pastime of more than one million people. Chess is a national sport in the countries of the former Soviet Union, which have several million club players. If you consider the percentage of the total population, the small country of Iceland (246,000 inhabitants) is the winner. The Chess Club of Reykjavik has around 500 members. The first international chess tournament, won by the German Anders-sen, took place in London 1851, where chess was and still is very popular.

This manual not only aims to familiarise the reader with the basic rules of the 'royal game', but also to reveal the richness of ideas that has made it so attractive. For the sake of clarity, I have summarised the chapters dealing with the opening of the game. However, I advise the reader to leave the 'Specialised Opening Theory' (lessons 11 to 21) until the end of the studies, and to put the main emphasis on 'Chess Tactics' (lessons 22 to 30). The student is well advised to set up each position on the board, and to play through the given moves several times, until he really understands their meaning. Under the heading 'Chess Strategy' (lessons 31 to 38) the reader gets to know the mastery of the game, which predominates in modern chess tournaments. He will be able to recreate and understand the moves of masters and experience the fascinating endeavours on the 64 squares – an occupation that is educational and promises intellectual enjoyment.

If you are ambitious and want to be successful in tournaments, you will have to practise extensively and invest a lot of time, apart from the competitive and personal qualities required. The basic prerequisites, however, are delivered by this book, which is suitable for self-study and has also been used successfully in many chess courses.

Rudolf Teschner

Basic Principles

1st Hour

Chess is a lake, in which a mosquito can bathe and an elephant drown.

Indian proverb

If a mosquito wants to bathe in it, the water needs to be calm, but if an elephant is to drown, it needs to be deep. Calmness and depth are the characteristics of the 'royal game', which, according to Sanskrit sources, was created 1400 years ago in the Far East, presumably India, as a competitive intellectual game between two forces. It reached Arabia via Persia, and was taken from there by the Moors via Spain to Europe. Initially a 'slow' game, the rules gradually developed to a more rapid confrontation of the opponents. The depth has remained, whereas the 'calmness' disappeared around the time of the Renaissance, when the Italians introduced the double move for the pawn and also castling (simultaneous movement of the king and rook).

The Legend of the Grain of Rice

To show his gratitude for the invention of chess, the Indian king Shiram asks his advisor, Sissa, to declare a wish. Sissa asks for grains of rice, one on the first of the 64 squares of the chessboard, two on the second, four on the third and on each following square double the amount of the previous. The king seems angry at the apparent modesty of the wise man, but promises to fulfil his wish. But soon he has to concede that neither his stocks nor all the reserves in the world would be able to accomplish this. He would have to find more than 18 trillion grains. To transport them, he would need an uninterrupted chain of wagons, which would reach 200,000 times around the equator. A nice legend which points out the dimensions of chess.

The Goal:
To Capture the King

What makes chess so different from any other game is the goal that both sides pursue: the capture of the hostile king. Both the monarchs are thus always at the centre of attention: they must never run the risk of being captured, and immediately have to evade any attack ('check') directed at them. If a king can no longer escape death ('checkmate'), the opponent has triumphed and the game is over. In chess, mind often triumphs over matter, for example when an attack involving a sacrifice forces checkmate. Generally, though, both sides need to pay strict attention to avoiding big material losses. Even the loss of a pawn can already be decisive. The opponent can then revert to the simplest plan that exists in chess: exchange all the other pieces, advance the remaining pawn to the opponent's back rank, promote it to a queen or rook, and then, with the help of his own king, succeed in checkmating its rival. The exchange of units of equal value serves to simplify a situation, to achieve a more favourable position, or to avoid a loss of tempo (through an otherwise necessary retreat).

The chessboard and the recording of moves

The board is arranged so that there is a dark square in the lower left hand corner. The horizontal lines ('ranks') carry the numbers 1 to 8 and the vertical lines ('files') have the letters a to h, so that each individual square is uniquely identified by a combination of a letter and a number. The white pieces are initially placed on the first and second ranks and the black pieces on the seventh and eighth ranks.

1

	a	b	c	d	e	f	g	h	
8	a8	b8	c8	d8	e8	f8	g8	h8	8
7	a7	b7	c7	d7	e7	f7	g7	h7	7
6	a6	b6	c6	d6	e6	f6	g6	h6	6
5	a5	b5	c5	d5	e5	f5	g5	h5	5
4	a4	b4	c4	d4	e4	f4	g4	h4	4
3	a3	b3	c3	d3	e3	f3	g3	h3	3
2	a2	b2	c2	d2	e2	f2	g2	h2	2
1	a1	b1	c1	d1	e1	f1	g1	h1	1
	a	b	c	d	e	f	g	h	

The novice is advised to mark the board as shown above, to make it easier to orient himself.

To record the moves, either the 'full' or the 'abbreviated' algebraic notation can be used. The full notation first states the square on which the piece is standing and then, after a hyphen, the square onto which it moves. The abbreviated method leaves out the square of origin and the hyphen. An example: K (for king) e1–e2 (full) or Ke2 (abbreviated). The capture of a piece is indicated by a small cross, for example Ke1xe2 or Kxe2. The P (for pawn) is left out.

Explanation of Symbols

0-0	short/kingside castling
0-0-0	long/queenside castling
–	moves
x	captures
+	checks the king
!	good move
?	bad move
=	equal position

Figurines

Whereas a player will normally use K (for king), Q (for queen) etc. when recording his moves, in publications it is customary to use pictorial representations, known as figurines:

king	K	♔
queen	Q	♕
rook	R	♖
bishop	B	♗
knight	N	♘

The Troops and their Movements

Each player has 16 men, namely eight pieces, which move and capture in various directions according to their status, and eight pawns, which can only move forwards by one square (or, if desired, by two squares from their starting point) and which capture in a different direction to their movement (one square diagonally to the right or left).

1. **The King** (the most important piece) may move one square in any direction, *but not onto a square threatened by the opponent*. If it is under attack, action has to be taken to rescue it.

2. **The Queen** moves any distance diagonally or in a straight line, forwards, backwards or sideways. It is by far the strongest of all the pieces. The Indians called it 'firzán' (minister) and its movements were very much restricted.

3. **The Rook** moves freely in all directions, but *only in a straight line*, not diagonally.

4. **The Bishop** moves freely in all directions, but *only diagonally*.

5. **The Knight** has the most peculiar movement. It jumps over two squares and changes the colour of its starting square. In contrast to the other pieces, *it is not restricted by either friendly or enemy pieces standing in its way*. It jumps over them.

Chess Diagrams

In graphic illustrations of the board and pieces, known as diagrams, the pieces are represented by symbols. The following list gives the description for the white (left) and black (right) pieces:

♔	King	♚
♕	Queen	♛
♖	Rook	♜
♗	Bishop	♝
♘	Knight	♞
♙	Pawn	♟

2

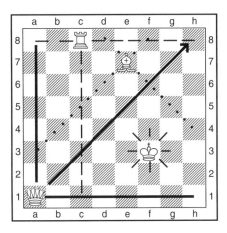

The arrows in diagram 2 show the possible moves for the king (f3), the queen (a1), the rook (c8) and the bishop (e7).

3

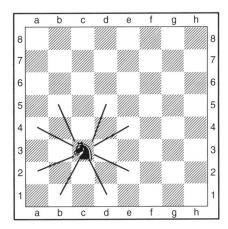

The Knight's Wheel. From its position on c3, the knight can jump to any of the squares marked by the arrows (b1, a2, a4, b5, d5, e4, e2 and d1).

11

Moving and Capturing with the Pieces

The range of movement ends just before any friendly piece that bars the way (except for the knight which can jump over them). If an enemy piece is in the way, the range extends onto the square occupied by the opposing piece. Your own piece can move onto this square by 'capturing' (and removing from the board) the opposing piece. The king is not allowed to move onto a square that is under attack by an opposing piece.

4

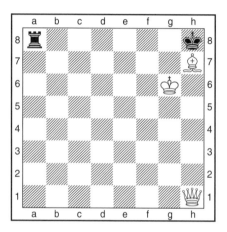

In diagram 4, the black king on h8 is *not* under attack by the white queen, because the white bishop on h7 is in the way. On the h-file, the white queen could move from h1 to h6 (but also to h2, h3, h4 or h5). On the first rank, it could go as far as a1, and from there attack the black king on h8, i.e. 'check' it. The queen would force the black rook, which stands on a8 and commands the entire a-file, to capture it by moving to the square a1. There would be no other escape for Black, because the king cannot move onto any of the squares g8, g7 and h7 belonging to its range of movement: the bishop at h7 is 'protected'

by the white king, the square g8 is controlled by the bishop, and the square g7 is even under attack from two directions, i.e. by the king at g6 and the queen at a1.

If it were White's turn to move in this position, he would of course not move his queen to a1, where it will be captured by the rook, but to a8, where it removes the rook from the board and simultaneously puts the black king in checkmate and brings the game to an end. (Thus checkmate ends the game immediately – the king is not captured.)

About the other pieces: the bishop on h7 can only move to g8, the king on g6 can move to f7, f6, f5, g5, h5 or h6, and the rook on a8 can move on the a-file up to a1 and on the eighth rank up to g8. The king on h8 is immobilised, since it cannot move onto any other square where it is not under threat.

Special Rules for Pawns

The pawns, of which each player has eight, generally **move** one square forward, but **capture** only on one square diagonally across. At the beginning of the game, all the white pawns are placed on the second rank and the black ones on the seventh. From this starting point, the pawn can, as desired, advance one **or** two squares (**never** can two pawns move one pace simultaneously).

If a pawn succeeds in reaching the back rank of the opponent (i.e. for Black the eighth, for White the first rank), it is promoted to **any desired** piece of one's own side, except for the king. So theoretically, one player could have **nine** queens on the board, i.e. the original one and eight promoted pawns. The further a pawn advances, the more powerful it becomes.

The Knight's Fork

5

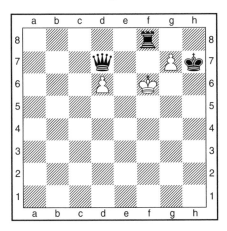

6

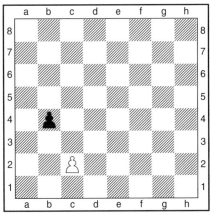

7

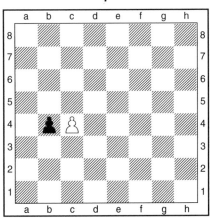

8

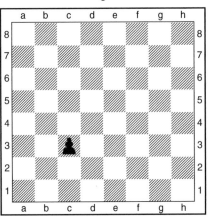

White wins by capturing the rook at f8, which is putting his king in check, with the pawn on g7, which is immediately promoted to a knight and gives check itself. In response, Black has to move his king to h6, g8 or h8. Then the knight captures the queen on d7 and White wins easily, because he can transform his d6 pawn into a new queen, once the knight at d7 has moved out of the way, and give checkmate within a few moves. With only the knight, this would not have been possible – not even with two knights!

Capturing En Passant

Finally there is one other special rule concerning capturing among pawns. If a pawn, coming from its starting rank, lands next to an enemy **pawn** by making a **double move**, then the rival one has the right, on the immediately following move, to capture it 'en passant' (in passing), just as if the pawn from the starting rank had only advanced by one square (see diagrams 6-8).

No. 6 is the starting position.

No. 7: The white pawn advances from the second to the fourth rank with a double move.

No. 8: The black pawn has captured 'en passant'.

Before Starting the Game

9

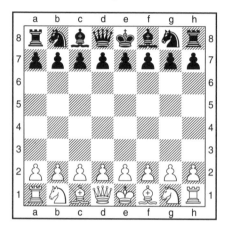

The starting position before beginning the battle should be carefully memorised. Kings and queens are facing each other – the white queen on a light square, the black queen on a dark square. White always starts, then the moves alternate; the right to move is also an obligation to move. A player can only win by checkmating the opponent's king. Normally, however, the disadvantaged party realises that it can no longer avoid checkmate and resigns beforehand. If no checkmate can be achieved, the game ends in a draw, when for example only the two kings remain on the board.

Stalemate. A special case of a draw is 'stalemate'.

10

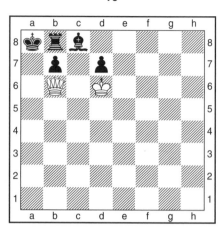

Black to move is stalemated, because his king is not in check (as opposed to checkmate, where the king has to be under attack), and neither the king nor any other black piece can make a permissible move.

2nd Hour

Castling

At the beginning of the 16th century, 'castling', a compound move of king and rook, was introduced into chess (first in Italy, then universally), 'a break-neck leap with the curious characteristic of becoming especially life-threatening if **not** performed' (H.W. Geissler).

Provided the squares between the king and rook are vacant, the king moves sideways by two squares towards the rook, and the rook takes over the square that the king has just crossed.

Castling counts as a single move. It is only permitted if neither the king nor the rook has been moved since the beginning of the game, the king is not in check and does not pass over or finish on a square attacked by an enemy piece.

11

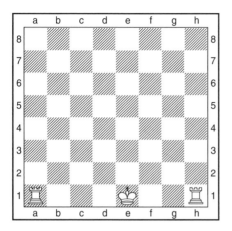

In diagram 11 (model), White has the choice of castling long (queenside) or short (kingside), provided the king and both rooks have not yet been moved.

12

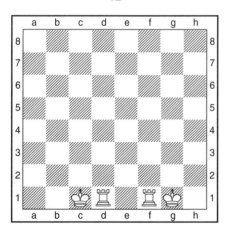

No.12 (model) shows how White could have castled on the left (long or queenside, symbol: 0-0-0), or on the right (short or kingside, symbol: 0-0). Generally speaking, castling is a very useful move, which makes the deployment of the forces

easier and quicker, and should be attempted as soon as possible. Here is an example from one of the most important chess openings, the Ruy Lopez (or Spanish Game): 1.e2–e4 e7–e5 2.♘g1–f3 ♘b8–c6 3.♗f1–b5 ♘g6–f6 4.0-0!. If a player is able to prevent the opponent from castling, he is usually in a favourable position.

13

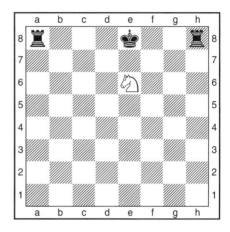

In No.13 the white knight prevents both opportunities to castle, because the black king can cross neither f8 nor d8.

Drawn Game

There are several reasons for a game to end in a draw.
1. If the remaining forces are insufficient to give checkmate. One pawn can be enough, if it is possible to promote it to a queen or rook.
2. If the material advantage is sufficient, but not the ability of the player. Checkmate has to occur within 50 moves, counting from the last move of a pawn or the last capture.

3. If one player accepts the draw offered by his opponent, because both realise that victory has become unlikely, for example if many pieces have been exchanged and the remaining ones are equally distributed.
4. If the same position with the same player having the right to move reoccurs for the third time (*draw by repetition*). The player with the right to move claims a draw, without executing the move which would repeat the position. In a tournament, the player calls the situation to the arbiter's attention.
5. If one player can check 'endlessly' (*perpetual check*). This is a situation where there is no escape for the king.
6. If a player, whose turn it is to move, has no legal move and his king is not in check, then it is stalemate, and the game ends in a draw (see diagram 10).

Perpetual Check

14

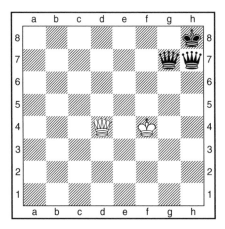

White to move gives 'perpetual check' starting with 1.♕d4–d8+ (the plus sign signifies check) and he continues by constantly attacking the king on the diagonal, file or rank, forcing one of the black queens to interpose, for example 1.♕d4–d8+ ♕h7–g8 2.♕d8–h4+ ♕g7–h7 3.♕h4–f6+ ♕g8–g7 4.♕f6–d8+ and so on.

The Value of the Pieces

A player, who wants to avoid falling behind, has to be careful not to give up any pieces unintentionally. The following table gives a guideline to the relative piece values: Pawn = 1, Bishop = 3, Knight = 3, Rook = 4½, Queen = 8. The one and a half point difference between the rook (a 'major piece') and the bishop or knight (both 'minor pieces') is called the 'exchange'. This means that you are the exchange up when you obtain a rook for a knight. If you give up a rook and obtain a bishop and a knight for it, you have achieved the same advantage. If you obtain a knight for a bishop, you have made an equal trade. You can also speak of a balanced trade, if you obtain a knight and two pawns for a rook. The queen is worth about three minor pieces, for example two bishops and a knight, or two rooks. We will see later on that this calculation gives only approximate values, and often – depending on the situation – it has to be adjusted.

Touch – move!

Right from the beginning, you should make it a habit not to take back any moves. Once you touch your own piece, it has to move; if you touch an enemy piece, you have to take it. If you have moved your own piece and let go of it, the move is irrevocable. If only for reasons of self-discipline, you should adhere to these official rules even in friendly games; first, to avoid arguments, and second, to become a stronger player. A good sight of the entire board, concentration, endurance and alertness are skills that a chess player has to practise.

Chess Diplomacy

The French King Louis XVI took chess lessons from the greatest player of his country, the composer François Danican Philidor. Soon the royal student wanted to know whether he was making progress. Philidor saved himself with diplomacy: 'Sir, there are three levels of chess players, namely those who don't play at all, those who play badly and those who play well. Your majesty has already advanced to the second level.'

3rd Hour

Checkmate (I)

If you have mastered checkmate, you have mastered the basics of chess technique. Generally speaking, a chess game follows the following pattern: in the opening, two to three moves with the pawns (usually the central pawns), the fastest possible and most effective 'development' of the pieces with the emphasis on the centre; in the middlegame, a concentrated attack on one wing, material gains (sometimes the attack on the king's wing leads directly to checkmate), simplification into the endgame and finally checkmate (which, if it is purely a question of routine, is generally left out). Before we start a game, we need to know how to end it. Dr. Tarrasch,

famous for his chess teachings in Germany at the turn of the century and well into the 1930s, wrote in his manual *Das Schachspiel* (also available in the series Praxis Schach from Edition Olms), that the beginner is well advised to suppress the understandable urge to play a game as soon as possible. The playing of games in the learning phase would be 'the sure way to incompetence'. A dogmatic but essentially correct sentence.

Typical Examples of Checkmate

Checkmate without a King

The bigger the material advantage, the easier it is to achieve checkmate, especially when the opponent is left with only a defenceless king.

15

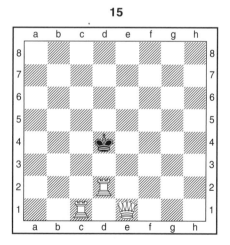

With a queen and two rooks, we can give checkmate in the middle of the board (diagram 15),

16

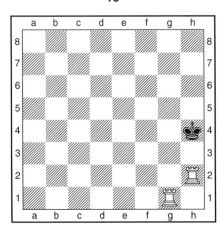

with two rooks on the edge (16),

and with a rook and a knight in the corner (17), each time without assistance from one's own king.

17

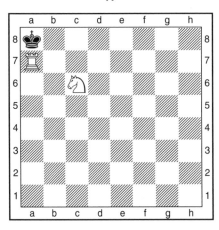

Checkmate is also possible in the middle of the board with a queen and two knights (18), with a queen and a bishop on the edge (19) and with two knights and a bishop in the corner (20), again without involving one's own king.

18

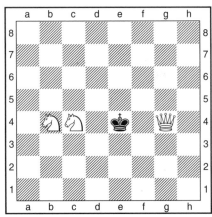

19

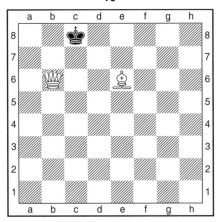

20

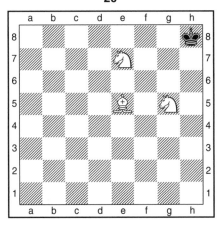

These are all 'pure' checkmates (a term from chess studies), i.e. none of the escape routes of the king are under double attack.

Checkmate with Assistance from the King

If the material advantage is not so great, the king has to assist in giving checkmate. With king and queen we can checkmate anywhere on the edge (21/22), with king and rook near a corner (23), and with king and two bishops in any corner (24).

23

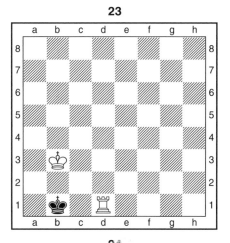

21

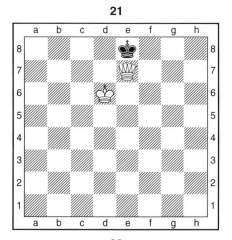

24

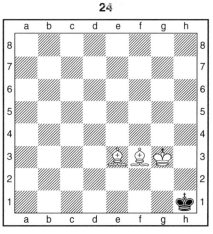

22

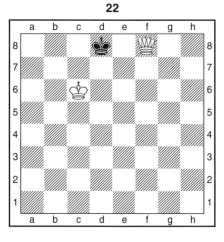

25

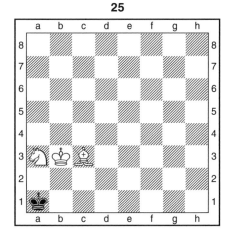

With a king, bishop and a knight, we can force checkmate only in the corner controlled by the bishop (25).

King and Queen against King
Watch out for stalemate!

Because we do not want to have played a (hopefully) good game in vain, we need to pay attention in the ending not to give stalemate unintentionally. It is particularly dangerous in the endgame when attacking the lone king with king and queen.

26

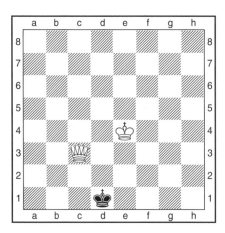

White, whose turn it is to move, intends to keep the black king on the edge of the board and then give checkmate. The moves 1.♔d3?, 1.♔e3? or 1.♔f3? are not suited to this purpose, because they do not leave the black king any room to breathe (the square e2) and the game ends abruptly in stalemate (a draw). The quickest way to achieve checkmate, without risking stalemate, is **1.♕c3–b2** (occupying the second rank and thus keeping the king on the edge) **1. ... ♔d1–e1 2. ♔e4–e3 ♔e1–f1** (or 2...♔d1 3.♕d2) **3.♕b2–f2 mate.**

*

With a little practice, it is possible to end the game in no more than ten moves from any position with this material combination.

The English master Joseph Blackburne once said: 'Never miss a check!'. That is to say, give check wherever possible – it could be checkmate! But this advice was meant to be ironic. In the present case, it is important to gradually force the king to the edge. Giving check is only sensible if it promotes this goal.

27

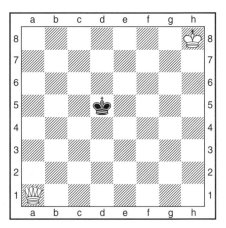

In the position shown in diagram 27, the white king first advances towards the black king: 1.♔h8–g7 ♔d5–e4 2.♔g7–f6 ♔e4–d5. Black stays in the middle of the board as long as possible. 3.♕a1–a4. The pursuit begins. White also employs 'zugzwang' (where a player is forced to move, even though any move is disadvantageous), which forces Black to retreat. 3. ... ♔d5–c5 4.♔f6–e6 ♔c5–b6 5.♔e6–d6 ♔b6–b7 6.♕a4–a5 ♔b7–b8 and now White has to watch out. 7.♔d6–c6! (7.♕a6? leads to stalemate) 7. ... ♔b8–c8 8.♕a5–c7 (or 8.♕a8) checkmate.

If Black plays ♔d5–d6 on the third move, then the pursuit looks as follows: 4.♕a4–b5 ♔d6–c7 5.♔f6–e6 ♔c7–c8 6.♔e6–d6 ♔c8–d8 7.♕b5–d7 (or b8) mate. Check, in this case, is only given if it is also checkmate.

King and Rook against King

If, instead of the queen, we only have a rook, checkmate will take a few more moves, because the chase will proceed not only to the edge but also, in most cases, to the corner of the board (see diagram 28).

28

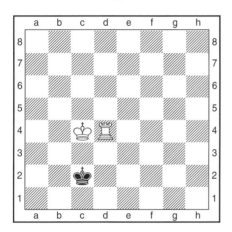

The ending may look like this:
1.♔c4–b4 ♔c2–b2 2.♖d4–d2+ ♔b2–c1
3.♔b4–c3 ♔c1–b1 4.♔c3–b3 ♔b1–c1 (or
4...♔a1 5.♖d1 mate) 5.♖d2–d8 (A waiting move, that often appears in this type of endgame. It puts Black in zugzwang.)
5. ... ♔c1–b1 6.♖d8–d1 mate.

In the following position, where it is not so straightforward for White to give checkmate (see diagram 29), he needs 16 moves to achieve this (he has, as we know, 50 moves after the last pawn move or capture, before the game is a draw):

29

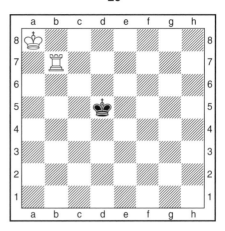

1.♖b7–d7+ ♔d5–c6 2.♖d7–d1 ♔c6–c7
3.♔a8–a7 ♔c7–c6 4.♔a7–a6 ♔c6–c5
5.♔a6–a5 ♔c5–c4 6.♔a5–b6 ♔c4–c3
7.♔b6–b5 ♔c3–c2 8.♖d1–d4 ♔c2–c3
9.♔b5–c5 ♔c3–b3 (or 9...♔c2 10.♔b4, see diagram 28) 10.♖d4–c4 ♔b3–a3
11.♖c4–b4 ♔a3–a2 12.♔c5–c4 ♔a2–a3
13.♔c4–c3 ♔a3–a2 14.♔c3–c2 ♔a2–a3
15.♖b4–h4 ♔a3–a2 16.♖h4–a4 mate. It is advisable to practice this procedure (you don't even need a partner), until checkmate can be securely achieved in the least possible number of moves, even against the best possible defence.

4th Hour

Checkmate (II)

Just as an athlete needs to improve his skill continuously in order to maintain his form, the chess player should also endeavour to perfect his technique (in checkmating, the exploitation of an advantage, attacking, the opening and so on). To this end, the elementary endings which we will now examine can be practised without a partner.

King and two Bishops against King

This endgame does not require a lot of effort. Suppose that we place the white king on e1, the white bishops on c1 and f1, and the black king on h8, we can easily create a prison with the bishops, from which the black king cannot escape. We play 1.♗f1–d3 ♚h8–g7 2.♗c1–g5 ♚g7–f7 3.♗d3–f5 and thus restrict the king (see Diagram 30).

30

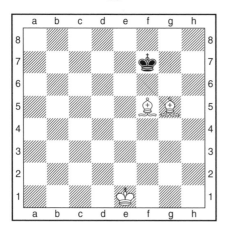

Now we only need to bring up the white king in order to drive the enemy king into the corner: 3. ... ♚f7–g7 4.♚e1–f2 ♚g7–f7 5.♚f2–g3 ♚f7–g7 6.♚g3–h4 ♚g7–f7 7.♚h4–h5 ♚f7–g7. Now the net can be tightened and the final pursuit begun. 8.♗f5–g6 ♚g7–g8 9.♚h5–h6 ♚g8–f8 10.♗g6–h5 (a waiting move that puts Black in zugzwang) 10. ... ♚f8–g8 11.♗g5–e7 ♚g8–h8 12.♗h5–g4 ♚h8–g8 13.♗g4–e6+ ♚g8–h8 14.♗e7–f6 mate.

King, Bishop and Knight against King

This endgame is far more difficult. Checkmate can only be achieved in a corner of the board that is controlled by the bishop (see Diagram 31).

31

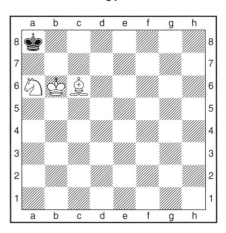

This is why the pursued king will flee towards the 'wrong' corner; from there, it has to be forced into the correct corner. For this, it is necessary to place the knight on the same colour square as the one controlled by the bishop, so that an impenetrable net is cast (Diagram 32).

32

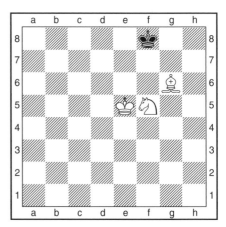

The ending may go like this: 1.♚e5–f6 ♚f8–g8 2.♘f5–d6 ♚g8–h8 3.♘d6–f7+

♚h8–g8 4.♗g6–f5 ♔g8–f8. This creates an important starting point. 5.♗f5–h7 ♔f8–e8 6.♘f7–e5. During the pursuit, the knight follows a fixed route, as if it wants to draw a 'W' on the board, by moving onto the squares f7–e5–d7–c5–b7. 6. … ♔e8–d8! An attempt to escape, which, however, does not succeed. Easier for White is 6...♔f8 7.♘d7+ ♔e8 8.♔e6 ♔d8 9.♔d6 ♔e8 10.♗g6+ ♔d8 11.♗f7 (a waiting move) 11...♔c8 12.♘c5 and so on. 7.♔f6–e6! ♔d8–c7 8.♘e5–d7. The knight sticks to its route. 8. … ♔c7–c6 9.♗h7–d3! Again the bishop and knight combine to cast an inescapable net. 9. … ♔c6–c7 10.♗d3–e4 ♔c7–c8. Back on the edge! 11.♔e6–d6 ♔c8–d8 12.♗e4–g6 ♔d8–c8 13.♘d7–c5 (up to here we have been following the comment on White's sixth move) 13. … ♔c8–d8 (or 13...♔b8 14.♘d7 ♔a7 15.♔c7 and so on) 14.♘c5–b7+ ♔d8–c8 15.♔d6–c6 ♔c8–b8 16.♔c6–b6 ♔b8–c8 17.♗g6–f5+ ♔c8–b8. Now beware: 18.♘c5 ♔a8 19.♘a6?? and Black is stalemated. 18.♗f5–d7. A waiting move. White has to arrange that his knight arrives on a6 with check. 18. … ♔b8–a8 19.♘b7–c5 ♔a8–b8 20.♘c5–a6+ ♔b8–a8 21.♗d7–c6 mate (see Diagram 31).
Lengthy, but educational and important.

King and two Knights against King

This endgame is impossible to win. However, if the weaker side still has a pawn, checkmate is often eventually achievable. Here it is possible to immobilise the enemy king in a corner, without causing stalemate, assuming the pawn has not advanced too far. This pawn, therefore, has to be blocked by one of the knights before the final entrapment, and prevented from advancing any further (see Diagram 33).

33

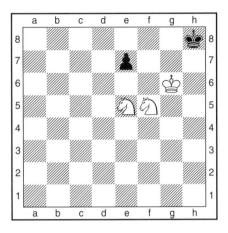

1.♘f5xe7? would give stalemate. Correct is 1.♘f5–h6 e7–e6 2.♘e5–f7 mate.

King and Knight against King

34

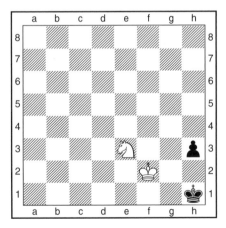

A lone knight can achieve checkmate only in exceptional circumstances. When, for example, the black king is being kept in a corner on White's first rank and is restricted by one of its own pawns (see Diagram 34).

Here 1.♘e3–f1! forces the pawn to advance to h2, so that 2.♘f1–g3 gives checkmate.

Useless Riches

There are cases where king and bishop (or knight) plus a pawn cannot win against a solitary king, because the pawn cannot be promoted. Often the problem is due to stalemate (Diagrams 35–37).

36

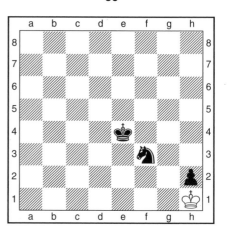

The same situation arises in No.36, where the black king cannot get close to the pawn without putting White in stalemate.

35

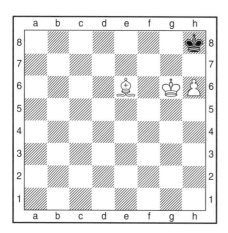

In diagram 35, in combination with a rook's pawn White has a 'wrong-coloured' bishop. Success could only be achieved with a dark-square bishop which would control the corner square and drive the king away.

37

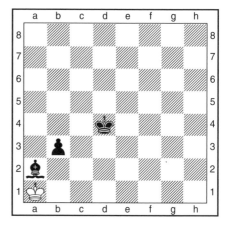

Again, in No.37 nothing can be done. The black king cannot move to c3 because of stalemate. One option would still be 1. ... ♚d4–c4 2.♚a1–b2 ♝a2–b1 3.♚b2xb1 ♚c4–c3, but after 4.♚b1–c1 a theoretically drawn pawn ending arises (4...b2+ 5.♚b1 ♚b3 stalemate), which we will look at more closely in the 5th Hour.

The taciturn Russian. The Argentine grandmaster, Miguel Najdorf (1910–1997), once made a peace offering to his Russian colleague, Isaak Boleslavsky, after only a few moves. A monosyllabic exchange ensued:

Najdorf: 'Would you like a draw?' Boleslavsky: 'No!' Najdorf: 'Are you playing for a win?' Boleslavsky: 'No.' Najdorf: 'So, a draw then?' Boleslavsky: 'No.' Najdorf: 'What do you want then?' Boleslavsky: 'To play.'

5th Hour

Pawn Endings (I)
King and Pawn against King

The pawn is the soul of the game.
Philidor

In his book *Basic Chess Endings* Reuben Fine agreed with Philidor's statement, and added that the pawn is not only the soul of the game, but in the endgame it is also ninety per cent of its body.

38

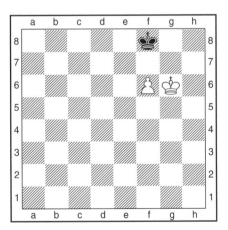

The endgame is the part of the chess game most suitable for exact calculation, and it has been the most extensively researched theoretically. If a material advantage, however small, is sustained until the last phase, it is often possible to determine the result of the game with the help of endgame theory. The advantage of one pawn alone can be decisive. Take a look at the easiest case (diagram 38).

White plays 1.f6–f7 and forces Black to respond 1. … ♚f8–e7 (because of zugzwang). Then 2.♔g6–g7 secures the promotion of the passed pawn to a new queen, which with the help of the king finally achieves checkmate.

Black to move. If, however, it is Black's turn to move, he will force a draw, by preventing the advance of the white king with 1. … ♚f8–g8 (the black king gains the 'opposition'). If White continues 2.f6–f7+, after 2. … ♚g8–f8 he can only chose between whether to give stalemate by 3.♔g6–f6, or to sacrifice the pawn with another move of the king (which, of course, would also lead to a draw). So please remember that the game will always end in a draw, if the pawn moves to the penultimate rank by giving check. We will now look at an 'absolute winning position' (see diagram 39).

39

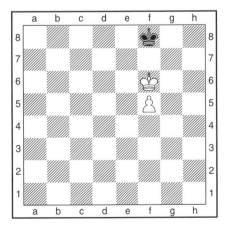

White wins

Here White always wins, no matter whose turn it is to move. If it is Black to move, he immediately has to surrender control of the promotion square f8 to the enemy. The sequel would be 1. ... ♚f8–e8 2.♔f6–g7 ♚e8–e7 3.f5–f6+ and so on. If it is White to move, he wins by creating the position in No.38 with 1.♔f6–g6 ♚f8–g8 2.f5–f6. After 2. ... ♚g8–f8 3.f6–f7 (the pawn advances to the penultimate rank without giving check) success is evident.

Things become more complicated, if we move the same position down by one rank (see diagram 40).

40

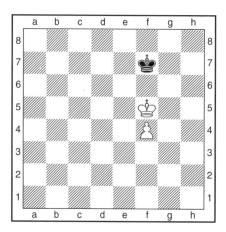

White can only achieve something, if his king is able to advance to the 6th rank (or more precisely, one of the squares e6, f6 or g6) without assistance from the pawn. This is only possible, if White has just gained the 'opposition', i.e. it is Black to move. After 1. ... ♚f7–g7 2.♔f5–e6 White already achieves his aim and he easily gains control of the promotion square f8 (for example 2. ... ♚g7–f8 3.♔e6–f6 ♚f8–e8 4.♔f6–g7 ♚e8–e7 5.f4–f5 and so on).

But if it is White to move, Black has the 'opposition' and he prevents the advance of the white king: 1.♔f5–e5 ♚f7–e7, or 1.♔f5–g5 ♚f7–g7. If White enlists the help of the pawn, position No.38 is eventually created with Black to move: 1.♔f5–g5 ♚f7–g7 2.f4–f5 ♚g7–f7 3.f5–f6 ♚f7–f8! (3...♚g8? loses) 4.♔g5–g6 ♚f8–g8 with a draw.

41

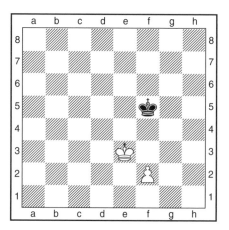

Also in diagram 41, the opposition decides the outcome. White wins with 1.♔e3–f3!, while Black to move forces a draw with 1. ... ♚f5–e5!.

A few special cases. Essentially everything has been said about this elementary ending. It remains only to point out a few special cases.

42

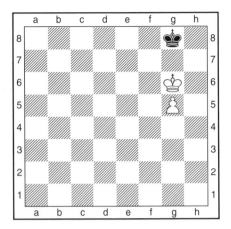

In diagram 42, White to move can only win with 1.♔g6–h6 ♚g8–h8 2.g5–g6 ♚h8–g8 3.g6–g7. With 1.♔g6–f6, which initially looks just as good, he would not be able to progress, because Black replies 1. ... ♚g8–h7!. If 2.g5–g6+? follows, then 2. ... ♚h7–h8! and the game is a draw (3.♔f6–f7 stalemate, or 3.g6–g7+ ♚h8–g8 4.♔f6–g6 stalemate). White has to return to the starting position with 2.♔f6–f7 ♚h7–h8 3.♔f7–g6 ♚h8–g8 and correct the situation with 4.♔g6–h6!.

43

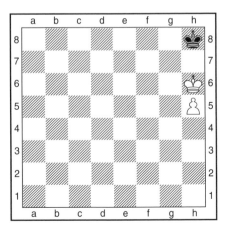

With a rook's pawn on the edge of the board (see diagrams 43–45), victory can only be achieved if two preconditions are fulfilled: the enemy king has to be so far removed that it can no longer reach the promotion square in time, or one's own king has to keep the enemy king away from the promotion square and support its pawn, without getting in its way. The opposition (see diagram 43) is of no use, because the black king, as can easily be seen, cannot be forced out of its corner.

44

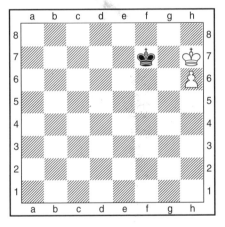

Even control of the promotion square does not help (diagram 44), because the king blocks the way of its own pawn. If it is White to move, after 1.♔h7–h8 ♚f7–g6 he must either give up the pawn (2.♔g8 ♚xh6), or curiously stalemate himself (2.h7 ♚f7). Only if the black king can be kept far enough away from the corner (see diagram 45), does the rook's pawn have a free run to the promotion square.

So how are we to understand Philidor's sentence quoted at the beginning? The pawns carry the marshal's baton in their kit bag; the biggest power on the chessboard lies hidden in them, because if all of them were promoted to queens, they would triumph over the entire original army!

45

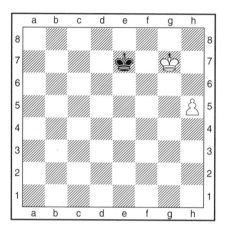

46

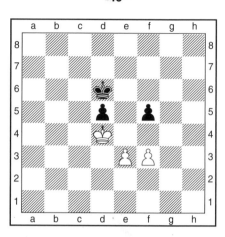

Isolated doubled pawns are especially awkward.

6th Hour

Pawn Endings (II)

As we know, a pawn – as opposed to the pieces – can move neither backwards nor sideways. This is why every move of a pawn needs careful consideration: it cannot be reversed. The value of a pawn changes considerably, depending on different circumstances.

Strategic Terms

Connected pawns are normally better than isolated pawns.

In diagram 46, White wins with 1.f3–f4. Black cannot avoid losing a pawn, for example 1. ... ♚d6–c6 2.♔d4–e5 or 1. ... ♚d6–e6 2.♔d4–c5. If we replace the f5 pawn at e6, the black pawns are also connected and the game will be drawn.

47

The doubled pawns c6/c7 are not only worthless, but can even be damaging. Black is in a hopeless situation even though he has an extra pawn: 1.♔d4–c5 ♚e6–d7 2.c2–c3 ♚d7–d8 (or 2...a6 3.c4 ♚d8 4.♔xc6 ♚c8 5.c5 ♚b8 6.♔d7 ♚b7 7.c6+ ♚b8 8.♔d8; 5...♚d8 6.♚b7 ♚d7 7.♔xa6 ♚c6 8.♚a7 does not change anything) 3.♔c5xc6 ♚d8–c8 4.c3–c4 ♚c8–

b8 5.♔c6–d7 ♚b8–b7 6.c4–c5 c7–c6 (or 6...♚a6 7.♔xc7 ♚xa5 8.c6 and White is much quicker) 7.♔d7–d6 a7–a6 8.♔d6–d7 and White wins.

If the pawn at c7 were not there, White would be unable to win (1.♔c5 ♚d7 2.c3 ♚c7 with an easy draw). Less is sometimes more!

A pawn is called *backward* when it has stayed behind its colleagues. The square immediately in front of such a pawn is a 'strong-point' for the opponent, who likes to establish one of his pieces there, because it cannot be driven away by a pawn. A backward pawn often becomes the object of enemy attacks and frequently it is worthless.

48

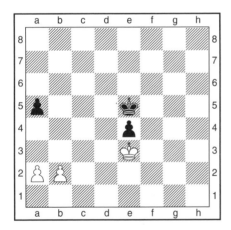

The weak move 1.a2–a3? loses the game. Black replies 1. ... a5–a4! and degrades the b2 pawn to a 'backward' pawn. The sequel could then be: 2.♔e3–e2 (after 2.b4 the black a-pawn captures 'en passant' on b3, see diagrams 6–8) 2. ... ♚e5–d4 3.♔e2–d2 e4–e3+ 4.♔d2–e2 ♚d4–e4 5.♔e2–e1 ♚e4–d3 6.♔e1–d1 e3–e2+ 7.♔d1–e1 ♚d3–e3 (after 7...♚c2? 8.♔xe2 ♚xb2 9.♔d2 ♚xa3 10.♔c1 a drawn

position, with which we are already familiar, would arise, due to the worthless pawn on the edge – see diagram 44) 8.b2–b4 a4xb3 (en passant) 9.a3–a4 b3–b2 10.a4–a5 b2–b1♕ (or ♖) mate.

The correct method is to advance the pawn which is not opposed by an enemy pawn on the same file (the Latvian grandmaster Aaron Nimzowitsch called it the 'candidate'): 1.b2–b3 ♚e5–d5 2.a2–a3 ♚d5–e5 3.b3–b4 would have easily held the draw.

49

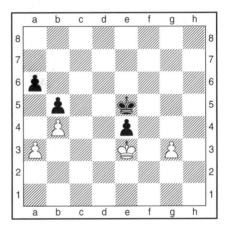

A pawn is 'passed' when it cannot be stopped by an enemy pawn on its way to the opponent's back rank. An 'outside' passed pawn is especially useful, since it diverts the enemy king and forces it to abandon its own subjects. In diagram 49, the white pawn at g3 is an outside passed pawn. White easily decides the game in his favour: 1.g3–g4 ♚e5–d5 2.g4–g5 ♚d5–e5 3.g5–g6 ♚e5–f6 4.♔e3xe4 ♚f6xg6 5.♔e4–d5, winning both the black pawns.

A passed pawn is 'protected' if it is guarded by a friendly pawn. Often its possession represents a decisive advantage, which is possibly only surpassed by 'two connected *passed pawns'* which nearly always form an invincible force.

All these terms are fundamentally important in chess strategy.

Disturbing

When Efim Bogoljubow (a German national of Russian origin, a challenger to the world champion Alexander Alekhine) was playing against Saviely Tartakower (born in Rostov-on-Don, a prominent Polish grandmaster and an intelligent aphorist), he found himself under fierce attack and announced checkmate in four moves for his opponent. Tartakower responded: 'I will not tolerate any disturbance!'

(Author's note: Technically he was right, because article 19.1c of the rules of the World Chess Federation states: 'It is forbidden to distract or disturb the opponent in any way.')

The Opening

7th Hour

Opening Strategy

The aim of the opening is to move all the pieces, including the rooks, to good positions where they are flexible, do not obstruct one another and pose a danger to the enemy pieces. More often than not, it is desirable to try to castle as soon as possible. The king is safest behind an uninterrupted chain of pawns, which does not easily lend itself to an enemy attack, as is possible when the pawns have been moved. 'Breathing space' for the king is usually only needed once the back rank, occupied by the king, is under threat of being attacked and the rooks want to leave their original rank.

More than two or three moves with pawns in the opening are usually unnecessary. It is generally advantageous to occupy the centre squares with one or two pawns, for White the squares e4 and d4, for Black e5 and d5. The opponent is thus restricted and his pieces are forced back. He will, therefore, fight for the centre. You should aim to establish at least one pawn in the centre, as this creates an important precondition for freely advancing the army into favourable positions. In addition it is important to make an exchange of pawns as soon as possible in the centre or at the edge of the board, in order to open a file for one or both rooks. Avoid bringing the queen into the game prematurely, in order not to risk losing time. Equally ill-advised is the early pursuit of pawns. The opponent can use the extra time to develop his army and seize the initiative.

Queen's Gambit

The Queen's Gambit can be used as an example of an opening performed in a controlled manner by both sides. A gambit is a sacrifice of material in the opening phase, which should help to open lines and bring out the pieces. The opponent is often well advised not to hang on too tightly to the material won.

1.d2–d4

White advances in the centre and also contemplates placing the e-pawn next to its colleague.

1. ... d7–d5

Black also establishes himself in the centre of the board and counters the hostile intentions.

2.c2–c4

White wants to remove the intruder and he simultaneously prepares the opening of the c-file for the future engagement of the major pieces (queen or rook). The move is not a genuine gambit, because Black is unable to hold onto his pawn, if he captures on c4. Thus: 2. ... d5xc4 (this move is playable, even if Black concedes the centre to White for now) 3.e2–e3 b7–b5? (correct is calm development, for example with 3...♘f6 4.♗xc4 e6) 4.a2–a4! and Black has to give back the pawn immediately, as 4...c6? 5.axb5 cxb5? 6.♕f3 loses a piece due to the weakening of the a8–h1 diagonal. After 4. ... b5–b4 5.♗f1xc4 White has a distinct development and spatial advantage.

2. ... e7–e6

A good developing move, which also serves to recapture on d5 with the e-pawn in the event of White taking on d5. Less good is 2. ... ♘g8–f6, because White would comfortably reach his goal with 3. c4xd5 ♘f6xd5 (or 3...♛xd5 4.♘c3 gaining a tempo) 4.e2–e4.

Now the development of the pieces begins.

3.♘b1–c3 ♘g8–f6 4.♗c1–g5 ♗f8–e7

The bishop move re-mobilises the knight, which was 'pinned' due to the danger to the queen. The move also enables kingside castling.

5.e2–e3

This makes room for the bishop on f1 and secures the position of the d4 pawn.

5. ... 0-0

Kingside (or short) castling, i.e. king to g8 and rook to f8.

6.♘g1–f3

The squares c3 and f3 are the most appropriate ones for the white knights. From here they influence the centre and do not obstruct their own army too much.

6. ... ♘b8–d7

Black does not want to obstruct his c-pawn, which should be involved in the fight for the centre.

7.♖a1–c1 c7–c6 8.♗f1–d3

White has quickly completed his deployment. It only remains for him to castle, move his queen to e2 and enable his rook, which will be on f1 after castling, to come into play at d1. Black still has to solve one problem: how to free his bishop imprisoned on c8? More on this later.

The 'Ten Commandments' of the Chess Opening

The 'ten commandments' formulated by the American grandmaster, Reuben Fine, are worthy of notice:

1. Open with the e- or d-pawn.
2. If possible make a good developing move that threatens something.
3. First develop the knights, then the bishops.
4. Choose the most suitable square for a piece and firmly allocate it.
5. Make one or two pawn moves in the opening, not more (sometimes three as in our example).
6. Do not develop the queen prematurely.
7. Castle as early as possible, preferably on the short or kingside.
8. Play to gain control of the centre.
9. Always try to secure at least one pawn in the centre.
10. Do not sacrifice material without a clear and sufficient reason.

Such rules are, of course, easier to lay down than to follow. However, a knowledge of them will be helpful in practice. Fine's 'ten commandments' lay the foundation for a methodical opening game.

8th Hour

Opening Sins: Loss of Time

One of the most common sins that beginners tend to commit in the opening is to lose time with unnecessary pawn moves and multiple moves with one piece, usually the queen. The consequences this can lead to, when the opponent puts the additional time to good use, are illustrated in the following, especially striking example.

1.e2–e4 e7–e5 2.d2–d4

It is basically correct to move both pawns to the centre, but this should not happen at any price. 2.♘g1–f3 is a good preparation.

2. ... e5xd4 3.♛d1xd4

Clearly, White wants to regain the pawn, but this does not necessarily make it desirable to bring out the queen so early. Here moves such as 3.♘g1–f3 or 3.c2–c3 (the Danish Gambit) come more into consideration.

3. ... ♘b8–c6

In this way Black develops his knight 'for free'.

4.♕d4–e3 ♘g8–f6 5.h2–h3?

The first real waste of time. White is unreasonably afraid of ♘f6–g4. Indicated was 5.♘b1–c3.

5. ... ♗f8–e7

Black rightly wants to castle quickly and then attack with the rook on the e-file.

6.a2–a3?

Another move driven by fear. The 'threat' of ♘c6–b4 was harmless because of the possible reply 7.♘b1–a3 or 7.♗f1–d3. These false threats should be ignored.

6. ... 0-0 7.♗f1–c4 ♖f8–e8! 8.♕e3–b3

And to top it all, White prepares a threat with insufficient means, which backfires.

8. ... d7–d5!

Black already wins at least a pawn with the superior game. White tries to avoid this – and quickly finds himself checkmated.

9.♗c4xd5

9.e4xd5 is followed by the immediate double check 9 ... ♗e7–b4+ (the rook from e8 and the bishop from b4 give check simultaneously – and a double check can be averted only by moving the king).

9. ... ♕d8xd5 10.e4xd5?

White has no other chance than to reconcile himself to the loss of the bishop with 10.♘b1–c3, if he wants to avoid immediate checkmate.

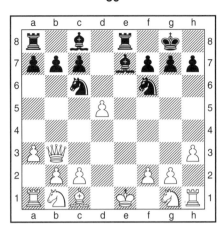

50

After White's 10th move

10. ... ♗e7–b4+

This double check is deadly.

11.♔e1–f1 (or ♔d1) 11. ... ♖e8–e1 mate.

Note that Black, as prescribed by the 'ten commandments', made no more than two moves with his pawns. This is why he had enough pieces in position at the right moment.

I cannot warn you strongly enough against going 'pawn-hunting' before you have castled. Here is a typical instance, from a correspondence game in 1922 between Luer and Rattmann.

1.e2–e4 ♘g8–f6 (the Alekhine Defence) **2. e4–e5 ♘f6–d5 3.♘g1–f3 d7–d6 4.d2–d4 ♗c8–g4 5.♗f1–e2 d6xe5**

Moves such as these, which make the opponent's pieces more mobile (here, as we will see in a moment, the white queen and white knight), are to be avoided. Black should immediately prepare to castle, i.e. play e7–e6 and then ♗f8–e7.

6.♘f3xe5 ♗g4xe2 7.♕d1xe2

Black already has to reckon with threats such as ♕e2–b5+ and ♕e2–f3 (which, however, White will carry out only if there are tangible benefits).

7. ... ♘d5–b6

This averts both attacks (8.♕b5+? c6, 8.♕f3 ♕d5).

8.0-0!

White offers the d-pawn as bait and prepares the intervention of the rook. Black's best reply was 8. ... ♘b8–d7. This brings the queen's knight into play and simultaneously confronts the dangerous white knight in the centre. On the contrary, 8...e6 would have been no good because of 9.♕f3 f6 (or 9...♕f6 10.♕xb7) 10.♕h5+ g6 11.♘xg6 hxg6 12.♕xh8 – a typical development. It emphasises the collaboration between queen and knight, the weakness of f7 before castling and the danger of being checked on the h5–e8 diagonal, once the f-pawn has advanced.

8. ... ♕d8xd4?

In view of Black's backward development, this is unforgivably irresponsible.

9.♖f1–d1

Black is indeed already lost (see diagram 51).

51

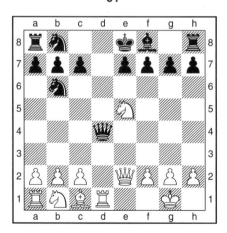

After White's 9th move

If 9...♕b4 there again follows 10.♕f3 f6 11.♕h5+ g6 12 ♘xg6, and 9...♕c5 is very nicely met by 10.♕h5! (10.♕f3? is not possible because of 10...♕xe5) 10...g6 11.♖d8+! ♔xd8 12.♘xf7+ ♔e8 13.♕xc5 ♔xf7 when White, under favourable circumstances, has won queen for rook and knight and he will gain **in addition** even more pawns.

9. ... ♕d4–h4 10.♗c1–g5!

An 'attraction sacrifice'. First the queen and then the king are brought under the spell of the knight.

10. ... ♕h4xg5 11.♖d1–d8+! ♔e8xd8 12.♘e5xf7+ and Black resigns. A case of a 'family fork'.

9th Hour

Opening Sins:

Endangering the King

If we follow the basic rules of the opening, as already discussed, our king will automatically be safe. But we also want to know how to attack an 'unprincipled' opponent.

At the beginning of the game, the two squares f7 (in the black camp) and f2 (white camp) are the most vulnerable, because they are protected only by the king. Also in danger are the diagonals h5–e8 and h4–e1 respectively. Just as metal attracts electricity, so weak points attract combinations (a phrase by Emanuel Lasker). There are many examples of this in chess literature.

The f7 Square

1.e2–e4 e7–e5 2.♗f1–c4 ♞g8–f6 3.d2–d4
c7–c6 4.d4xe5 ♞f6xe4 5.♞g1–e2 ♞e4xf2
Black 'reasons' as follows: if the white king
takes the knight, the queen check at h4
wins the bishop on c4. He does not pay
sufficient attention to the weakness on f7.
6.0-0 ♞f2xd1?
He is so tempted by the queen that he
forgets about his own king. Correct is 6. ...
♗f8–c5 7.♗c4xf7+ ♚e8xf7 8.♞e2–d4 with
an unclear position.
7.♗c4xf7+ ♚e8–e7 8.♗c1–g5 mate. A
game by Captain MacKenzie.
Not worth imitating is the primitive attempt
1.e2–e4 e7–e5 2.♗f1–c4 ♗f8–c5 3.♕d1–
h5? A premature excursion for the queen,
which Black can easily counter with 3...♕e7
and ♞f6, when the white queen's move
turns out to be a complete waste of time. 3.
... ♞g8–f6?? An acute case of 'check
blindness'. 4.♕h5xf7 mate. 'Fool's mate'
belongs in the same category: 1.f2–f4 e7–
e6 2.g2–g4?? ♕d8–h4 mate.

Legall's Mate

Named after the 18th century French
player Legall de Kermeur, this checkmate
is a standard example: **1.e2–e4 e7–e5
2.♞g1–f3 d7–d6 3.♗f1–c4 h7–h6?** An
unnecessary waste of time. After 3...♞f6?
Black fears the response 4.♞g5. He could,
however, have proceeded safely without
loss of time with 3...♗e7 (this controls the
g5 square and simultaneously prepares for
castling). If White now plays 4.♞c3, Black
replies 4...♞f6, when 5.♞g5 is now harmless, as 5...0-0 (kingside castling) comfortably protects the square f7 a second time.
4.♞b1–c3 ♗c8–g4? (diagram 52)

52

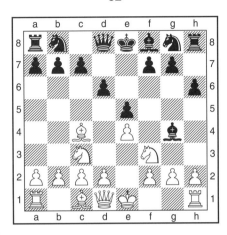

Before this ♞g8–f6 should be played. Now
White carries out a combination which
relies on two weaknesses, the square f7
and the unprotected bishop on g4.
5.♞f3xe5!
The knight only seemed to be 'pinned'
because of the queen standing behind it. If
Black now captures the knight on e5 with
the pawn (d6xe5), after 6.♕d1xg4 White
wins an important pawn under favourable
conditions. But this was the lesser evil for
Black.
**5. ... ♗g4xd1? 6.♗c4xf7+ ♚e8–e7 7.♞c3–
d5** mate.

Danger on the Diagonal

A few examples on the theme 'How not to
play chess' (the title of a book published in
1910 by the strong Russian master, Znosko-
Borovsky).
1.e2–e4 c7–c6 2.d2–d4 d7–d5 3.♗f1–d3
♞g8–f6 It would have been tactically more
sensible to exchange on e4 (3...dxe4
4.♗xe4) and then gain a tempo by 4...♞f6,
attacking the unprotected bishop.

4.e4–e5 ♘f6–d7? The knight should retreat to g8, so that the line for the bishop at c8 remains open.

5.e5–e6! f7xe6??

Suicidal. 5...♘f6 was essential, although after 6.exf7+ ♚xf7 7.♘f3 the king is in a bad position and castling is no longer possible.

6.♕d1–h5+ g7–g6 7.♕h5xg6+ h7xg6 8.♗d3xg6 mate.

That White can also become a victim of the diagonal after only a few moves is shown in a miniature game between Gibaud and Lazard (Paris, 1924).

1.d2–d4 ♘g8–f6 2.♘b1–d2 (Not a good place for the knight. It contributes little and obstructs its own pieces.) 2. ... e7–e5 3.d4xe5 ♘f6–g4 4.h2–h3?? (A disastrous pawn move.) 4. ... ♘g4–e3! White resigns, since if he saves his queen (5.fxe3), there follows 5...♕h4+ 6.g3 ♕xg3 mate.

This shows that there is always a certain danger when the f-pawn advances and exposes the king. This becomes clear if Black, after 1.e2–e4 e7–e5 2.♘g1–f3, protects his e-pawn with 2. ... f7–f6 (the standard move is 2...♘c6).

White can then prepare the dangerous intervention of his queen by sacrificing his knight with 3.♘f3xe5. If Black captures (f6xe5), he loses his rook on h8 after 4.♕d1–h5+ g7–g6 (even worse for him is 4...♚e7 5.♕xe5+ ♚f7 6.♗c4+) 5.♕h5xe5+. Black must decline the Greek gift on the third move, take action against the threat of 4.♕h5+ g6 5.♘xg6 and also try to recover the lost pawn.

This is achieved with 3. ... ♕d8–e7, because 4.♕h5+ would be an instructive mistake: 4...g6! 5.♘xg6 ♕xe4+ followed by ♕xg6 and Black has the advantage.

White therefore plays 4.♘e5–f3 and achieves a clear positional advantage after 4. ... ♕e7xe4+ (or 4...d5 5.d3) 5.♗f1–e2, followed by kingside castling with the threat of ♖f1–e1, whereas the black position has been permanently damaged by the irrevocable advance of the f-pawn.

10th Hour

Opening Sins – Loss of Material

Strategy and tactics, two terms known not only in military theory, are also applicable in chess. 'Strategy' refers to the general game plan, while 'tactics' concern the individual moves which aim to enforce the plan with reference to the opponent's actions. If the tactics are faulty, the plan cannot be executed. Experience shows that a shrewd player, even when playing without strategy, can be superior to a tactically weak strategic player.

Some of the dangers already facing a player at the beginning of the game, the recognition of which requires a good sight of the board (which can only be acquired through constant practice), are the loss of pieces through checks, double attacks and pinning. The following are some of the shortest games ever played in tournaments.

Dr.Lehmann-Schulz (Berlin Championship, 1950)

1.c2–c4 d7–d5 2.c4xd5 ♘g8–f6 3.e2–e4 ♘f6xe4? Black should try a gambit and play 3....c6. He thus gains time in return for his lost pawn (4.dxc6 ♘xc6) and puts pressure on the d4 square.

4.♕d1–a4+. Black resigns because he loses his knight at e4.

R.F.Combe – W.R.Hasenfuss
(Chess Olympiad, Folkestone 1933)
1.d2–d4 c7–c5 2.c2–c4 c5xd4 3.♘g1–f3 e7–e5 4.♘f3xe5? The same mistake as above – with the colours reversed. 4. ... ♛d8–a5+. White resigns. A technically experienced tournament player will not bother to continue if he loses a piece without any compensation.

The following is another example of the premature loss of a knight.

Dr.Rahn – Rellstab (German Championship, Bad Oeynhausen 1941)
1.e2–e4 c7–c5 2.♘g1–f3 d7–d6 3.d2–d4 c5xd4 4.♘f3xd4 ♘g8–f6 5.♘b1–c3 g7–g6 6.♗c1–e3 ♘f6–g4? A 'finger-slip'. Correct is 6...♗g7, as prepared on the fifth move, if only to be able to castle. The knight at g4 is protected, but...

53

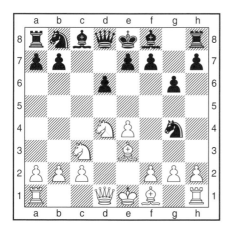

...7.♗f1–b5+! exploits the inflexibility of the black king. Black is in a dilemma. Only with 7...♘c6 8.♘xc6 bxc6 9.♗xc6+ ♗d7 10.♗xa8 ♘xe3 11.fxe3 ♛xa8 can he still put up a little resistance. The next 'blunder' belongs in the same category.

Halicz – Lanz (Vienna 1932)
1.d2–d4 ♘g8–f6 2.♘g1–f3 c7–c5 3.♗c1–f4 Here there are a number of safe moves such as 3.d5, 3.c4, 3.e3, 3.c3, or 3.g3 followed by 4.♗g2.
3. ... c5xd4 4.♘f3xd4? The queen should recapture, although this is not very pleasant in view of 4...♘c6. Now Black wins a piece with a 'pawn fork', a double attack by a pawn. 4. ... e7–e5! White resigns, because 5.♗xe5 ♛a5+ would cost the bishop. The fork is a very popular mechanism for taking the opponent by surprise, and it always has to be kept in mind. Here is another example.

Ozols – Reid (Chess Olympiad, Stockholm 1937)
1.c2–c4 e7–e5 2.♘b1–c3 ♘b8–c6 3.g2–g3 ♗f8–c5 4.♗f1–g2 d7–d6 5.e2–e3 ♘g8–f6 6.♘g1–e2 ♗c8–e6? Black underestimates, as often happens, the advance of the d-pawn.

54

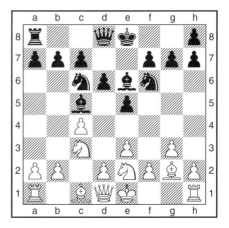

7.d2–d4! (White did not make use of this in the game!) and Black has to either give up his bishop at c5 or allow the pawn fork 8.d4–d5, i.e. he loses a piece in either case.

And finally an instructive example, where White combines a fork with pinning.

Elm – Steffens (Essen 1934)
1.d2–d4 ♘g8–f6 2.c2–c4 e7–e5 3.d4xe5 ♘f6–g4 4.♗c1–f4 ♘b8–c6 5.♘g1–f3 ♗f8–c5 6.e2–e3 ♕d8–e7 7. a2–a3 a7–a5 (Despite the threat of b2–b4, Black should regain the sacrificed pawn on e5. However, he needed to anticipate a tactical subtlety: 7...♘gxe5! 8.♘xe5 ♘xe5 9.b4 ♗d6! 10.c5 ♘d3+! 11.♗xd3 ♗xf4, and White cannot capture the piece in return, because the e3 pawn is pinned by the enemy queen – the white pawn, after all, has to protect the king!).
8.♘b1–c3 (The threat of 9.♘d5 is now extremely inconvenient.) 8. ... ♘g4xe5? (This loses inevitably. Black did not really have any choice other than 8...d6) 9.♘f3xe5 ♘c6xe5 10.♘c3–d5! A centralised knight straight out of the text book. It not only threatens to capture the queen, but also to make a 'fork' on c7 (where it gives check and also attacks the rook in the corner at a8). 10. ... ♕e7–d6 (Even though it is badly placed, the queen has to protect e5 and c7 simultaneously.) 11.♕d1–h5! Black resigns. The pinned knight at e5 dare not move, but the f7 pawn is also pinned and cannot defend the knight.

Is your head spinning? Don't worry – it happens to everyone who first attempts to find his way around the 64 squares.

11th Hour

Specialised Opening Theory (I)

Open Games

Without a certain understanding of openings, a player competing in club tournaments would quickly find himself in a losing position. The essence of four hundred years of experience should not be disregarded altogether. The Spanish priest, Ruy Lopez, who visited Rome in 1559 and defeated all his opponents on the 64 squares, published a chess manual two years later. Among other things, he discussed the opening 1.e2–e4 e7–e5 2.♘g1–f3 ♘b8–c6 3.♗f1–b5, which is called the Ruy Lopez or Spanish Opening. Even today, it is aimed at by most players when opening with the king's pawn. Ruy Lopez was a favourite of the Spanish king Philip II.
Since then, opening theory has been expanded to such an extent that it now has a scientific character. Numerous questions, however, remain unanswered – proof of the inexhaustible nature of the Royal Game. The openings are roughly divided into three types, 'open' (1.e2–e4 e7–e5), 'semi-open' (1.e2–e4 *not* e7–e5) and 'closed' (*not* 1.e2–e4). This description, as has been known for a long time, is not really very appropriate. Whether the game is going to open up very soon or remain closed, rarely depends on the first few moves. Moreover, some variations change from one type to the other. We will first look at the 'open games', which are preferred by the majority of players.

Italian Game

One of the oldest openings, which already existed in the 15th century, is called the Italian Game (originally Giuoco Piano, or quiet game). It arises after the moves 1.e2–e4 e7–e5 2.♘g1–f3 ♞b8–c6 3.♗f1–c4 ♝f8–c5 (see diagram 55). Depending on his temperament and disposition, White has a choice of three continuations.

55

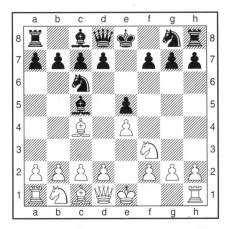

A. **4.d2–d3** (the original Giuoco Piano) **4. ... d7–d6 5.♘b1–c3 ♞g8–f6 6.♗c1–g5** (In such symmetrical positions, it is, for once, advisable not to castle too early. After 6.0-0 the pinning move 6...♝g4 would be unpleasant for White, especially as Black can answer 7.h3 with 7...h5. Accepting the sacrifice would be very dangerous for White. The preventive move 6.h3 costs valuable time – Black would have nothing to fear after 6...♝e6.) **6. ... h7–h6 7.♗g5xf6** (To 7.♗h4 Black's simplest reply is 7...♝g4 8.h3 ♝xf3 9.♕xf3 ♞d4 10.♕d1 c6) **7. ... ♕d8xf6 8.♘c3–d5 ♕f6–d8** (8...♕g6 is also possible, leading to a very intricate game, since 9.♘xc7+? ♚d8 10.♘xa8 ♕xg2 11.♖f1 ♝g4 would

allow Black a strong attack. White's best reply is 9.♕e2.)
9.c2–c3 White now threatens to gain a certain positional advantage with 10.b4 ♝b6 11.a4 a6 12.♘xb6 cxb6 because the black pawn formation has suffered. A good defence is 9. ... a7–a6 10.d3–d4 e5xd4 11.c3xd4 ♝c5–a7.

B. **4.c2–c3** (The most frequently used.) White threatens to attack the e5 square with 5.d4, and he also prepares an attack on the weak f7 square with ♕b3. In reply **4. ... ♞g8–f6** has proven itself, in order to initiate counterplay in the centre. The sequel could be: **5.d2–d4 e5xd4** (not 5...♝b6 because of 6.dxe5 ♘xe4 7.♕d5!) **6.c3xd4 ♝c5–b4+ 7.♗c1–d2** (Already in the 17th century, the Calabrese, Gioacchino Greco (†1634), explored the sacrifice 7.♘c3 with developments that marked him as the forerunner of the brilliant American, Paul Morphy (1837–1884). His main variation goes: 7...♘xe4 8.0-0! ♘xc3 9.bxc3 ♝xc3 10.♕b3 ♝xa1 11.♗xf7+ ♚f8 12.♗g5 ♞e7 13.♘e5 with a decisive attack. Black made the most plausible moves, but not the best. He missed the important counterattack d7–d5 on the ninth or tenth move. Nowadays, it is usual to play differently on the eighth move: 8...♝xc3 9.d5 ♝f6 10.♖e1 0-0 11.♖xe4 ♞e7 12.♗g5 (the Møller Attack, which promises no more than a draw).
7. ... ♝b4xd2+ (Dangerous is 7...♘xe4 8.♗xb4 ♘xb4 9.♗xf7+ ♚f7 10.♕b3+ d5 11.♘e5+ ♚e6! 12.♕xb4 c5 13.♕a3) **8.♘b1xd2 d7–d5** Very often it is this double advance that strengthens Black's game. Here it breaks up the white centre and provides an outpost at d5. **9.e4xd5 ♘f6xd5 10.♕d1–b3 ♞c6–e7 11.0-0 0-0 12.♖f1–e1 c7–c6** with equal chances for the two sides.

C. 4.b2–b4 Evans Gambit

An opening that was very popular in the 19th century. White gives up his b-pawn in order to occupy the centre more quickly. After **4. ... ♗c5xb4 5.c2–c3 ♗b4–a5 6.d2–d4 e5xd4 7.0-0** it would be very risky to capture also on c3 (the 'compromised' Evans Gambit), for example 7...dxc3 8.♕b3 ♕f6 9.e5 ♕g6 10.♘xc3 ♘ge7 11.♗a3 0-0 12.♖ad1 ♖e8 13.♗d3 ♕h5 14.♘e4 ♘xe5 15.♘xe5 ♕xe5 16.♗b2 ♕e6 17.♕b5 (from the *Handbuch des Schachspiels* by Paul Rudolph von Bilguer).

7. ... ♘g8–e7 8.c3xd4 d7–d5! with a roughly equal game.

The safest is probably 5. ... ♗b4–e7 6.d2–d4 ♘c6–a5 7.♘f3xe5 ♘a5xc4 8.♘e5xc4 d7–d5.

Although the Italian Game is not one of the fashionable openings, it offers enough ammunition for both the adventurous as well as the patient player. Please try it!

12th Hour

Specialised Opening Theory (II)

Two Knights Defence

Psychology plays an important part in chess combat. If we know that our opponent prefers to use a specific opening, it is desirable to avoid it (unless we know an effective response of which he is probably not aware). If he likes the 'Italian' game, we can spoil his concept with the 'Prussian' defence. Black of course is not required to accept the opponent's plan and respond to **1.e2–e4 e7–e5 2.♘g1–f3 ♘b8–c6 3.♗f1–c4** with 3. ... ♗f8–c5. The reply **3. ... ♘g8–f6** which was thoroughly investigated by Berlin masters, especially Bilguer and Max

Lange, back in the mid-19th century, immediately launches a counter-attack. This is why players with White have been persuaded to choose 3.♗f1–b5 over 3.♗f1–c4. Whether rightly so, is another matter. We should take a closer look at some of the main lines.

A. 4.♘f3–g5

Dubious and dangerous for both sides. According to the basic rules, this is premature, because it moves the knight a second time before development is complete and also removes it from the centre, i.e. the knight is 'decentralised'. It is true that Black is obliged to sacrifice a pawn, but he can force the white pieces to retreat and quickly gain a lead in development. According to Tarrasch, White gives up his 'birthright of attack' for next to nothing.

4. ... d7–d5 (see diagram 56)

The Traxler Gambit 4. ... ♗f8–c5 is too involved and complicated. But the move is often seen in correspondence chess. White does best to continue 5.♗c4xf7+ ♔e8–e7 6.♗f7–b3 ♖h8–f8 7.0-0 d7–d6 8.♘b1–c3 ♕d8–e8 9.♘c3–d5+ ♔e7–d8 10.c2–c3! h7–h6 11.d2–d4 e5xd4 12.e4–e5! (from a correspondence game Porreca–Balbe, 1968/69) when he clearly stands better.

Even the amazing move 4. ... ♘f6xe4 is not easy to counter (5.♘xe4? d5). Thus 5.♘g5xf7 ♕d8–h4 has nothing to offer. But Black gets into difficulties after 5.♗c4xf7+ ♔e8–e7 6.d2–d4! d7–d5 7.♘b1–c3 (Lopuchin) 7. ... ♘e4xc3 8.b2xc3, since ♗a3+ is threatened (8...♗f5 9.♕f3; 8...♕d6 9.a4! ♔d8 10.♗g8! ♔e8 11.♗xh7 with a big advantage).

56

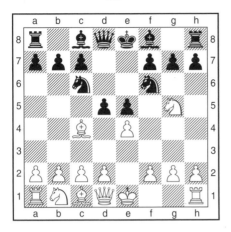

5.e4xd5 ♘c6–a5 In order to chase the bishop off the dangerous a2–g8 diagonal. The simple response 5. ... ♘f6xd5 is too dangerous, firstly because of the immediate sacrifice 6.♘g5xf7 ♚e8xf7 7.♕d1–f3+ ♚f7–e6 8.♘b1–c3 ♘c6–b4 9.a2–a3 (proposed by the Italian, Polerio, already around 1600) 9. ... ♘b4xc2+ 10.♚e1–d1 ♘c2–d4! (the acceptance of the rook sacrifice loses outright: 10...♘xa1 11.♘xd5 ♚d7 12.d4 ♗d6 13.dxe5 ♗xe5 14.♖e1!, Estrin) 11.♗c4xd5+ ♚e6–d6 12.♕f3–f7 with unclear complications. A draw is likely. Even more unpleasant than the immediate sacrifice on f7 is 6.d2–d4 e5xd4 7.0–0. Then some resistance is possible only with 7. ... ♗c8–e6 8.♖f1–e1 ♕d8–d7 9.♘g5xf7 ♚e8xf7 10.♕d1–f3+ ♚f7–g8 11.♖e1xe6 ♖a8–d8 12.♗c1–g5! (Euwe), but White stands clearly better.

Worthy of notice is the suggestion by the German master, Alexander Fritz (1857–1932), 5. ... ♘c6–d4. Theoretically, it is not possible to gain a clear advantage for White, for example 6.d5–d6 ♕d8xd6! 7.♗c4xf7+ ♚e8–e7, or 6.c2–c3 b7–b5 (or 6...♘f5 7.d4 exd4 8.0-0) 7.♗c4–f1 ♘f6xd5 with an unclear position.

6.♗c4–b5+ c7–c6 After 6...♗d7 there would follow 7.♕e2!. **7.d5xc6 b7xc6 8.♗b5–e2** White has won a pawn, but his development comes to a standstill. **8...h7–h6 9.♘g5–f3** (according to Bobby Fischer, world champion from 1972 to 1975, the old Steinitz suggestion 9.♘h3 is better than its reputation; neither 9...♗c5 10.0-0 g5 11 ♚h1 g4 12.♘g1 ♘e4 13.♗xg4! nor 9...♗f5 10.0-0 ♕d7 11.♖e1! is fully satisfactory for Black) **9. ... e5–e4 10.♘f3–e5 ♗f8–d6** White will now support his knight with his d- or f-pawn, which Black will capture 'en passant' with an equal game.

B.   4.♘b1–c3

This protects the e4 pawn and develops a piece, but Black can comfortably break up the centre with a temporary sacrifice:

4. ... ♘f6xe4! 5.♘c3xe4

Tempting but weak is the counter-sacrifice 5.♗xf7+ ♚xf7 6.♘xe4 d5 7.♘eg5+ ♚g8 (see diagram 57). Black has lost the right to castle, but he has acquired a strong centre and the bishop pair, which will be useful for attacking. He will soon castle 'artificially' by playing h7–h6 followed by ♚g8–h7 and then bringing his rook to f8 after moving his bishop from this square.

5. ... d7–d5 6.♗c4–d3! d5xe4 7.♗d3xe4 ♗f8–d6 8.♗e4xc6+ b7xc6 9.d2–d4 The position offers roughly equal chances. As compensation for his damaged pawns, Black has the bishop pair.

57

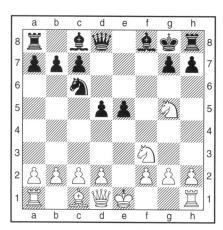

Analysis of 5.♗xf7+

58

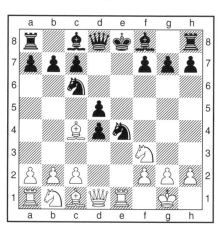

C.   4.d2–d4 This immediate action in the centre offers the best chances, although no final judgement can yet be made about the complex developments. **4. ... e5xd4** (not 4...♘xe4 5.dxe5 with the threats of 6.♕d5 and 6.♗xf7+ followed by 7.♕d5+) **5.0-0** Black counters the immediate advance of the centre pawn 5.e5 with the typical 5...d5 6.♗b5 ♘e4 7.♘xd4 ♗d7. The position now calls for precise play by both sides. Here the sortie 5.♘g5 provides just as little advantage as on the previous move, if Black responds 5...d5 6.exd5 ♘e5 7.♕xd4 ♘xc4 8.♕xc4 ♕xd5 9.♕e2+ ♗e6 10.0-0 0-0-0 11.♘xe6 ♖e8!. **5. ... ♘f6xe4** The Max Lange Attack 5...♗c5 6.e5 d5 (also possible is 6...♘g4) 7.exf6 dxc4 8.♖e1+ ♗e6 9.♘g5 is unresolved. Black should not carelessly capture on f6, because after 9...♕xf6 10.♘xe6 fxe6 11.♕h5+ the bishop on c5 would be lost. Correct is 9...♕d5 10.♘c3 ♕f5 11.♘ce4 0-0-0 with an acceptable game. **6.♖f1–e1 d7–d5** (see diagram 58)

7.♗c4xd5 A combination based on the knight at e4 being pinned.
7. ... ♕d8xd5 8.♘b1–c3 ♕d5–a5 9.♘c3x e4 ♗c8–e6 10.♘e4–g5. White now regains the sacrificed pawn by capturing on e6. The prospects are roughly equal.
There are, of course, numerous variations on both sides, which no one can memorise completely; but that, after all, is what makes chess so attractive!

13th Hour

Specialised Opening Theory (III)

Ruy Lopez: 1.e2–e4 e7–e5
2.♘g1–f3 ♘b8–c6 3.♗f1–b5

The great teacher, Dr. Tarrasch, spoke in his book *Die moderne Schachpartie* (1912), about the 'milking cow' of the tournament player. He had in mind the Ruy Lopez or Spanish Opening **(1.e2–e4 e7–e5 2.♘g1–f3 ♘b8–c6 3.♗f1–b5).** With this opening, White usually stays in control for a long time; it has since lost nothing in popularity, but rather gained. Nearly every master player, who opens with the king's pawn, is aiming for the Ruy Lopez.

In fact, the bishop move is very logical. Black tries to maintain the balance in the centre with his pawn on e5. White now turns indirectly against this pawn with his bishop move. He undermines the pawn by preparing to remove the piece protecting it. However, as yet this is no real threat, so long as the white pawn on e4 is not directly or indirectly protected.

White's aim, however, is not actually the winning of the e5 pawn (Black can easily prevent this), but the beneficial exchange of the white d-pawn for the black e-pawn.

59

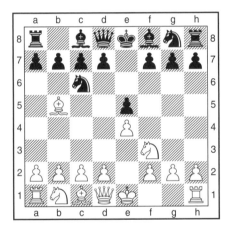

If Black were forced to exchange on d4, he would lose his outposts on d4 and f4. White would thus gain space in the centre and restrict Black's game. If Black avoids this as well, White can make use of another stratagem: he can try to break up the black pawn formation and make use of this in the endgame.

If Black wants to defend himself against all these dangers, he has to act cautiously. Any carelessness can have disastrous consequences.

3. ... a7–a6 is the most usual, to force the bishop to declare its intentions. Here it is important to realise that White cannot now win a pawn, since after 4.♗b5xc6 d7xc6! 5.♘f3xe5 Black has the reply 5. ... ♛d8–d4. The queen simultaneously attacks two unprotected enemy pieces and regains the pawn with a good game (two effective bishops). It is more advisable for White to exchange his valuable bishop for the knight on c6 only if he achieves something definite and lasting in return, as for example damaging the opponent's pawn structure or gaining time. Thus kingside castling would be far preferable to 5.♘f3xe5.

Most popular is **4.♗b5–a4.** This keeps open the option of capturing on c6, and indirectly keeps aiming at the king on e8. Black could now push the bishop further back with b7–b5. However, this move is a concession, because it loosens the pawn structure on the queen's wing. At the next opportunity White can conveniently play a2–a4. Also the bishop is still well placed on b3, at least better than if it had been played on the third move to c4, where it is always threatened by d7–d5. It is more advantageous for Black to delay b7–b5 and to develop quietly with 4. ... d7–d6 or 4. ... ♘g8–f6.

A.   4. ... d7–d6

Now White has to watch out for the 'Noah's Ark trap', which has already claimed numerous victims. The logical move 5.d2–d4 has the disadvantage that the white bishop is in danger of being imprisoned: after **5. ... b7–b5! 6.♗a4–b3 ♘c6xd4 7.♘f3xd4 e5xd4** White has to play either 8.♗d5 ♜b8 9.♗c6+ ♗d7 10.♗xd7+ ♛xd7 11.♛xd4 without gaining any advantage, or sacrifice a pawn with 8.c3. After the careless **8.♛d1xd4 c7–c5 9.♛d4–d5**

♗c8–e6 10.♕d5–c6+ ♗e6–d7 11.♕c6–d5 c5–c4! the white bishop is cut off and is lost in exchange for two pawns – for Black a sufficient advantage to win.

White can avoid falling into this trap and continue **5.♗a4xc6+ b7xc6 6.d2–d4.** If Black exchanges on d4, White recaptures with the queen and achieves a certain spatial advantage. Should Black defend the square e5 with 6...f7–f6, he ends up being restricted. On the other hand, White has given up his important light square bishop.

This is why **5.0-0 ♘g8–f6 6.♗a4xc6+ b7xc6 7.d2–d4** is more popular, or **5.c2–c3** as a preparation for d2–d4. Adventurous players may now choose the Siesta Variation 5. ... f7–f5, to which White's best response is 6.e4xf5 ♗c8xf5 7.d2–d4. However, Black also has a more solid method at his disposal: **5. ... ♗c8–d7 6.d2–d4 g7–g6 7.0-0 ♗f8–g7 8.d4xe5 d6xe5 9.♗c1–g5 ♘g8–f6 10.♘b1–d2 ♕d8–e7** and White has not made much progress.

B.   4. ... ♘g8–f6 (see diagram 60)

60

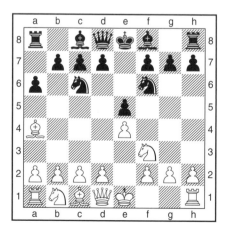

Black defends with a counter-attack on e4. It has been shown that **5.0-0** is now an appropriate move for White. He abandons the pawn on e4, but secures his king and prepares the involvement of the rook on e1. This has long been a standard procedure. If Black captures on e4, this is known as the Open Variation; if he does not capture, but prepares kingside castling with ♗f8–e7 this is the Closed Variation. Both variations are playable; they have been tested and examined in many variations. A few indications will have to suffice.

5. ... ♘f6xe4 6.d2–d4

6.♖e1 ♘c5 7.♗xc6 dxc6 8.♘xe5 is not so effective.

6. ... b7–b5

It is very risky to open the e-file completely and play 6...exd4, as shown by the game Capablanca–Ed.Lasker, New York, 1915: 7.♖e1 d5 8.♘xd4 ♗d6 (the sharp Riga Variation is the only attempt to justify this way of playing) 9.♘xc6 ♗xh2+ 10.♔h1! (10.♔xh2 ♕h4+ leads to a draw) 10...♕h4 11.♖xe4+! dxe4 12.♕d8+ ♕xd8 13.♘xd8+ ♔xd8 14.♔xh2 ♗e6 15.♗e3 f5 16.♘c3 ♔e7 17.g4 g6 18.♔g3 with an advantageous endgame.

7.♗a4–b3 d7–d5 8.d4xe5 ♗c8–e6 9.c2–c3 ♗f8–c5 with a roughly equal game.

A hint: If you are uncomfortable with the Open Ruy Lopez and want to avoid being burdened with variations, you can protect the e-pawn with 5.♕d1–e2.

5. ... ♗f8–e7

The majority of tournament players choose this classical continuation.

6.♖f1–e1 Black now has to reckon seriously with the loss of the pawn after 7.♗a4xc6 followed by ♘f3xe5. 6...d6 is met by 7.♗xc6+ bxc6 8.d4 and Black has nothing better than to exchange on d4 and leave the opponent with a spatial advantage, if he does not want to suffer a disrupted pawn position without any compensation: 8...♗g4? 9.dxe5 ♗xf3 (9...dxe5? 10.♕xd8+ ♗xd8 11.♘xe5, winning a pawn) 10.♕xf3 dxe5.

6. ... b7–b5 7.♗a4–b3 d7–d6 is the usual continuation, as 8.d2–d4 would again be premature because of 8. ...♘c6xd4 9.♘f3xd4 e5xd4, similar to the 'Noah's Ark trap'. Thus: **8.c2–c3 0-0** (the pin 8. ...♗c8–g4 is less good, as White does not play d2–d4, but is content with 9.d2–d3!, and he later disturbs the bishop at g4 with a manoeuvre such as ♘b1–d2–f1–e3.)

9.h2–h3 (After 9.d2–d4 the reply 9. ...♗c8–g4 is more unpleasant, because the pressure on d4 forces White to declare his intentions. Black threatens to capture on f3 and break up the white king's wing, if White does not want to lose a pawn.) **9. ... ♘c6–b8** This retreat is attributed to the Hungarian master, Gyula Breyer (1894–1921), who liked such bizarre moves. At one time this continuation more or less superseded the old Chigorin Variation 9. ... ♘c6–a5 10.♗b3–c2 c7–c5, although nowadays it occurs more rarely. Breyer's retreat also frees the c-pawn, but avoids placing the knight on the edge of the board.

10.d2–d4 ♘b8–d7 11.♘b1–d2 ♗c8–b7 12.♗b3–c2 ♖f8–e8 13.♘d2–f1 ♗e7–f8 14.♘f1–g3 (as in the third game of the Fischer–Spassky match, Sveti Stefan, 1992). If Black does not want to be restricted to defence, he has to play a gambit. The Marshall Attack lends itself to this aim: **7. ... 0-0** (not 7...d6) **8.c2–c3 d7–d5!?** (with this Black sacrifices his e-pawn) **9.e4xd5 ♘f6xd5 10.♘f3xe5 ♘c6xe5 11.♖e1xe5 c7–c6 12.d2–d4 ♗e7–d6 13.♖e5–e1 ♕d8–h4** and it is difficult to judge the chances of the two sides. In a game Veselin Topalov–Ivan Sokolov (Li-

nares 1995), after 7...0-0 White inserted the move of the rook's pawn 8.a4 and kept the upper hand after 8...b4 9.c3 d5 10.exd5 ♘xd5 11.♘xe5 ♘xe5 12.♖xe5 c6 13.d4 ♗d6 14.♖e1 ♕h4 15.g3 ♕h3 16.♗e3 ♗g4 17.♕d3 bxc3 18.♘xc3 ♖fb8 19.♗d1 ♖xb2 20.♗xg4 ♕xg4 21.♘xd5 cxd5 22.♖eb1 ♖xb1+ 23.♖xb1 a5 24.♖b5 ♕f3 25.♕b3.

The strategic and tactical problems arising from this opening are so complex and difficult that many Black players avoid it by replying to 1.e2–e4 not with e7–e5, but by choosing a 'semi-open' defence such as 1. ... c7–c5, 1. ... c7–c6 or 1. ... e7–e6.

14th Hour

Specialised Opening Theory (IV)

Sicilian Defence: 1.e2–e4 c7–c5

In the category of semi-open games the Sicilian Defence (1.e2–e4 c7–c5) plays the most important role. At one time, it even surpassed the open games (1.e2–e4 e7–e5). Other responses to the double move of the king's pawn gain in importance when employed by popular players, then disappear again, only to resurface newly polished in some future tournament. The Sicilian is the oldest of the semi-open defences. It was examined by Italian masters back in the 17th century (see diagram 61).

61

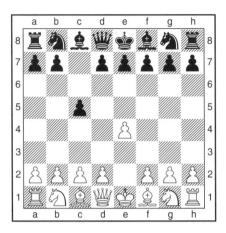

The move **1. ... c7–c5** has an aggressive character. It avoids the symmetry and leaves White with a spatial advantage (especially in the centre of the board), but does not, strictly speaking, achieve as much as the double move of the king's pawn. The basic tendency has a strategic nature and is effective in the long run. If White advances in the centre with the double move of his queen's pawn, then Black, by exchanging on d4, opens the c-file, on which his rook and queen will assert themselves. Furthermore, he keeps his two central pawns, whereas White has exchanged one of his for a black wing pawn. Should Black later succeed in advancing his d-pawn to d5 and exchanging it for the white e-pawn, this is almost always good for him. White's chances lie in attacking as soon as possible in the centre and on the king's wing. He could, for example, play an early f2–f4 (although rarely before castling) and threaten e4–e5,or perhaps f4–f5.

This defensive system is sharp and extremely versatile. Both sides have many opportunities to vary, as the following examples illustrate.

The position after **1.e2–e4 c7–c5 2.♘g1–f3 d7–d6 3.d2–d4 c5xd4 4.♘f3xd4 ♘g8–f6** is very common.

4. ... g7–g6 is also possible, although White could then play 5.c2–c4 and make the potential freeing advance d6–d5 considerably more difficult (on the other hand, 5.c4 delays White's development).

5.♘b1–c3 a7–a6

Also at this point, 5. ... g7–g6 is often played, with the intention of developing the king's bishop on the wing. This, the Dragon Variation can continue as follows: 6.♗e3 ♗g7 (6...♘g4? 7.♗b5+!) 7.f3 0-0 8.♕d2 ♘c6 9.0-0-0, or more quietly 6.♗e2 ♗g7 7.0-0 0-0 8.♗e3 ♘c6 9.♕d2.

The move a7–a6 is often unavoidable in the Sicilian Defence. It secures the square c7 for the queen against a white knight appearing on b5; the move b7–b5, prepared by the rook's pawn, can also be useful in more than one sense (see diagram 62). White can now choose between several continuations of equal value.

62

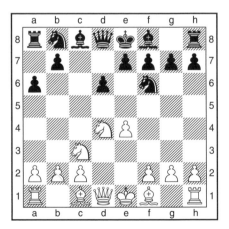

I. 6.♗f1–e2

Black can now transpose into the Scheveningen Variation, a domain of Garry Kasparov, by responding 6. … e7–e6 7.0-0 ♗f8–e7. He can also play 6. … e7–e5 'à la Najdorf' (after Miguel Najdorf, 1910–1997, the Polish-Argentinean grandmaster). The d6 pawn becomes 'backward' (it remains behind its neighbouring pawns) and the square d5 will be weakened, but Black often succeeds in carrying out the move d6–d5 and in freeing himself. Here is a practical example: 7.♘d4–b3 ♗f8–e7 8.♗c1–e3 ♗c8–e6 9.♕d1–d2 (planning queenside castling) 9. … 0-0 10.f2–f4 ♕d8–c7 (or 10…exf4 11.♗xf4 ♘c6 12.0-0-0 ♘e5, Dolmatov–Heissler, Germany 1991) 11.f4–f5 ♗e6–c4 12.0-0-0 b7–b5 13.g2–g4 and White has attacking chances, Smagin–Kaminski, Dortmund 1992.

II. 6.f2–f4

Black has a choice between both moves of the e-pawn. White obtains a promising attack after 6. … e7–e5 7.♘d4–b3 ♕d8–c7 8.a2–a4 ♘b8–d7 9.♗f1–d3 g7–g6 10.0-0 ♗f8–g7 11.♕d1–e1, but Black is not without chances: he is very solidly placed.

III. 6.♗c1–g5

Now the reply 6. … e7–e5 is less advisable, because 7.♗g5xf6 ♕d8xf6 8.♘c3–d5 ♕f6–d8 9.♘d4–f5 leads to a blockade of the light squares. Black does better to develop with 6. … e7–e6. The impetuous advance 7.f2–f4 b7–b5 (thoroughly examined by Lev Polugayevsky) 8.e4–e5 d6xe5 9.f4xe5 ♕d8–c7! has not yet been clarified (10.e5xf6 ♕c7–e5+).

IV. 6.♗f1–c4

White immediately puts the bishop in an effective position, where, however, it is exposed to attack. An example: 6. … e7–e6 7.a2–a3 ♗f8–e7 8.♗c4–a2 (White has to anticipate a pseudo-sacrifice on e4) 8. … 0-0 9.0-0 b7–b5 10.f2–f4, followed by ♖f1–f3 and ♖f3–h3.

V. 6.♗f1–d3

A methodical move with the idea 6. … e7–e6 7.f2–f4 b7–b5 (7…♕c7 is more careful) 8.e4–e5! d6xe5 9.f4xe5 ♘f6–d5 10.♕d1–g4 (see diagram 63).

63

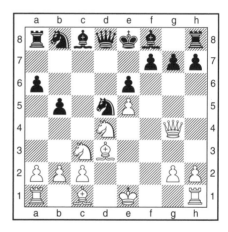

White has a lot of space on the king's wing and a strong attack (Parma-Gheorghiu, The Hague 1961). The move 6.♗f1–d3, which is neglected by theory, was also successful in the game Kholmov–O'Kelly, Havana 1968: 6…♘c6 7.♘xc6 bxc6 8.0-0 g6 9.♕e2 ♗g7 10.♗d2 0-0 11.♖ae1 ♘d7 12.b3 with a good game (12…e5 13.♘a4 ♖e8 14.♖d1 ♕c7 15.♗c4!).

VI. 6.g2–g3

Calm, but very effective. The bishop appearing on g2 makes the response planned by Black on the queen's wing more difficult. White will soon castle and gain more space by advancing his kingside pawns. After 6. ...e7–e5 7.♘d4–e2 ♘b8–d7 8.♗f1–g2 b7–b5 9.a2–a4 b5–b4 10.♘c3–d5 Black has to accept a cramped position.

VII. 6.♗c1–e3

This is all the fashion at the moment. White retains his options for further development. The best response seems to be the immediate 6. ... ♘f6–g4. The consequences of 7.♗e3–g5 h7–h6 8.♗g5–h4 g7–g5 9.♗h4–g3 ♗f8–g7 are unresolved. In Frolov–Sakaev, Alushta 1994, the following happened: 10.♕d2 ♘c6 11.♘b3 f5 12.exf5 ♗xf5 13.0-0-0 0-0 14.h4 a5, after which 15.♗b5 is recommended by Sakaev and Nesis.

Less prudent for Black would be 6. ... e7–e5, after which White can choose 7.♘d4–b3 ♗f8–e7 8.♗f1–c4 (Shirov), or 7.♘d4–f3 ♗f8–e7 8.♗f1–c4 0-0 9.0-0 ♘b8–c6 10.♖f1–e1 ♘c6–a5 11.♗c4–f1 ♗c8–e6 12.♘c3–d5 ♗e6xd5 13.e4xd5 b7–b5, Topalov–Gelfand, Linares 1994.

Both sides are faced with difficult problems in this complex opening. The stronger player will prevail.

White can counter Black's aspirations by playing 2.♘b1–c3 and postponing the advance of his pawn to d4. Famous players of the Closed Variation of the Sicilian are the former world champions Vasily Smyslov and Boris Spassky. The opening moves could develop as follows: 1.e2–e4 c7–c5 2.♘b1–c3 ♘b8–c6 3.g2–g3 g7–g6 4.♗f1–g2 ♗f8–g7 5.d2–d3 d7–d6 6.♘g1–e2 e7–e5 (Mikhail Botvinnik). The idea is to reply to 7.f2–f4 with 7. ... f7–f5.

The learner should play through the variations given and try out those that most appeal to him and suit his way of playing. The opening, after all, is supposed to secure a position for the player that suits his taste and character.

15th Hour

Specialised Opening Theory (V)

French Defence: 1.e2–e4 e7–e6

Since the beginning of the tournament era, in the middle of the 19th century, the French Defence has been practised. It places great demands on the defensive skills and patience of the commander of the black pieces. He responds to **1.e2–e4** with **e7–e6** and prepares the advance d7–d5. Meanwhile, he endures restrictions in the centre and on the king's wing. In addition, there is the concern of how to make use of the bishop, imprisoned on c8. Black's chances (after 1.e4 e6 2.d4 d5 and now or later e4–e5) consist in undermining the white central pawns and using them to open lines. The moves f7–f6 and c7–c5 serve this aim. If Black manages to exchange the pawns on d4 and e5, and occupy or control them with his own pieces or pawns, he will gain the advantage in the centre. White aims to secure control over the squares d4 and e5, and so to confine the black pawns to d5 and e6. White often exchanges the pawn on d4 for the c5 pawn and tries to station a piece on d4, usually a knight which can threaten vulnerable squares from there.

Initially, the fight is generally centred around the square d4. After **1.e2–e4 e7–e6 2.d2–d4 d7–d5 3.e4–e5** Black advances **3. ... c7–c5**: he attacks the first link in the pawn chain. As the defender, he is entitled to this, in so far as White has made a move (3.e5) which contributes nothing to the development of his pieces. Subsequently, White will have to defend the square d4 or exchange on c5, and Black will keep his sights trained on d4: **4.c2–c3 ♘b8–c6 5.♘g1–f3 ♕d8–b6** (see diagram 64)

64

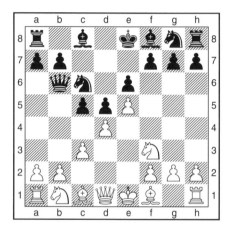

6.♗f1–e2

Also possible is 6.♗d3 cxd4 7.cxd4, since grabbing the pawn 7...♘xd4? would be a grave mistake due to 8.♘xd4 ♕xd4? 9.♗b5+, as often committed by inexperienced players – the black queen is lost. Black should first play 7...♗d7, to prevent the check by the bishop on b5. White can respond 8.♗e2, protecting his d4 pawn with the loss of a tempo, or sacrifice a pawn with the aim of gaining an advantage in development, which, according to the former world champion, Mikhail Tal (1936–1992), offers some opportunities: 8...♘xd4 9.♘xd4 ♕xd4 10.♘c3, after which 10...♕xe5, capturing a second pawn but opening the e-file, would be extremely dangerous: 11.♖e1 ♕d6 12.♘b5 and so

on. 10...a6 is more careful.

6. ... c5xd4 7.c3xd4 ♘g8–h6 8.b2–b3 (8.♗xh6? ♕xb2!) **8. ... ♘h6–f5 9.♗c1–b2 ♗f8–b4+ 10.♔e1–f1** Losing the right to castle, generally a disadvantage, is easy to tolerate here, since White can comfortably 'castle artificially', and so bring his rook at h1 into play. 10.♘bd2? is not possible because of 10...♘xd4.

10. ... h7–h5 (so that the knight at f5 cannot be forced away by g2–g4) **11.h2–h4**. White will now continue g2–g3 followed by ♔f1–g2 with good prospects, but Black can hold on.

3.♘b1–c3 is a natural move. White develops and simultaneously defends his central pawn. If Black now exchanges on e4 (3. ... d5xe4), he avoids the constraining e4–e5, but abandons his post in the centre. His position remains strong and is difficult to attack, as Tigran Petrosian (1929–1984, world champion from 1963–1969) repeatedly confirmed in important games. There is no doubt, though, that White has the more comfortable game. An example: **3. ... d5xe4 4.♘c3xe4 ♘b8–d7 5.♘g1–f3 ♘g8–f6** (also possible is 5...♗e7 6.♗d3 ♘gf6 7.♘xf6+ ♗xf6 8.0-0 c5) **6.♘e4xf6+ ♘d7x6 7.♗c1–g5 ♗f8–e7 8.♗f1–d3** (at this point moves such as 8.♗c4 or 8.♗b5+ ♗d7 9.♗xd7+ ♕xd7 10.♗xf6 gxf6 11.c3 have been tried, Spassky–Petrosian, Moscow 1967. But White did not have any luck with 8.♕d3 ♗e7 9.♗xf6 ♗xf6 10.♕b5+ ♗d7 11.♕xb7 ♖b8!, Tal–Petrosian, Curaçao 1962) **8. ... b7–b6! 9.♘f3–e5 ♗c8–b7 10.♗d3–b5+ c7–c6! 11.♗b5–e2** (suggested by Hans Kmoch).

The Estonian grandmaster, Paul Keres (1916–1975), advised the attacker to castle on the queenside and he presented the following instructive analysis:

(moves 1–6 as before) 7.♗f1–d3 ♗f8–e7 8.♕d1–e2 0-0 9.♗c1–g5 c7–c5 10.d4xc5 ♕d8–a5+ 11.c2–c3 ♕a5xc5 12.0-0-0 ♖f8–d8 13.♘f3–e5 (see diagram 65)

65

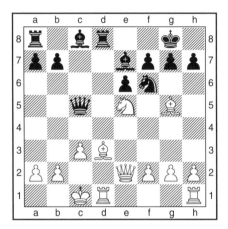

Now 13...♗d7 fails to 14.♗xf6 ♗xf6 15.♘xd7 ♖xd7 16.♗xh7+.

A 'beginner's mistake' is 9...b6? 10.♗xf6 ♗xf6 11.♕e4, winning a rook following the double attack on h7 and a8.

Classical Defence:
3.♘b1–c3 ♘g8–f6 4.♗c1–g5 ♗f8–e7

The McCutcheon Variation 4. ... ♗f8–b4 is rarely encountered. *The Encyclopaedia of Chess Openings* (1981) presents the following moves as the essence of many analyses: 5.e5 h6 6.♗d2 ♗xc3 7.bxc3 ♘e4 8.♕g4 g6 9.♗d3 ♘xd2 10.♔xd2 c5 11.♘f3 ♘c6 12.♖ab1 cxd4 13.cxd4 ♕a5+ 14.♔e3!? b6 15.♕f4 ♗a6 16.♖hc1; Kasparov judges the position to be unclear. Nowadays White usually plays e4–e5 already on the fourth move, whereby he incidentally avoids this method.

5.e4–e5 ♘f6–d7 Formerly, an exchange would be made on e7 with roughly equal chances. More exciting is the gambit **6.h2–h4** introduced by Alexander Alekhine (1889–1946, world champion from 1927–1935 and 1937–1946). One idea after **6. ... f7–f6** is to continue **7.♕d1–h5+ ♔e8–f8** (7...g6 8.exf6! gxh5 9.fxe7) **8.e5xf6 ♘d7xf6 9.♕h5–e2**. The acceptance of the pawn sacrifice 6...♗xg5 7.hxg5 ♕xg5 8.♘h3 is unresolved. The very complex consequences of 6...c5 7.♗xe7 ♕xe7 8.♘b5 also call for a clear understanding of the variations.

In modern practice, Nimzowitsch's move **3. ... ♗f8–b4** is the most popular. After **4.e4–e5 c7–c5 5.a2–a3 ♗b4xc3+ 6.b2xc3 ♘g8–e7** White has a large choice of tested moves. An example: 7.♕g4 ♔f8 (7...♘f5 8.♗d3 h5 9.♕f4 ♕h4 10.♘e2 ♕xf4 11.♘xf4 and White has better chances in the endgame) 8.h4 ♕c7 9.♕d1! cxd4 10.cxd4 ♕c3+ 11.♗d2 ♕xd4 12.♘f3 with advantage to White, Garry Kasparov–Predrag Nikolic, Horgen 1994. This entire variation is very complex and needs a lot of experience and knowledge of the relevant theory.

Tarrasch Variation: 3.♘b1–d2

With this White prevents the pinning move ♗b4, but blocks his queen's bishop and does not put the d5 square under fire.

Black can, therefore, without any great danger continue **3. ... c7–c5**. The weakness of the d5 pawn after **4.e4xd5 e6xd5** (also playable is 4...♕xd5 5.♘gf3 cxd4 6.♗c4 ♕d6 7.0-0 ♘c6 8.♘b3) **5.♘g1–f3** is tolerable.

A position with a chain of pawns on both sides is created after 3.♘b1–d2 ♘g8–f6 4.e4–e5 ♘f6–d7 5.f2–f4 (or 5.♗d3 c5 6.c3 ♘c6 7.♘e2) 5. ... c7–c5 6.c2–c3 c5xd4

7.c3xd4 ♛d8–b6 8.♘d2–f3 ♝f8–b4+
9.♚e1–f2 with a difficult game for both
sides.

For a player who is skilled in rapidly turning
a defensive position into an attack, as soon
as the opportunity arises, the French
Defence is ideal.

16th Hour

Specialised Opening Theory (VI)

Caro-Kann Defence: 1.e2–e4 c7–c6

This solid system of defence, examined
towards the end of the 19th century by the
masters Horatio Caro (who lived and
played mainly in Berlin) and Marcus Kann
(Vienna), has long played only a subordi-
nate role. But when stars such as Tartakower, Capablanca and Flohr achieved
practical successes with this opening, it
increased in importance. And when the
former world champion, Mikhail Botvinnik,
used it in his matches with Smyslov and
Tal, many great players, such as Petrosian,
Keres and Karpov, employed the move 1.
... c6 in their opening programme. The
idea of the move is sensible: Black wants
to establish a pawn on the central square
d5 (with an immediate 1...d5 2.exd5 ♛xd5
3.♘c3 this would not be possible) and at
the same time avoid the imprisonment of
his queen's bishop (which supporters of
the French Defence tolerate).

After **1.e2–e4 c7–c6 2.d2–d4 d7–d5** White
has the choice of either protecting (1),
advancing (2) or exchanging (3) his e4
pawn.

66

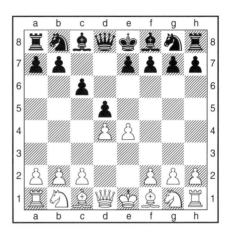

1. 3.♘b1–c3 (or 3.♘b1–d2) is the usual
way of protecting the pawn; 3.♝d3? dxe4
4.♝xe4 ♘f6 costs time. The classical
continuation is **3. ... d5xe4 4.♘c3xe4
♝c8–f5** (equally effective is 4...♘d7,
followed by ♘gf6, although Black has to
beware of the crafty 5.♘g5 h6? 6.♘e6)
5.♘e4–g3 ♝f6–g6 6.h2–h4. White can
act more calmly as well, for example 6.♘f3
♘d7 (Black does not want to allow the
white knight onto e5 although this is not in
fact a problem, as shown by the game
Ashley–Korchnoi, San Francisco 1995:
6...♘f6 7.♘e5 ♘bd7 8.♘xg6 hxg6 9.♝d3
♛c7 10.♛f3 e6 11.♝e3 c5 with a good
game.) 7.♝c4 e6 and Black retains a
strong position.
**6. ... h7–h6 7.h4–h5 ♝g6–h7 8.♘g1–f3
♘b8–d7! 9.♝f1–d3 ♝h7xd3 10.♛d1xd3
e7–e6**

67

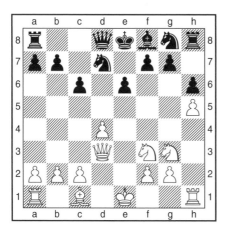

11.♗c1–d2 ♘g8–f6 12.♕d3–e2 c6–c5
This or similar positions have often occurred. In the game Timmerman–Scheeren, Rotterdam 1995, Black was not quite able to hold the balance: 13.0-0-0 c5xd4 14.♘f3xd4 ♕d8–b6 15.♖h1–h4 ♗f8–c5 16.♘d4–b3 0-0 17.♘b3xc5 ♕b6xc5 18.♘g3–e4 and so on. More modern is the method in Anand–Adams, Linares 1994 (up to the tenth move as above): **11.♗c1–f4 ♗f8–b4+ 12.c2–c3 ♗b4–e7 13.0-0-0 ♘g8–f6 14.♔c1–b1 a7–a5 15.♘f3–e5 a5–a4 16.c3–c4 0-0** with roughly equal chances.

2. The Restricting 3.e4–e5

The advance **3.e4–e5** is very common in modern usage, although experience does not provide a clear judgement about its value. **3. ... ♗c8–f5** is accepted as a good response. The game Tal–Pachman, Bled 1961, was unique: **4.h2–h4 h7–h6** (The bishop needs a retreat square, as can be seen from 4…e6? 5.g4 ♗e4 6.f3 ♗g6 7.h5 when it is trapped.) **5.g2–g4 ♗f5–d7** (After

5…♗h7! Black feared 6.e6 fxe6 7.♗d3, but he can play 6…♕d6!) **6.h4–h5 c6–c5 7.c2–c3 e7–e6 8.f2–f4** (After eight moves, White has not yet moved a single piece! Black, whose queen's bishop has been constrained, is very restricted and the position is closed so that White's backward development is not so important.) **8. ... ♕d8–b6 9.♘g1–f3 ♘b8–c6 10.♘b1–a3 c5xd4 11.c3xd4 0-0-0 12.♘a3–c2.** White subsequently attacked with ♗d3, ♖b1, ♗d2 and b2–b4 (see diagram 68).

68

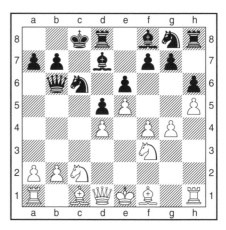

Recently White has taken to treating the position very calmly: 4.♘g1–f3 e7–e6 5.c2–c3 c6–c5 6.a2–a3 c5xd4 7.c3xd4 ♘g8–e7 8.♗c1–e3 ♘e7–c6 9.♗f1–d3 and Black, who does not have any pressure on d4, was in trouble, Short–Gulko, 9th match game, New York 1994.

The position after 3.e4–e5 brings to mind the closed variation of the French Defence. The move 3. … c7–c5, which is common in that variation, has also been tried in the Caro-Kann, even with a loss of time (the e-pawn is still on e7 and the c-pawn has been moved twice). The following happened in the 8th game of the Tal–Botvinnik world championship match, Moscow 1961: 3...c5 4.dxc5 e6 5.♕g4 ♘c6 6.♘f3 ♕c7 7.♗b5 ♗d7 8.♗xc6 ♕xc6 9.♗e3 ♘h6 10.♗xh6 gxh6 11.♘bd2 ♕xc5 12 c4! with the better game for White.

Here is a different example from the Mitropa Cup in Bükfürdö (Hungary) 1995. Grosar (Slovenia)–Van der Werf (Netherlands): 3...c5 4.dxc5 ♘c6 5.♗b5 e6 6.♘f3 ♗xc5 7.c4 ♘ge7 8.♘c3 a6 9.♗xc6+ bxc6 10.0-0 ♘g6 11.♘a4 ♗a7 12.♗e3 ♗xe3 13.fxe3 0-0 14.♕d4 with a positional advantage.

3. Panov Attack

3.e4xd5 c6xd5 4.c2–c4 (the quiet move 4.♗f1–d3 is also not at all bad) **4. ...♘g8–f6 5.♘b1–c3 e7–e6** (more complicated is 5...g6 6.cxd5 ♗g7 7.♕b3, Charlow–Malisauskas, Berlin 1994) **6.♘g1–f3 ♗f8–e7 7.c4xd5 ♘f6xd5 8.♗f1–d3** White exerts pressure, but Black stands firm. A similar position can arise from the Queen's Gambit.

As in any opening, unsolved problems crop up on every move. This is just as well. The idea is to join the fray open-mindedly and use the theoretical instructions merely as guidelines.

Beware, a trap!

A typical opening trap occurs after **1.e2–e4 c7–c6 2.♘b1–c3** (White omits 2.d4 for the moment) **2. ... d7–d5 3.♘g1–f3 d5xe4** (3...♗g4 is also good) **4.♘c3xe4.** Now **4. ... ♗c8–f5** would be stereotyped and wrong, because the white king's knight is already poised to leap to e5, for example **5.♘e4–g3 ♗f5–g6 6.h2–h4 h7–h6 7.♘f3–e5 ♗g6–h7 8.♕d1–h5 g7–g6** (see diagram 69).

69

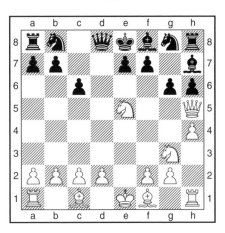

After Black's 8th move

9.♗f1–c4 (threatening checkmate). **9. ... e7–e6 10.♕h5–e2**, threatening 11.♘xf7. Instead of 4...♗f5, Black does better to play 4...♘d7 followed by ♘gf6.

This concludes our deliberations on the fashionable Caro-Kann Defence: it does not offer an infallible solution, but it secures Black a safe and defensible position.

17th Hour

Specialised Opening Theory (VII)

Other Semi-Open Games

The group of semi-open games (not e7–e5 in response to 1.e2–e4) comprises a few openings, which are not so often used, such as the Alekhine Defence (1. ... ♘g8–f6), the Pirc Defence (1. ... d7–d6), the Scandinavian Defence (1. ... d7–d5) and the Nimzowitsch Defence (1. ... ♘b8–c6). The theoretically uninitiated player is advised to specialise in one of these methods when commanding the black pieces. On the one hand, he will always be in familiar territory, and on the other hand he will reduce the danger of running into a novelty in the opening. Chess is so unbelievably varied, that there is no danger of falling victim to monotony or repetition.

Alekhine Defence: 1.e2–e4 ♘g8–f6

The aim of this knight move is to tempt the white central pawn forward, in order later to facilitate the exchange of the d-pawn for the white e-pawn. White should take care not to loosen his position with too many pawn moves and not to neglect the development of his pieces. He is well advised to be content with a small spatial gain. A winning recipe of the elite is to only aim for a truly achievable goal. This may often be only small, but nevertheless a useful one in practice.

One Main Variation

1.e2–e4 ♘g8–f6 2.e4–e5
After 2.♘b1–c3 e7–e5 we find ourselves in the Vienna Game, which means that Black has avoided the dangerous Ruy Lopez, and he can also try 2. ... d7–d5.
2. ... ♘f6–d5 3.d2–d4 d7–d6 4.♘g1–f3 ♗c8–g4 The following sharp continuation originates with the Danish grandmaster, Bent Larsen: 4. ... d6xe5 5.♘f3xe5 ♘b8–d7, after which the sacrifice 6.♘e5xf7 ♔e8xf7 7.♕d1–h5+ ♔f7–e6 is difficult to judge. Not advisable is 4. ... ♘b8–c6 5.c2–c4 ♘d5–b6 6.e5–e6 f7xe6 (6...♗xe6? loses a piece to the pawn fork 7.d5) 7.♘f3–g5!.
5.♗f1–e2 e7–e6 6.0-0 ♗f8–e7 7.c2–c4 ♘d5–b6 8.e5xd6 c7xd6 9.b2–b3
White develops his bishop at b2 and his queen's knight at d2, and is slightly better placed – the method of the former world champion Vasily Smyslov (see diagram 70).

70

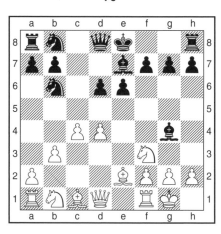

The aggressive advance (after 1.e4 ♘f6 2.e5 ♘d5) **3.c2–c4 ♘d5–b6 4.d2–d4** (4.c5 ♘d5 5.♗c4 e6 is a sharp gambit. White intends to sacrifice a pawn with 6.♘c3, for example 6...♘xc3 7.dxc3 ♗xc5 8.♕g4 ♔f8 [but not 8...0-0? 9.♗h6] 9.♗f4 d5 10.0-0-0 ♘c6 and both sides have chances.) **4. ... d7–d6 5.f2–f4** leads to the Four Pawns Attack. Also simple and good is 5.exd6 exd6 6.♘c3 ♘c6 7.♗e3 ♗e7 8.♗d3 0-0 9.♘ge2 ♗g4. **5. ... d6xe5** (Black opens the d-file and wants to put pressure on the d4 square.) **6.f4xe5 ♘b8–c6 7.♗c1–e3 ♗c8–f5 8.♘b1–c3** (8.♗d3? ♗xd3 9.♕xd3 would be a mistake because of 9...♘xe5) **8...e7–e6 9.♘g1–f3 ♘c6–b4** This move has superseded the older method 9...♕d7 10.♗e2 0-0-0 11.0-0 f6 12.d5! ♘xe5 13.♘xe5 fxe5, but wrongly so in the opinion of the Russian theorist, Vladimir Bagirov, who thinks that it is possible to parry the normal moves 14.♖c1 or 14.a4. **10.♖a1–c1 c7–c5 11.♗f1–e2 ♗f8–e7 12.0-0 0-0** White can now play 13.a3 cxd4 14.♘xd4 ♘c6 15.♘xf5 or 13.dxc5 ♘d7 14.a3 ♘c6 15.b4 ♘dxe5 16.♘xe5 ♘xe5 17.♘b5 (Hort–Knezevic, Slncev Brjag 1974) with slightly the better position.

Pirc Defence:
1.e2–e4 d7–d6 2.d2–d4 ♞g8–f6

Black intends to act defensively in the centre, fianchetto his king's bishop, quickly castle and, if possible, create play on the queen's wing. His position is very firm and difficult to disturb.

Moreover, this defence has the advantage that Black can aim for the same position if the opponent opens with the queen's pawn, i.e. 1.d2–d4 d7–d6 2.e2–e4 (here White could take the play along 'Indian' channels with 2.c4) 2. ... ♞f6 and so on.

After **3.♞b1–c3 g7–g6** White can choose between different structures. Theory suggests 4.f2–f4 as the most aggressive system, 4.♞g1–f3 is calm and good, 4.f2–f3 is solid, and 4.♝f1–e2 followed by the advance of the h-pawn is interesting. Here is a short game, opened with the Byrne Variation.

4.♝c1–g5 ♝f8–g7 5.f2–f4 0-0 6.e4–e5 A sharp advance, which was first played in a game Unzicker–Pirc, Opatija 1953. The standard move is 6.♞f3. **6. ... ♞f6–e8(?)** This is how Pirc played in the afore-mentioned game. Later Raymond Keene discovered that 6. ... ♞f6–g4 is much stronger with the threats of ♞g4–e3 and f7–f6. **7.♞g1–f3 ♞b8–d7 8.h2–h4** Sacrificing the bishop. The h-file is where things will be decided. Unzicker continued more solidly 8.♝c4 ♞b6 9.♝b3 d5 10.0-0 and also won. **8. ... h7–h6** (8...h5 is more circumspect) **9.h4–h5 h6xg5 10.♞f3xg5 ♞d7–b6 11.♝f1–d3 f7–f6** Here inspiration is needed. **12.h5xg6 f6xg5 13.♖h1–h8+!**

71

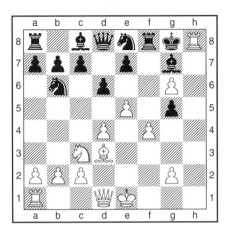

With his third piece sacrifice White makes the h8 square available, which would not be the case after 13.♕h5 ♖xf4 14.♕h7+ ♚f8. Black resigned in the game Nettheim-Hamilton, Australia 1958. He is check-mated after 13...♝xh8 14.♕h5 ♖xf4 15.♕h7+ ♚f8 16.♕xh8.

Scandinavian Defence:
1.e2–e4 d7–d5

This was very popular in Nordic chess circles at the beginning of the 20th century; the aim is to break up the centre at once. The Leipzig master and chess author, Jacques Mieses (1865–1954), also achieved some fine successes with it. After (1.e2–e4 d7–d5) **2.e4xd5! ♕d8xd5 3.♞b1–c3 ♕d5–d8 4.♞g1–f3** White has won an important tempo, so that strategically speaking there is not much to be said in favour of this defence. Mieses, therefore, advocated the move **3. ... ♕d5–a5**, in order to keep the queen in the game. However, Black has to be careful that his queen does not get drawn into the crowd. Thus 4.d2–d4 e7–e5 (one of the fundamental ideas of this variation) 5.d4xe5

♕a5xe5+ **6.♗f1–e2 ♗c8–g4 7.♕d1–d5** again leads to a clear tempo advantage for White. **4.d2–d4 ♘g8–f6** (Mieses's move) **5.♘g1–f3 ♗c8–g4** (or 5...♘c6 6.♗b5 ♗g4 7.h3) **6.h2–h3! ♗g4–h5** (the lesser evil is the exchange against the knight) **7.g2–g4 ♗h5–g6 8.♘f3–e5** and the black queen has to retreat (because of the threat of 9.♘e5–c4).

This is why followers of the Scandinavian Defence prefer the gambit move **1.e2–e4 d5–d5 2.e4xd5 ♘g8–f6.** As usual, White does best not to hold on to the pawn too tightly, but to let it go with a good game, for example 3.d2–d4, or 3.c2–c4 c7–c6 4.d2–d4 transposing into the Panov Attack (see Caro-Kann Defence). The following variation originates with Emanuel Lasker (1868–1941), the world champion from 1894–1921: 3.c2–c4 c7–c6 4.d5xc6 ♘b8xc6 5.d2–d3 e7–e5 6.♘b1–c3 ♗c8–f5 7.♘g1–f3 ♕d8–d7 8.♗f1–e2 ♖a8–d8 and now White has to give back the pawn. This can be comfortably achieved with 9.0–0! ♗f5xd3 10.♗e2xd3 ♕d7xd3 11.♕d1–a4 (see diagram 72).

White has the superior position. However, according to Boleslavsky Black can continue more strongly with 7...♗b4 8.♗e2 e4!, and White has problems, for example 9.dxe4 ♘xe4!, or 9.♘h4 ♗e6 10.0–0 exd3 11.♗xd3 ♗xc3 12.bxc3 ♘e5!.

Nimzowitsch Defence:
1.e2–e4 ♘b8–c6

This is not often played. With 2.♘g1–f3 White can direct the game towards more common channels. The occupation of the centre **2.d2–d4** looks more logical, although it does not disprove the defence. The most important variation is probably **2. ... e7–e5 3.d4xe5 ♘c6xe5 4.♘g1–f3 ♕d8–f6 5.♗f1–e2 ♗f8–b4+ 6.♘b1–d2 ♘e5xf3+ 7.♗e2xf3 ♘g8–e7 8.0–0 0–0 9.♘d2–b3** and White has the more comfortable game. Black aims at a difficult positional game with **2. ... e7–e6 3.♘g1–f3 d7–d5.** White can enter into the spirit of it and insist on gaining space: **4.e4–e5 b7–b6 5.c2–c3 ♘c6–e7 6.♗f1–d3 a7–a5 7.♕d1–e2** (see diagram 73).

72

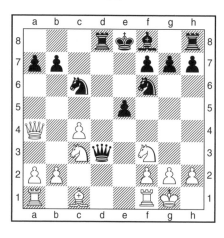

73

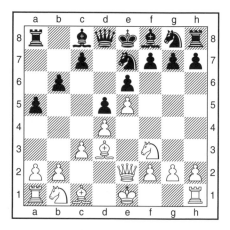

The exchange of the light square bishops, which Black was aiming for on a6, has been prevented by White; he has the better position.

Please choose what is most suited to your own taste, and then: play it!

18th Hour

Specialised Opening Theory (VIII)

Closed Games. The Queen's Gambit: 1.d2–d4 d7–d5 2.c2–c4

Up till now we have looked at what happens when the game is opened with the most popular move, the double advance of the king's pawn. In tournament play, other opening moves, belonging to the 'closed games', are also commonly made. It is a matter of taste and temperament, and also of feeling which type of opening is preferred. The majority of top players do not rely on one particular type of opening, in order to make it more difficult for the opponent to prepare for a game.

Everyone can be forced, when playing Black, to defend himself against a 'closed' opening. This is why it is essential to gain some theoretical knowledge in this area as well. First, we will look at the double move of the queen's pawn.

'Orthodox' Queen's Gambit: 1.d2–d4 d7–d5 2.c2–c4 e7–e6 3. ♘b1–c3 ♘g8–f6

The 'Indian' defences, which arise when Black begins with 1. … ♘g8–f6, will be discussed later.

1.d2–d4 d7–d5 2.c2–c4 Careful souls will first play 2.♘g1–f3, because they are afraid of the Albin Counter-Gambit 2.c2–c4 e7–e5. Wrongly so – but White should not make the mistake of holding on at all costs to the pawn, gained after 3.d4xe5, to the detriment of his development. He should also know that after 3. … d5–d4 the seemingly logical developing move 4.e2–e3 is incorrect because of 4. … ♗f8–b4+ 5.♗c1–d2 d4xe3! 6.♗d2xb4 e3xf2+ 7.♔e1–e2 f2xg1♘+!, an amusing turn (because of the threat ♗g4+, White is forced to play 8.♔e1 and after 8…♕h4+ he is lost). Here is an example of a good set-up for White: 4.♘f3 ♘c6 5.♘bd2 ♗e6 6.g3 ♕d7 7.♗g2 ♘ge7 8.0-0 ♘g6 9.a3 ♗e7 10.♕a4 ♖d8 11.b4 0-0 12.♗b2 and so on.

2. … e7–e6 The classical response. Also very popular is the Slav Defence 2. … c7–c6 (see below), while the acceptance of the gambit, 2. … d5xc4, is also playable. **3.♘b1–c3 ♗f8–e7 4.♘g1–f3 ♘g8–f6 5.♗c1–g5 0-0 6.e2–e3 h7–h6** The Tartakower Variation, which has thus been initiated, is one of the most reliable weapons against the Queen's Gambit.

7.♗g5–h4 In order to gain time, White can also play 7.♗xf6 ♗xf6 8.♕b3 c6 9.0-0-0 ♘d7 10 e4. However, many players do not like to exchange their queen's bishop for the knight.

7. … b7–b6 8.♗f1–d3 ♗c8–b7 9.0-0 c7–c5.

Black has freed himself somewhat. In the Queen's Gambit this is nearly always the case when he can carry out the double move of his c-pawn without disadvantage. Here is an example from modern practice (moves 1 to 7 as before):

(see diagram 74)

74

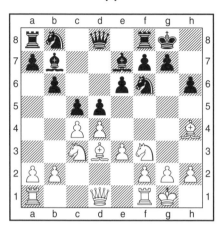

8.♗e2 ♗b7 9.♗xf6 ♗xf6 10.cxd5 exd5 11.b4 c6 12.0-0 ♕d6 13.♕b3 ♘d7 14.♖fe1 ♗e7 15.♖ab1 a5 16.bxa5 ♖xa5 17.a4 ♖e8 18.♗f1 ♗f8 (in Karpov–Bönsch, Baden-Baden 1992, Black still had a difficult game after 18...♗a6 19.♗xa6 ♖xa6 20.e4 dxe4 21.♘xe4) 19.♕c2 g6 20.e4 and White has the better chances, Karpov–Georgiev, Tilburg 1994.

A hundred years ago, Dr. Siegbert Tarrasch called the move 3. ... c7–c5 immediately after 3.♘b1–c3 'the only correct one'. He did not see the isolated d-pawn, which Black suffers (after 4.c4xd5 e6xd5), as a disadvantage. Today many world-class players share this opinion. Here is an example from a world championship match: 5.♘f3 ♘c6 6.g3 ♘f6 7.♗g2 ♗e7 8.0-0 0-0 9.♗g5 cxd4 10.♘xd4 h6 11.♗e3 ♖e8! with equal play, 18th championship game, Petrosian–Spassky, Moscow 1969.

Slav Defence to the Queen's Gambit

1.d2–d4 d7–d5 2.c2–c4 c7–c6 This popular move has the advantage, compared to 2. ... e7–e6, of not shutting in the queen's bishop. On the other hand, Black takes away the useful square c6 from his knight. Neither can he play c7–c5 in one go, although does not give up the idea of later playing c6–c5. The basic ideas may be explained by the following game.

3.♘g1–f3 After 3.♘c3 White has to reckon with 3...e5 (4.dxe5 d4). **3. ... ♘g8–f6 4.♘b1–c3** The exchange variation 4.cxd5 cxd5 5.♘c3 ♘c6 6.♗f4 e6 offers a small, but not to be underestimated, chance to keep the tempo advantage for a little while longer. **4. ... d5xc4** Not so good is 4...♗f5 5.cxd5 cxd5 6.♕b3 and Black has no choice other than to return his bishop to its initial square (as 'compensation' White has freed the c6 square for the knight at b8). **5.a2–a4** Especially adventurous players prefer the gambit 5.e2–e4 b7–b5 6.e4–e5 ♘f6–d5 7.a2–a4.

5. ... ♗c8–f5 Smyslov's move 5...♘a6 is occasionally played, for example 6.e4 (The original variation 6.♘e5 ♘g4! 7.♘xc4 e5! stems from Smyslov) 6...♗g4 7.♗xc4 ♗xf3 8.gxf3 e6. White has a strong centre and the bishop pair. Also possible is 7...e6 8.♗e3 ♗b4 9.♕c2 ♗xf3 10.gxf3 0-0 11.0-0 c5 12.d5 ♗xc3 13.bxc3 exd5 14.♖fd1 ♕c8 15.exd5 as in Hübner–Smyslov, Tilburg 1979. White has the more promising position.

6.e2–e3 (The older method is: 6.♘f3–e5 ♘b8–d7 7.♘e5xc4 ♕d8–c7 8.g2–g3 e7–e5 9.d4xe5 ♘d7xe5 10.♗c1–f4 ♘f6–d7 with slightly the better game for White; 7...♘b6 is also playable instead of 7...♕c7.) **6. ... e7–e6 7.♗f1xc4 ♗f8–b4 8.0-0 ♘b8–d7 9.♕d1–e2 ♗f5–g6** (A good alternative is 9. ... ♘f6–e4 10.♗c4–d3, an unclear pawn sacrifice. Also popular is 9. ... ♗f5–g4 10.h2–h3 ♗g4xf3 11.♕e2xf3 0-0 12.♖f1–d1 ♕d8–a5 13.e3–e4 e6–e5 14.d4–d5, Kasparov–Bareev, Novgorod 1994. The position offers White good prospects.)

10.e3–e4 (a pawn sacrifice, which Black declines) **10. ... 0-0 11.♗c4–d3 a7–a6 12.e4–e5 ♘f6–d5 13.♗d3xg6 f7xg6 14.♘c3–e4 c6–c5 15.♖f1–d1**, Yermolinsky–Finegold, Reno 1999. Black has a few problems (see diagram 75).

75

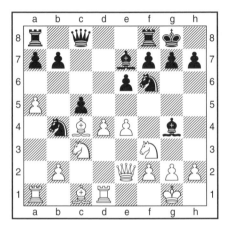

The Meran Variation arises when White does not develop his queen's knight on the fourth move, but secures his c-pawn and simultaneously develops his king's wing with **4.e2–e3**. After the sequel **4. ... e7–e6** (4. ... ♗c8–f5 is also possible) **5.♘b1–c3 ♘b8–d7 6.♗f1–d3 d5xc4 7.♗d3xc4**, the move **7. ... b7–b5** reveals Black's development plan: the queen's bishop will go to b7 and the position will be normalised by playing an early c6–c5. White, on the other hand, aims to quickly advance his e-pawn, so that his queen's bishop can also be brought out. The sequel could be: **8.♗c4–d3 a7–a6 9.e3–e4 c6–c5 10.d4–d5** (An important alternative is 10.e4–e5 c5xd4 11.♘c3xb5 ♘d7xe5 [or 11...axb5 12.exf6] 12.♘f3xe5 a6xb5 13.♕d1–f3 with difficult complications.) **10. ... e6–e5** (Strategically doubtful. After this, White can delight in a strong, protected passed pawn in the centre. Better would be 10. ... c5–c4 11.d5xe6 c4xd3 12.e6xd7+ ♕d8xd7 13.0-0 ♗c8–b7. Black has a nearly equal game. However, in the game Karpov–Lutz, Dortmund 1994, White remained in control after 14.♖e1 ♗e7 15.e5 ♘d5 16.♘e4 0-0 17.♕xd3 ♕g4 18.♘fg5. An alternative for Black is 10. ... ♕d8–c7 11.0-0 ♗c8–b7 12.d5xe6 f7xe6 13.♗d3–c2 c5–c4 14.♕d1–e2 (or 14.♘g5 ♘c5) 14. ... ♗f8–d6, Kramnik–Shirov, Novgorod 1994.

11.b2–b3 c5–c4 A doubtful pawn sacrifice, to try and force the opponent onto the defensive. **12.b3xc4 ♗f8–b4 13.♗c1–d2 b5xc4 14.♗d3–c2** (diagram 76)

76

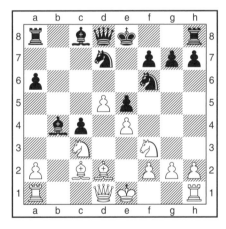

White's game is preferable (14. ... ♕d8–a5 15.♘c3–e2 ♘f6xe4 16.♗c2xe4 c4–c3 17.♘e2xc3, Uhlmann-Pomar, Stockholm 1962).

19th Hour

Specialised Opening Theory (IX)
Indian Defences: 1.d2–d4 ♘g8–f6

It is questionable whether India, the country where chess originated, has anything to do with the modern opening strategies called 'Indian'. Since the middle of the 19th century, games opening 1.d2–d4 ♘g8–f6 were known to be played in India, but this also happened elsewhere. When Dr. Saviely Tartakower, a clever chess player and author, called this opening 'Indian' around 1920, he might have wanted to give this 'unusual' opening an exotic ring. It was at this time that the 'hypermodern school', which searched for new ways in chess and found them, was formed. It was influenced by inventive masters such as Richard Réti and Aaron Nimzowitsch. One idea was to control or fight for the centre without the assistance of the pawns. The hypermodernists discovered that it was sometimes better not to occupy the centre with pawns, but to use remote pieces to control it.

After 1.d2–d4 the move 1. ... ♘g8–f6 initially prevents the double advance of the white king's pawn and also influences the d5 square. White cannot exchange the black d-pawn with c2–c4, as is the case in the Queen's Gambit (i.e. when 1. ... d7–d5 has been played). The hypermodern school instructed that the central pawns were especially valuable. This is why they should be held back at the beginning. Depending on Black's further behaviour, the game branches into the Nimzo-Indian (1.d2–d4 ♘g8–f6 2.c2–c4 **e7–e6 3.♘b1–c3 ♗f8–b4**), the Queen's Indian (1.d2–d4 ♘g8–f6 2.c2–c4 **e7–e6 3. ♘g1–f3 b7–b6**)

or the King's Indian (1.d2–d4 ♘g8–f6 2.c2–c4 **g7–g6**).

Nimzo-Indian Defence:
1.d2–d4 ♘g8–f6 2.c4–c4 e7–e6 3.♘b1–c3 ♗f8–b4

The move **3. ... ♗f8–b4** (after 1.d4 ♘f6 2.c4 e6 3.♘c3) continues the fight for the e4 square and also aims to castle as soon as possible. White can follow several strategies of roughly equal value. Nowadays the old move 4.♕d1–c2, which intends to preserve the pawn position on the queen's wing, has again become fashionable.

4.e2–e3 is a neutral move; you could argue, however, that it accepts the doubled pawns that arise after 4. ... ♗b4xc3+ 5.b2xc3, when White can rely on the bishop pair. More usual is **4. ... c7–c5** (see diagram 77).

77

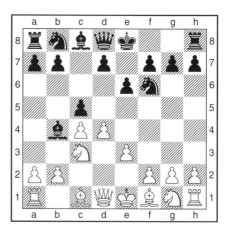

Also not bad is 4. ... b7–b6 5.♘g1–e2 ♗c8–a6 6.a2–a3 ♗b4xc3+ 7.♘e2xc3 d7–d5. If White plays 5.♘g1–f3, then there follows 5. ... ♗c8–b7 6.♗f1–d3 0-0 7.0-0 ♗b4xc3 8.b2xc3 ♗b7–e4. With 4. ... c7–c5

Black follows the same recipe as White with 2.c2–c4: the c-pawn attacks the centre, so that the queen's knight can be introduced more effectively.

5.♘g1–f3 0-0 6.♗f1–d3 d7–d5 Finally this move is played after all. Otherwise Black would have to reckon with the pawn advance d4–d5, which would restrict his game. **7.0-0 ♘b8–c6** The 'normal position' of this variation. With 8.a2–a3 ♗b4xc3 9.b2xc3 White can gain two bishops against bishop and knight, which can be advantageous all the way to the endgame. A modern example shows that Black is not without chances. Boris Gelfand–Victor Korchnoi, Horgen 1994: 9...dxc4 10.♗xc4 ♕c7 11.♗a2 e5 12.h3 b6 13.♕c2 (somewhat questionable; preferable, according to Korchnoi, is 13.d5 e4 14.dxc6 exf3 15.♕xf3 ♕e5! 16.e4! ♕xe4 17.♕xe4 ♘xe4 18.♖e1) 13. ... ♗a6 14.♖d1 e4 and Black can be very satisfied.

Queen's Indian Defence:
1.d2–d4 ♘g8–f6 2.c4–c4 e7–e6
3.♘g1–f3 b7–b6

In this defence Black moves his queen's bishop to the long a8–h1 diagonal (hence the name Queen's Indian). This method is very appropriate when White develops his king's knight on the second or third move but holds back his queen's knight: 1.d2–d4 ♘g8–f6 2.♘g1–f3 b7–b6, or 1.d2–d4 ♘g8–f6 2.c2–c4 e7–e6 3.♘g1–f3 b7–b6. Not so favourable is 1.d2–d4 ♘g8–f6 2.c2–c4 b7–b6 3.♘b1–c3! ♗c8–b7 4.f2–f3, because the bishop immediately runs into a wall and White is able to play e2–e4. The two main variations begin on the fourth move. White has to decide whether to fianchetto his bishop or develop it in the centre.

1.d2–d4 ♘g8–f6 2.c2–c4 e7–e6 3.♘g1–f3 b7–b6

a) **4.g2–g3 ♗c8–b7 5.♗f1–g2 ♗f8–e7 6. 0-0 0-0 7.♘b1–c3 ♘f6–e4** Not advisable is 7. … c7–c5 8.d4–d5!, but 7. … d7–d5 8.♘f3–e5 c7–c6 is also possible. **8.♕d1–c2 ♘e4xc3 9.♕c2xc3** To speculate on a double attack against the weak squares h7 and b7 with 9.♘g5? would be fatal: 9...♘xe2+ and Black wins. **9. … f7–f5 10.d4–d5** with the idea of **10. … e6xd5 11.♘f3–e1.** Black maintains the balance after **11. … ♕d8–c8 12.c4xd5 ♘b8–a6.**

b) **4.e2–e3 ♗c8–b7 5.♗f1–d3 d7–d5**
After 5. … ♗f8–b4+ 6.♘b1–d2 0-0 7.0-0 d7–d5 (otherwise e3–e4) 8.b2–b3 ♘b8–d7 9.♗c1–b2 ♕d8–e7 10.♕d1–c2 White stands slightly better.

An instructive variation arises after 5. ... ♗f8–e7 6. ♘b1–c3 c7–c5 7.0-0 c5xd4 8.e3xd4 0-0 9.d4–d5! e6xd5 10.c4xd5 ♘f6xd5 11.♘c3xd5 ♗b7xd5 12.♗d3xh7+ ♔g8xh7 13.♕d1xd5 with advantage to White. Black should play d7–d5 on the sixth or eighth move.

78

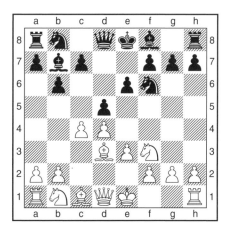

6.b2–b3 ♗f8–d6 7.0-0 0-0 8.♗c1–b2 ♘b8–d7 9.♘b1–d2 ♕d8–e7 10.♖a1–c1

♖a8–d8 with chances for both sides (Spassky–Tal, Montreal 1979).
In practice, Black often uses the opportunity, after ♘g1–f3, to transpose into the Queen's Gambit with 3. ... d7–d5.

King's Indian Defence:
1.d2–d4 ♘g8–f6 2.c2–c4 g7–g6

An aggressive opening, often played today. If you choose it, you have to be prepared for a lengthy defence, and be alert and able to seize the opportunity for a counter-attack. Great names, such as David Bronstein, Svetozar Gligoric, Yefim Geller, Bobby Fischer and Garry Kasparov have won some glorious games with it. But if you want to play it, you need to burden your memory with numerous variations.
Here is a topical main variation:
1.d2–d4 ♘g8–f6 2.c2–c4 g7–g6 3.♘b1–c3 ♗f8–g7 4.g2–g3 d7–d6 5.♗f1–g2 0-0 6.♘g1–f3 ♘b8–c6
The classical method goes: 6...♘bd7 7.0-0 e5 8.e4 c6 9.♖b1 a5 10.h3 a4 11.♗e3 exd4 (the commander of the black pieces suggests 11...♕a5 12.♕c2 b5 as an alternative) 12.♘xd4 ♖e8 13.♕c2 ♘c5 14.♖fe1 ♘fd7 15.b4 axb3 16.axb3 ♕e7 17.♖bd1 h5 and now White should play 18.f4 with slightly the better prospects, Gavrikov–Kasparov, Horgen 1994. Right from the beginning there are numerous possibilities to deviate from this path.
7.0-0 a7–a6 The Argentinean, Oscar Panno, created this idea of gaining counterplay with b7–b5. **8.d4–d5 ♘c6–a5 9.♘f3–d2 c7–c5 10.♕d1–c2 ♖a8–b8 11.b2–b3 b7–b5 12.♖a1–b1 b5xc4 13.b3xc4 ♗c8–d7** Black has achieved his goal, but many problems remain unresolved. In the game Kir. Georgiev–Neved-

nichy, Serbia 1994, there followed 14.♗b2 ♕c7 15.♘d1 ♖b4 16.♗c3, and in Cvitan–Nevednichy, Biel 1994, 14.♖xb8 ♕xb8 15.♗b2 ♕c7 16.♘d1 ♖b8 17.♗c3 occurred. In both cases White maintained an advantage.

The Four Pawns Attack is neglected in practice, but is not without danger: **1.d2–d4 ♘g8–f6 2.c2–c4 g7–g6 3.♘b1–c3 ♗f8–g7**
Black has the opportunity to transpose into the Grünfeld Defence with 3. ... d7–d5. White's simplest reply is 4.cxd5 ♘xd5 5.e4 ♘xc3 6.bxc3 c5 7.♗c4 ♗g7 8.♘e2 0-0 9.0-0 ♘c6 10.♗e3, when the fight remains open.
4.e2–e4 d7–d6 5.♗f1–e2 0-0 6.f2–f4 (The quiet 6.♘f3 has more followers.) **6. ... c7–c5 7.d4–d5 e7–e6 8.♘g1–f3 e6xd5 9.e4xd5** 9.c4xd5 leads to very complicated play and demands special preparation. The sharp pawn sacrifice 9.e4–e5!? which originates from the Estonian, Ivo Nei, presents Black with difficult problems, for example: 9...♘g4 10.cxd5 dxe5 11.h3 e4 12.hxg4 exf3 13.gxf3 ♖e8 14.f5, Vaiser–Kasparov, Moscow 1981. According to the game Li Zunian–Gheorghiu, Dubai Olympiad 1986, 9...♘e4! 10.cxd5 ♘xc3 11.bxc3 ♘d7 12.0-0 dxe5 13.fxe5 ♘xe5 14.♗e3 ♘xf3+ 15.♗xf3 ♕b6! is best. In the game Nei–Polugayevsky, Tbilisi 1967, White obtained a promising attack after 9...♘fd7 10.cxd5 dxe5 11.0-0! exf4 12.♗xf4 ♘f6 13.♕d2 ♗g4 14.h3 ♗xf3, but now he should have recaptured not with the bishop, but with the rook.
9. ... ♗c8–f5 (one way to equalise is Byrne's move 9...♘e8 10.0-0 ♘c7 11.♗d3 f5) **10. 0-0 ♘f6–e4 11.♘c3xe4 ♗f5xe4 12.♘f3–g5 ♖f8–e8 13.♗e2–d3 ♗e4xd3 14.♕d1xd3** with a complex game (see diagram 79).

79

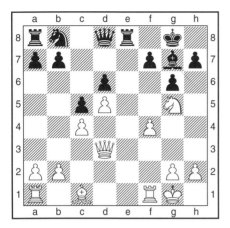

With the seemingly obvious move 14...
♘d7, Black would now invite the strong
attack 15.f5!, which he can, and must avoid
only with 14...h6 (the sacrifice 15.f5 hxg5
16.fxg6 ♗d4+! 17.♔h1 f6 is insufficient).
It is clear that the 'Indian' systems are fully
equivalent to the classical openings and
lead to interesting play.

20th Hour

Specialised Opening Theory (X)

Dutch and Benoni Defences

Apart from the Indian defences, which we
discussed in lesson 19, there are several
others, which try to avoid or delay the
symmetrical move d7–d5. They share the
same fighting character, which presents
both sides with difficult problems. If you
consider yourself the stronger player, you
might want to employ them, because they
increase the tension on the board and
thereby improve Black's chances.

Dutch Defence: 1.d2–d4 f7–f5

A similar method to the one we know from
the Sicilian Defence (1.e2–e4 c7–c5).

There the battle revolves around the
square d4, whereas here it is around the
other central square e4, which Black later
wants to occupy. The Dutch Defence
involves a fundamental risk, because f7–f5
affects the security of the king. Neither
does it further the development of a piece,
whereas c7–c5 makes room for the queen.
The Dutch is thus not a 'fashionable opening', but this does not mean it has been
disproved. The long-standing world champion, Mikhail Botvinnik, liked to use it
during his best period.

What is White's most promising continuation? Combinative players like to employ
the sharp Staunton Gambit (1.d2–d4 f7–f5)
2.e2–e4, in order after 2. ... f5xe4 3.♘b1–
c3 ♘g8–f6 to definitely give up a pawn with
4.f2–f3! (faulty is 3...d5? 4.♕h5+ followed
by 5.♕xd5). If Black captures on f3, the
knight recaptures with pleasant compensation for the pawn. 4. ... d7–d5 seems
best, for example 5.♗c1–g5 ♗c8–f5
6.f3xe4 d5xe4 7.♗f1–c4 ♘b8–c6 with the
intention of castling queenside. Both sides
have chances (see diagram 80).

80

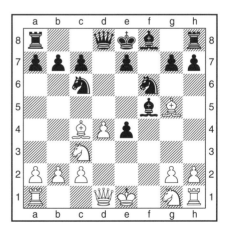

Calm and enduring is the system devised by Wilhelm Steinitz (1836–1900), the first world champion. White prepares, step by step, the advance of his e-pawn: **2.c2–c4 e7–e6 3.e2–e3 ♞g8–f6 4.♝f1–d3**, followed by ♞g1–e2, f2–f3 and e3–e4. Black can try to disturb White's plan by putting pressure on the square d4 and playing 4. ... ♞b8–c6. In a game Teschner–Franz, Riga 1959, the sequel was 5.♞b1–c3 ♝f8–b4 6.♞g1–e2 0-0 7.0-0 b7–b6 (not 7...d6, since after 8.♞b1 the exchange on c3 has been avoided and the bishop at b4 is in danger) 8.f2–f3 d7–d5 9.♛d1–c2 and White threatens 10.c4xd5.

The structure **2.c2–c4 e7–e6 3.g2–g3** is the most common and proved itself in the Bronstein–Botvinnik world championship match, Moscow 1951. The 22nd game continued **3. ... ♞g8–f6 4.♝f1–g2 ♝f8–e7 5.♞b1–c3 0-0 6.e2–e3 d7–d5 7.♞g1–e2** (the contours of the Steinitz system are recognisable) **7. ... c7–c6 8.b2–b3 ♞f6–e4** (see diagram 81).

81

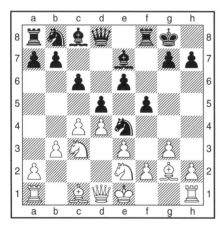

After Black's 8th move

Black has adopted the 'Stonewall' set-up, which is difficult to destroy. After the sequel **9.0-0 ♞b8–d7 10.♝c1–b2 ♞d7–f6** according to Alexander Kotov 11.f2–f3 ♞e4xc3 12.♞e2xc3 with the intention e3–e4 would have been most logical. In any case Black has a difficult life, although White also has to work hard, if he does not want to lose his grip accidentally.

Benoni Defence: 1.d2–d4 c7–c5

Here Black accepts being cramped in the centre. If White goes along with this and plays 2.d4–d5, he allows his opponent certain advantages. Black can open the e-file with e7–e6 (if White captures on e6, this strengthens the black centre); he can develop his king's bishop at g7 and exert pressure on the diagonal up to a1; he also has the possibility of advancing his b-pawn. Finally, he can play e7–e5 as early as the second move, creating a complex position. Modern masters usually turn to the Benoni system only after 1.d2–d4 ♞g8–f6 2.c2–c4 with c7–c5, so that White does not have the chance to restrict the bishop at g7 with a later c2–c3. Occasionally, similar positions can also be reached via the King's Indian, for example after 1.d2–d4 ♞g8–f6 2.c2–c4 g7–g6 3.♞b1–c3 ♝f8–g7 4.e2–e4 d7–d6 5.g2–g3 0-0 6.♝f1–g2 e7–e5 7.d4–d5 c7–c5.
Here are two examples of the opening, with and without the move c2–c4.
Mikhail Botvinnik–Lothar Schmid (Leipzig Olympiad 1960) **1.d2–d4 c7–c5 2.d4–d5 d7–d6 3.e2–e4 g7–g6 4.♞g1–f3 ♝f8–g7 5.♝f1–e2 ♞g8–f6 6.♞b1–c3 ♞b8–a6** A typical manoeuvre. The knight goes to c7, where it controls important squares such as e6, d5 and b5, and supports the advance of the b-pawn. **7.0-0 ♞a6–c7 8.a2–a4 a7–a6 9.♞f3–d2!** If the square c4 is

free, the knight is ideally placed there, aiming at the b6 and d6 squares and supporting e4–e5. According to Schmid, 9…b6 (in order to avoid a4–a5) followed by ♖b8 and b6–b5 would now have been correct. **9. … ♗c8–d7 10.♘d2–c4 b7–b5 11.e4–e5!** (see diagram 82).

82

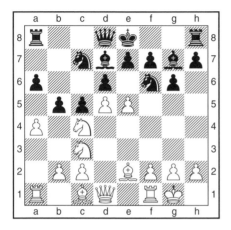

White has seized the initiative and he won in excellent style.

Jonathan Penrose–Mikhail Tal (Leipzig Olympiad 1960) **1.d2–d4 ♘g8–f6 2.c2–c4 e7–e6 3.♘b1–c3 c7–c5** (the Modern Benoni) **4.d4–d5 e6xd5 5.c4xd5 d7–d6 6.e2–e4 g7–g6 7.♗f1–d3** (According to the game Kasparov-Nunn, Lucerne Olympiad 1982, 7.f2–f4 ♗f8–g7 8.♗f1–b5+ ♘f6–d7 9.a2–a4! is advantageous to White.) **7. … ♗f8–g7 8.♘g1–e2** A promising method introduced by the Finnish player Kaarle Ojanen. **8. … 0-0 9.0-0 a7–a6** Here, according to Hans Müller from Vienna, the method used in the earlier section, ♘b8–a6 followed by ♘a6–c7, would have been suitable. **10.a2–a4** (White does not easily allow the move b7–b5.) **10. … ♕d8–c7 11.h2–h3 ♘b8–d7 12.f2–f4 ♖f8–e8 13.♘e2–g3 c5–c4 14.♗d3–c2**

♘d7–c5 15.♕d1–f3 ♘f6–d7 16.♗c1–e3 White managed to carry out the moves e4–e5 and f4–f5, even though this involved a pawn sacrifice: 16…b5 17.axb5 ♖b8 18.♕f2 axb5 19.e5! dxe5 20.f5!. White has opened important lines and gained the e4 square for his knights. The 23–year-old Latvian, who had just become world champion, was unable to repel the attack. All these examples show that deviations from the 'standard' path 1. … d7–d5 increase the danger of errors – for both sides! As Saviely Tartakower put it: 'Mistakes are the spice of chess'.

21st Hour

Specialised Opening Theory (XI)

No Central Pawn

To conclude our discussions on openings, we will look at those which do *not* begin with the double move of one of the two central pawns. Some of them lead to the openings already encountered – the moves simply occur in a different order. Others introduce new ideas, or use methods that have been successfully applied by Black, with an extra move for White.

English Opening: 1.c2–c4

The opening with the c-pawn is nowadays considered equally good as 1.e2–e4 or 1.d2–d4. There are also other openings which should not be regarded as being weaker, such as 1.♘g1–f3 or 1.g2–g3.

With **1.c2–c4** White aims at the central square d5, without disclosing what he intends to do with his valuable central pawns. He gives Black the opportunity to occupy the centre himself with **1. … e7–e5**. White then plays the Sicilian with an extra tempo. Great masters such as Alexander

Alekhine and others considered such an opening to be advantageous to White. After **2.♘b1–c3 ♘g8–f6** White can go into the Bremen Variation with **3.g2–g3**. Black can open up the game with **3. ... d7–d5 4.c4xd5 ♘f6xd5** with the continuation **5.♗f1–g2 ♘d5–b6 6.♘g1–f3 ♘b8–c6 7.0-0 ♗f8–e7 8.d2–d3**, and a position arises which, with colours reversed, corresponds to the Dragon Variation of the Sicilian Defence, but with an extra tempo for White (see diagram 83).

83

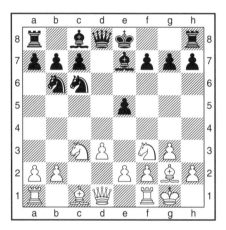

Black has the option of changing direction towards the King's Indian by **3. ... d7–d6 4.♗f1–g2 g7–g6 5.♘g1–f3 ♗f8–g7 6.d2–d4 ♘b8–d7**.

According to the books, a safe method for Black is also to advance his c-pawn two squares. An example is provided by the start of the game Korchnoi–Ftacnik, Ostrava 1994: **1.c2–c4 ♘g8–f6 2.♘b1–c3 c7–c5 3.♘g1–f3 e7–e6 4.g2–g3 b7–b6 5.♗f1–g2 ♗c8–b7 6.0-0 ♗f8–e7 7.♖f1–e1 ♘f6–e4 8.♘c3xe4 ♗b7xe4 9.d2–d3 ♗e4–b7 10.e2–e4 ♘b8–c6 11.d3–d4 c5xd4 12.♘f3xd4 ♘c6xd4 13.♕d1xd4 0-0 14.♗c1–f4** (White could also fianchetto

his queen's bishop and, to this end, play 14.b3, e.g. 14...♗c5 15.♕c3 ♕e7 16.a3 a5 17.♗b2 with good prospects, Vaganian–Yermolinsky, Tilburg 1993.) **14. ... d7–d6 15.♕d4–d3 ♕d8–c7** and White has the more comfortable game.

The reply **1.c2–c4 ♘g8–f6** normally transposes into Indian set-ups. After 2.d2–d4 e7–e6 3.♘b1–c3 ♗f8–b4 we reach the Nimzo-Indian Defence. White can avoid this by playing **2.♘b1–c3 e7–e6 3.e2–e4**. It seems best for Black to respond **3. ... c7–c5**, since although **4.e4–e5 ♘f6–g8** forces the knight back to its initial square, it also leaves holes in the white ranks, as shown in the game Mikenas-Kan, Leningrad 1960: **5.d2–d4 c5xd4 6.♕d1xd4 ♘b8–c6 7.♕d4–e4 d7–d6 8.♘g1–f3 ♕d8–a5 9.e5xd6 ♘g8–f6! 10.♕e4–f4 ♕a5–b4** and Black regains the pawn under favourable circumstances. 10.♕d3 needs to be tested.

The move ♗f8–b4 has, for years, played an important role in the English Opening. Here is an example from world championship candidates match, Vladimir Kramnik–Gata Kamsky, New York 1994 (2nd game): **1.♘g1–f3 ♘g8–f6 2.c2–c4 e7–e6 3.♘b1–c3 ♗f8–b4 4.g2–g3 0-0 5.♗f1–g2 c7–c5 6.0-0 ♘b8–c6 7.d2–d4 c5xd4 8.♘f3xd4 ♕d8–e7 9.♘d4–c2 ♗b4xc3 10.b2xc3 ♖f8–d8 11.♗c1–a3 d7–d6 12.♖a1–b1**. According to *Chess Informator*, this is an innovation; the usual move 12.♕d2 is also good. **12. ... ♕e7–c7** (12...e5 would be dubious, because of 13.♘e3!) **13.♘c2–d4 ♘c6xd4** (if 13...♘e5, then 14.♘b5 ♕xc4 15.♗xd6), and now White should have captured with the queen, when Black would still have had to work hard to equalise (for example 14.♕xd4 e5 15.♕d3 ♗e6 16.♖xb7 ♕xc4 and so on).

1.c2–c4 e7–e6 can transpose into the orthodox Queen's Gambit. After **1.c2–c4**

c7–c6 Slav positions arise (if White plays **2.e2–e4**, after **2. … d7–d5** we reach Caro-Kann Defence!). The universality of the move 1.c2–c4 is extraordinary. Not just for this reason, the aphorist Dr. Tartakower gave it the title 'the strongest opening move in the world'.

Réti Opening:
1.♘g1–f3 d7–d5 2.c2–c4

When Réti's series of moves was introduced into tournament play in the 1920s, it seemed like a reassessment of all values. It is typical of the 'hypermodern' school, which, as here with White, holds back the central pawns. With the black pieces, we can recognise the same idea in the Modern Benoni (1.d2–d4 ♘g8–f6 2.c2–c4 e7–e6 3.♘b1–c3 c7–c5 4.d4–d5), with one tempo less. The cramping **2. … d5–d4** is not without danger, because Black loses time and opens up lines for his better developed opponent. There can follow **3.e2–e3 ♘b8–c6 4.e3xd4! ♘c6xd4 5.♘f3xd4 ♛d8xd4 6.♘b1–c3 c7–c6 7.d2–d3 ♗c8–g4 8.♛d1–a4** (see diagram 84).

84

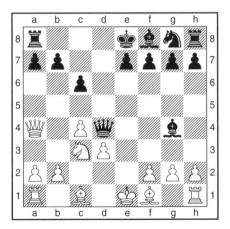

Black will find it hard to prevent White advantageously playing ♗c1–e3 and d3–d4. For this reason Black usually avoids 2. … d5–d4 and makes a neutral move such as c7–c6 or e7–e6.

If Black captures on c4, White can favourably continue 3.♘b1–a3 followed by 4.♘a3xc4. The New York system, introduced by Emanuel Lasker (1868–1941), is more sensible: **2. … c7–c6 3.b2–b3 ♘g8–f6 4.g2–g3 ♗c8–f5 5.♗f1–g2 e7–e6 6.♗c1–b2 ♘b8–d7 7.0-0 h7–h6.** A characteristic of the Réti Opening is the development of both bishops on the wing. Black may also chose a structure similar to the Queen's Gambit, for example **2. … e7–e6 3.g2–g3 ♘g8–f6 4.♗f1–g2 ♗f8–e7 5.0-0 0-0 6.b2–b3 c7–c5 7.c4xd5 ♘f6xd5 8.♗c1–b2 ♘b8–c6**, where White has the opportunity to transpose into the Catalan Queen's Gambit by 6.d2–d4.

All these systems require White to play the move c2–c4. This also applies to the flank opening 1.g2–g3.

Flank Opening: 1.g2–g3

The title 'Korchnoi Opening' would not be out of place, because one of the greatest players of our time, the Swiss grandmaster Victor Korchnoi, originally from St Petersburg (the former Leningrad), has achieved many successes with it. The idea is to make a favourable transposition into systems that lead to a complex game. Thus, for example, after **1.g2–g3 d7–d5 2.♘g1–f3 ♘g8–f6 3.♗f1–g2 c7–c5 4.0-0 e7–e6 5.c2–c4 ♘b8–c6 6.c4xd5 ♘f6xd5 7.d2–d4**

(see diagram 85)

85

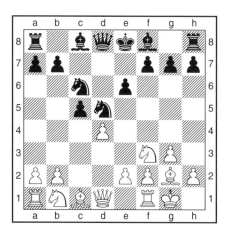

a variation, quite advantageous to White, of the Catalan Queen's Gambit arises. In the game Korchnoi–Teschner, interzonal tournament, Stockholm 1962, after 7...cxd4 8.♘xd4 ♗c5 9.♘xc6 bxc6 10.♘c3 0-0 11.♘a4 ♗b6 12.b3 ♗a6 13.♗a3 ♖e8 14.♕c2 Black was saddled with the weakness of his c6 pawn and had to resign on move 41 (14...♖c8 15.♖fd1 ♕g5 16.e4 ♘f6 17.♗c5 and so on).

A King's Indian set-up arises after **1.g2–g3 ♘g8–f6 2.♗f1–g2 g7–g6 3.e2–e4 d7–d6 4.d2–d4 ♗f8–g7 5.♘g1–e2** (Benkö–Fischer, Curaçao 1962). The following arrangement is called the King's Indian Attack: **1.g2–g3 d7–d5 2.♘g1–f3 g7–g6 3.♗f1–g2 ♗f8–g7 4.0-0 c7–c5 5.d2–d3 ♘b8–c6 6.c2–c3 ♘g8–f6 7.♘b1–d2 0-0 8.e2–e4 e7–e5**, as played in the game Petrosian–Teschner, Stockholm 1962, where White continued with the pawn advance 9.a2–a3 followed by b2–b4.

Bird Opening: 1.f2–f4

The game can also be opened in the style of the Dutch Defence with the double move of the f-pawn. White (as advocated by André Danican Philidor) wants to develop his g1 knight at f3, without blocking the f-pawn. He often follows up with b2–b3 and ♗c1–b2, in order to control the e5 square and enable the bishop to develop its full potential on the long diagonal. An energetic response is the From Gambit **1. ... e7–e5**. If White accepts the pawn sacrifice, Black has attacking chances thanks to his advantage in development **(2.f4xe5 d7–d6 3.e5xd6 ♗f8xd6)**. White can, if he wants, transpose into the King's Gambit with **2.e2–e4**. The play develops more quietly with **1. ... d7–d5 2.♘g1–f3 ♘g8–f6 3.e2–e3** after which Black can take up the fight for the square e5 with 3. ... ♗c8–g4, for example 4.h2–h3 ♗g4xf3 5.♕d1xf3 ♘b8–d7 6.d2–d4 ♘f6–e4 7.♗f1–d3 f7–f5 8.0-0 e7–e6 9.c4–c4 c7–c6. Both sides have chances.

The author hopes to have provided the reader with an understanding of the diverse nature of the opening and at the same time laid the foundations for him to prepare his own programme with the help of these explanations. In practice, it is useful to be prepared for all plausible responses, when playing both White and Black – not least in order to save time for the difficult middlegame.

Table of Openings

A. Open Games: 1. e2–e4 e7–e5

2. f2–f4				**King's Gambit**
2. …	e5xf4			King's Gambit Accepted
		3. ♘g1–f3		King's Knight's Gambit
		3. … d7–d5	4. e4xd5 ♘g8–f6	
		3. ♗f1–c4		King's Bishop's Gambit
		3. … ♘g8–f6	4. ♘b1–c3 c7–c6!	
2. …	♗f8–c5			King's Gambit Declined
		3. ♘g1–f3 d7–d6	4. ♘b1–c3 ♘g8–f6	
2. …	d7–d5			Falkbeer Counter-Gambit
		3. e4xd5 e5–e4	4. d2–d3 ♘g8–f6	
2. ♘b1–c3				**Vienna Game**
2. …	♘g8–f6	3. f2–f4 d7–d5	4. f4xe5 ♘f6xe4	
2. d2–d4				**Centre Game**
2. …	e5xd4	3. ♕d1xd4 ♘b8–c6 4. ♕d4–e3 ♘g8–f6		
		3. ♘g1–f3		**Centre Gambit**
		3. … ♘b8–c6	4. c2–c3	**Göring Gambit**
			4. … ♘g8–f6	5. e4–e5 ♘f6–e4
2. ♗f1–c4				**Bishop's Opening**
2. …	♘g8–f6	3. d2–d3 ♗f8–c5	4. ♘g1–f3 d7–d6	
2. ♘g1–f3				**King's Knight's Game**
2. …	♘g8–f6			**Petroff Defence**
		3. ♘f3xe5 d7–d6	4. ♘e5–f3 ♘f6xe4	
		3. d2–d4 e5xd4	4. e4–e5 ♘f6–e4	5. ♕d1xd4 d7–d5
2. …	d7–d6			**Philidor Defence**
		3. d2–d4 ♘b8–d7		Hanham Variation
			4. ♗f1–c4 c7–c6!	5. c2–c3 (or 5. 0–0, or 5. ♘b1–c3)
2. …	f7–f5			**Latvian Gambit**
		3. ♘f3xe5 ♕d8–f6	4. ♘e5–c4 f5xe4	5. ♘b1–c3
2. …	d7–d5			**Queen's Pawn Counter-Gambit**
		3. ♘f3xe5 d5xe4	4. ♗f1–c4 ♕d8–g5	5. ♗c4xf7+
2. …	f7–f6?	3. ♘f3xe5		**Damiano Defence**
2. …	♘b8–c6	3. ♗f1–c4 ♘g8–f6		**Two Knights Defence**
		3. … ♗f8–c5		**Giuoco Piano**
			4. c2–c3 ♘g8–f6	5. d2–d4 e5xd4 6. c3xd4 ♗c5–b4+
			4. b2–b4	**Evans Gambit**
			4. … ♗c5xb4 5. c2–c3	Accepted
			4. … ♗c5–b6	Declined
		3. d2–d4		**Scotch Game**
		3. … e5xd4	4. ♘f3xd4 ♘g8–f6	
			4. ♗f1–c4	Scotch Gambit
			4. … ♘g8–f6	5. 0–0 ♘f6xe4

3. ♘b1–c3 ♘g8–f6	**Four Knights Game**
3. c2–c3	**Ponziani Opening**
3. ... ♘g8–e7 4. d2–d4 e5xd4 5. c3xd4 d7–d5!	
3. ♗f1–b5	**Ruy Lopez / Spanish Game**
3. ... a7–a6	Morphy Defence
3. ... ♘g8–f6	Berlin Defence
3. ... d7–d6	Steinitz Defence

B. Half–open Games: 1. e2–e4 not e7–e5

1. ... e7–e6		**French Defence**
2. d2–d4 d7–d5 3. e4xd5		Exchange Variation
3. ♘b1–c3 ♗f8–b4		Winawer Variation
3. ... d5xe4		Rubinstein Variation
3. ... ♘g8–f6		Classical Variation
3. ♘b1–d2		Tarrasch Variation
3. ... ♘g8–f6	4. e4–e5	
3. ... c7–c5	4. e4xd5	
3. e4–e5		Advance Variation
3. ... c7–c5	4. c2–c3 ♘b8–c6	
1. ... c7–c5		**Sicilian Defence**
2. ♘b1–c3		Closed Variation
2. ... ♘b8–c6 3. g2–g3 g7–g6		
2. ♘g1–f3 e7–e6 3. d4 cxd4 4. ♘xd4 ♘f6 5. ♘c3 d6		Scheveningen Variation
2. ... d7–d6 3. d2–d4 c5xd4 4. ♘xd4 ♘f6 5. ♘c3 a6		Najdorf Variation
2. ... d7–d6 3. d2–d4 c5xd4 4. ♘xd4 ♘f6 5. ♘c3 g6		Dragon Variation
2. ... ♘b8–c6 3. d4 cxd4 4. ♘xd4 ♘f6 5. ♘c3 d6 6. ♗g5		Richter-Rauzer Attack
2. ... ♘g8–f6		Rubinstein Variation
3. e4–e5 ♘f6–d5	4. ♘b1–c3 e7–e6	
1. ... d7–d5		**Scandinavian Defence**
2. e4xd5 ♛d8xd5 3. ♘b1–c3 ♛d5–a5 4. d2–d4		
2. ... ♘g8–f6		Gambit Variation
3. c2–c4 c7–c6		
1. ... c7–c6		**Caro-Kann Defence**
2. d2–d4 d7–d5 3. ♘b1–c3 d5xe4 4. ♘c3xe4 ♗c8–f5		Classical Variation
3. e4xd5 c6xd5	4. c2–c4	Panov Attack
	4. ♗f1–d3	Exchange Variation
3. e4–e5 ♗c8–f5		Advance Variation
1. ... ♘g8–f6		**Alekhine Defence**
2. e4–e5 ♘f6–d5 3. c2–c4 ♘d5–b6 4. d2–d4 d7–d6 5. f2–f4		Four Pawns Attack
3. d2–d4 d7–d6 4. ♘f3 ♗g4 5. ♗e2		Modern Variation
1. ... d7–d6		**Pirc Defence**
2. d2–d4 ♘g8–f6 3. ♘b1–c3 g7–g6		
1. ... g7–g6		**Modern Defence**
2. d2–d4 ♗f8–g7		

C. Closed Games: Not 1. e2–e4

1. d2–d4 d7–d5 2. ♘g1–f3	**Queen's Pawn Game**
2. ... ♘g8–f6 3. e2–e3 c7–c5 4. c2–c3	**Colle Variation**
2. c2–c4	**Queens Gambit**
2. ... d5xc4	Queens Gambit Accepted
2. ... e7–e6 3. ♘b1–c3 ♘g8–f6	Orthodox Defence
2. ... c7–c6	Slav Defence
2. ... e7–e5	Albin Counter-Gambit
3. d4xe5 d5–d4	
2. ... ♘b8–c6	Chigorin Defence
3. ♘b1–c3! d5xc4 4. ♘g1–f3	
2. ... ♘g8–f6	Marshall defence
3. c4xd5 ♘f6xd5 4. ♘g1–f3	
2. ♘b1–c3	**Veresov Opening**
2. ... ♘g8–f6 3. ♗c1–g5	
2. e2–e4	**Blackmar-Diemer Gambit**
2. ... d5xe4 3. ♘b1–c3 ♘g8–f6 4. f2–f3	
1. ... ♘g8–f6	**Indian Defence**
2. c2–c4 g7–g6 3. ♘b1–c3 ♗f8–g7	**King's Indian Defence**
3. ... d7–d5	**Grünfeld Defence**
2. ... e7–e6 3. ♘b1–c3 ♗f8–b4	**Nimzo-Indian Defence**
3. ♘g1–f3 b7–b6	**Queen's Indian Defence**
2. ... e7–e5	**Budapest Defence**
3. d4xe5 ♘f6–g4 4. ♗c1–f4	
3. ... ♘f6–e4 4. ♕d1–c2!	Leipzig Variation
1. ... f7–f5	**Dutch Defence**
1. ... c7–c5	**Benoni Defence**
1 ... ♘g8–f6 2. c2–c4 c7–c5	**Modern Benoni**
1. ... e7–e5?!	**Englund Gambit**
1. ... ♘b8–c6	**Nimzowitsch Defence**
1. ♘g1–f3 d7–d5 2. c2–c4	**Zukertort-Réti Opening**
1. c2–c4	**English Opening**
1. ... e7–e5 2. ♘b1–c3 ♘g8–f6 3. g2–g3	Bremen Variation
3. ♘g1–f3 ♘b8–c6	English Four Knights
1. f2–f4	**Bird Opening**
1. ... e7–e5	**From Gambit**
1. ... d7–d5 2. ♘g1–f3 c7–c5	**Dutch for White**
1. b2–b4	**Sokolsky/Orang-Utan Opening**
1. ... ♘g8–f6 2. ♗c1–b2 e7–e6 3. b4–b5 d7–d5	

Chess Tactics

22nd Hour

Combinations (I)

Having looked at the basic principles of the game of chess and the most important openings, we will now discuss the various types of combinations, which occur in all phases of the game almost automatically. Again and again a player will come across certain types of formations, which have already occurred in a similar form. The more 'standard combinations' you know and the better you are able to apply them to a given situation, the better you will play.

Pins

Many combinations are of a geometrical nature – especially the pin, which we will examine first. It is actually a special form of the double attack (see 23rd Hour) and can occur when two pieces of the same side are on the same file, rank or diagonal, which is controlled by an enemy long-range piece (queen, rook or bishop). The piece which is under direct attack physically protects the piece standing behind it, which is either very valuable or unprotected.

In diagram 86, we see a standard type of pin. It would be bad to attack the knight with 1.f2–f4?, because it responds with the fork 1. ... ♘e5–f3+ and wins the bishop, since the king has to move. Correct is **1.♗d2–c3**. The knight is attacked and simultaneously pinned. If the king protects it with **1. ... ♔g7–f6**, it will be attacked again by **2.f2–f4** and won.

86

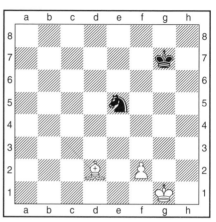

A similar situation arises in diagram 87. As in the previous example, the immediate attack 1.f2–f3? would be completely unsuitable, since the knight does not hesitate to move to f2 and win the rook. A practised player will first pin the knight before trying to win it, i.e. **1.♖d3–e3 f7–f5 2.f2–f3.**

87

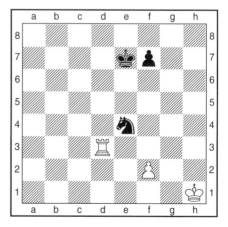

If it is not the king that is protected by the pinned piece, but any other piece or pawn, the pin is 'artificial' and its existence is conditional.

88

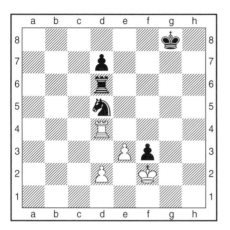

89

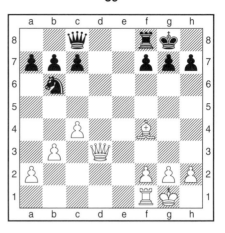

In diagram 88, it would be wrong for White to rely on the 'pin' and try to win the knight with 1.e3–e4?. Black replies 1. ... ♘d5–f6! and laughs at White. The black rook is protected indirectly because of the knight fork on e4 (2.♖d4xd6 ♘f6xe4+ 3.♔f2xf3 ♘e4xd6). White should prepare the attack with **1.d2–d3!** (the pawn protects the square e4 as a precaution). Black has no way of protecting the rook at d6 or moving it to safety. One move later, 2.e3–e4 will indeed win the knight. If the pawn at f3 were not there, Black could avoid the pin by giving check with his rook on f6, before moving the knight to safety.

In diagram 89, White can make use of the strong move **1.♕d3–g3**. He attacks the pawn at c7 a second time, but more importantly he pins the g7 pawn. Because the white queen is on the same file as the black king, the g7 pawn can only move

forwards, but is unable to capture (one square diagonally in front). If Black saves his c7 pawn and plays **1. ... c7–c6**, then **2.♗f4–h6** exploits the situation. As a consequence of the attack on g7, the white queen threatens to checkmate on this square. Black has to reply **2. ... g7–g6** and allow his rook at f8 to be captured by the bishop. He has lost the 'exchange' (see page 16).

It is always dangerous when a long-range enemy piece is on the same file as the king (and often also the queen). In such circumstances, you should always move out of the way with the valuable piece, so in this case play 1. ... ♔g8–h8 and abandon the c7 pawn.

Another example of this can be found in diagram 90. The black king is in an unfavourable position in more than one sense. It is on the same file as the rook at f1 and consequently the f5 pawn is pinned. The king is also, and this is less perceptible, on the same diagonal as the white queen.

90

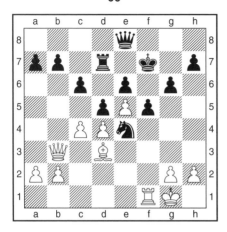

With **1.c4xd5** White achieves a decisive advantage. After **1. ... e6xd5? 2.♗d3xe4** he would win the black knight, as both protecting pawns have been put out of action. It would be just as wrong to insert 1. ... ♘e4–d2, because White can interpose the check 2.d5xe6+. The lesser evil would be 1. ... c6xd5. White then pins the rook with 2.♗d3–b5 and wins the exchange. 2. ... ♘e4–d2 would not change anything, because 3.♕b3–a4 attacks the rook a second time.

91

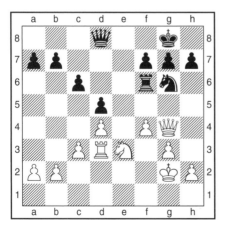

The pin in diagram 91 is quite well hidden (similar situations occur quite often in practice). Black achieves a decisive material gain with **1. ... ♘g6xf4+!**. Because White does not want to lose the rook on d3, he has to give up his queen after **2.g3xf4 ♖f6–g6**. The advantage gained (Black wins queen and pawn for rook and knight), is sufficient to win the game.

92

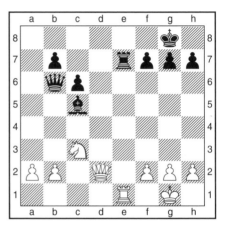

In diagram 92 the threatened white pieces, the rook on e1 and the pawn on f2, are protected, but with **1. ... ♗c5xf2+!** the queen is forced into a pin, **2.♕d2xf2**, so that **2. ... ♖e7xe1** achieves checkmate.

Diagram 93 shows the effectiveness of a 'cross-pin'. The only way for Black to defend simultaneously against mate on g7 and the threatened, unprotected rook on b2 is with **1. ... ♕a5–e5**. But after **2.♖f1–e1!** the queen is stretched to the limit. It is pinned on the e-file as well as the diagonal and is lost.

93

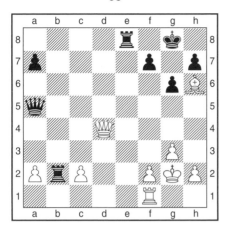

Diagram 94 is taken from a game Alexander–Krummhauer, Berlin 1951. It shows that it sometimes takes imagination to recognise a pin in the planning stages.

94

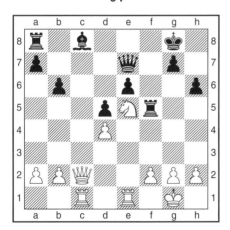

Imagine this position without the white knight, and you will see that the e6 pawn is pinned (the unprotected black queen is on same file as the white rook) and thus ♕c2xf5 is possible. Knowing this, White continues **1.♘e5–g6** (1.♘e5–c6 would be

equally effective) **1. ... ♕e7–f6 2.♘g6– e7+! ♕f6xe7 3.♕c2xf5**. As R. Urschel discovered, there is an equally good 'alternative solution': 1.♕xc8+ ♖xc8 2.♖xc8+ ♖f8 (2...♔h7 3.♖h8+ ♔xh8 4.♘g6+) 3.♘g6 ♕g5 4 ♖xf8+ ♔h7 5.♘f4 and wins easily.

Sometimes a pin is used simply to make a certain square available for a piece. In diagram 95 White sacrifices his queen, so that his knight can reach g6 without harm.

95

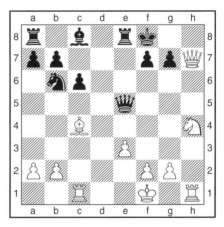

1.♕h7–g8+! ♔f8xg8 (Black has to resign himself to 1...♔e7 2.♕xf7+ ♔d8 3.♖d1+ ♗d7 4.♘g6, if he does not want to be mated immediately) **2.♘h4–g6** and Black resigns. Because the f7 pawn is now pinned, the knight is untouchable. Black can only delay, but not avoid, mate by the rook on h8 (Abrahams–Thynne, Liverpool 1930). A similar development occurred in England a second time two years later (see diagram 155).

To conclude, diagram 96 demonstrates one of the most famous combinations in chess literature, in which White used the

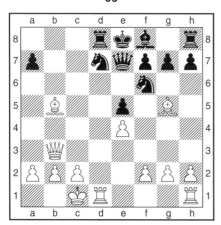

96

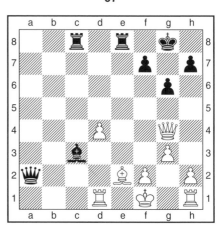

97 ✓

pinning effect of his two bishops in order to mobilise his reserves as quickly as possible (Morphy–Consultants, Paris 1858): **1.♖d1xd7! ♖d8xd7 2.♖h1–d1 ♕e7–e6** (neither would 2…♕b4 save the situation, as shown by 3.♗xf6 gxf6 [3…♕xb3? 4.♗xd7 mate] 4.♗xd7+ ♔d8 5.♕xf7) **3.♗b5xd7+ ♘f6xd7 4.♕b3–b8+! ♘d7xb8 5.♖d1–d8** mate. A problem-like finish. White is left with only the two pieces he needs to give checkmate.

23rd Hour

Combinations (II)
Double Attacks

So-called 'double attacks' are among the most common combinations, from which no player, despite constant vigilance, can ever be completely safe. Even great masters fall victim to them every now and again, especially when they are tired after a difficult fight or are short of time.

Diagram 97 is taken from the game Keres–Fischer, Candidates Tournament, Yugoslavia 1959. This illustration may serve as a warning, not to leave any piece unguarded, wherever possible, or to move it to an unprotected square. The Estonian grandmaster Paul Keres wanted to connect his rooks by moving his king to g2, but the bishop on e2 is 'hanging'. Correct would be a move such as 1.♗e2–f3 or first 1.d4–d5. White decided to move his bishop away from the attack with gain of tempo and so he threatened the rook on e8: **1.♗e2–b5?** But this lost a piece to the reply **1. …♕a2–d5!** when he had to lay down his arms immediately. A shocking mistake with fatal consequences for the course of the tournament.

No. 98 shows a double attack as a geometrical pattern. White forces the two enemy pieces onto the same diagonal or file. **1.♗h7–g8+!** winning the queen in three variations: **1. … ♕e8xg8 2.♕b4–b3+** (this type of double attack is also called a 'skewer'), or **1. … ♔d5–c6 2.♕b4–a4+**, or **1. … ♔d5–e5 2.♕b4–e1+**.

98

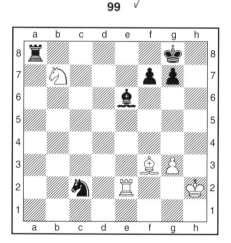

This is the end phase of a study by Alexey Troitsky from *Shakhmatny Zhurnal*, 1898: White: ♔h2, ♕b3, ♗g8 – Black: ♔e4, ♕e8. After 1.♗h7+ ♔d4 (1...♔f4 2.♕g3 mate) 2.♕b4+ ♔d5 (2...♔e3 or 2...♔e5 3.♕e1+) we arrive at the position in diagram 98.

99

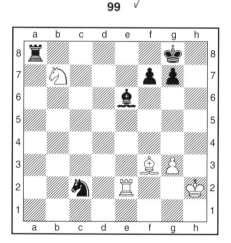

Sometimes one double attack prepares a decisive second attack, as in diagram 99 (Réti–Alekhine, Baden-Baden 1925). **1. ... ♘c2–d4 2.♖e2–f2** (the lesser evil was 2.♖xe6) **2. ... ♘d4xf3+ 3.♖f2xf3 ♗e6–d5**,

with a bishop fork: White loses his knight, because his pieces are so awkwardly placed that they cannot protect each other. Double attacks are most frequently overlooked when they are preceded by a pseudo-sacrifice, similar to the situation in No. 98.

100

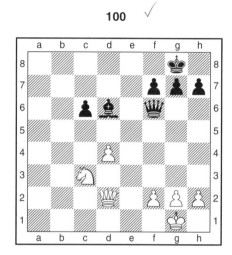

Diagram 100 shows a schematic example. **1.♘c3–e4?** allows a textbook development, in which Black wins a pawn because the knight is standing on an unprotected square: **1. ... ♗d6xh2+ 2.♔h1xh2 ♕f6–h4+ 3.♔h2–g1 ♕h4xe4**. Black created the second point of attack for his queen with the sacrifice of the bishop.

In No. 101 (Tal–Petrosian, Candidates Tournament, Curaçao 1962), White provided the opponent with an opportunity for a double attack with his last move ♖a1–a2? (played in order to protect the a-pawn once again by ♖d1–a1): **1. ... ♖a4xc4!** wins the bishop, because for his own rook Black wins the enemy rook on a2 after 2.♕d3xc4 ♗c6–d5.

101

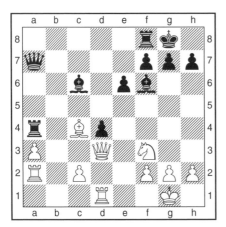

Tactical developments, which cannot be clearly visualised up to the end, are better left alone. Thus in No.102 it is tempting to win a pawn with the help of two pseudo-sacrifices.

102

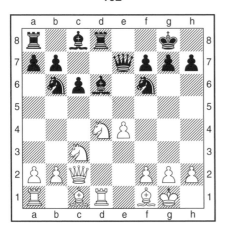

1. ... &d6xh2+ 2.&g1xh2 &d8xd4 3.&d1xd4 &e7–e5+ and Black recovers the sacrificed material with interest. However, because Black exposes his back rank and the rook on a8 is not involved, the situation is unclear if White displays his presence of mind with **4.&c1–f4!**, for example 4. ... &e5xd4 (after 4...&xf4+ 5.&g1 White threatens mate on d8 and is the exchange up) 5.&a1–d1 &g6–g4+ 6.&h2–g1 &d4–f6 7.f2–f3 g7–g5 8.&f4–c1 with chances for both sides.

103

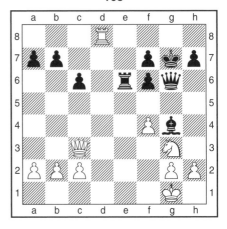

No. 103 is taken from the game Chigorin–Janowski, Paris 1900. The threat of checkmating on f8, for example with 1.&c3–a3, could be averted by 1. ... f6–f5. White therefore looks for a double threat and he begins with the pawn fork **1.f4–f5! &g4xf5**. With this he has created a second vulnerable point on f5, so that now **2.&c3–c5** is instantly conclusive due to the double attack on f8 and f5.

The double attack in No.104 is created extremely effectively. Especially peculiar is the fact that the combination is based on a knight fork, although as yet there is no knight on the board. The passed pawn on b7 has been chosen for the task.

104

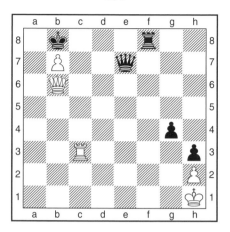

White first directs the black rook so that the pawn can be promoted, then diverts the king away from the promotion square and into the fork: **1.♖c3–c8+! ♖f8xc8 2.♕b6–a7+! ♔b8xa7** (futile is 2...♔c7 3.bxc8♕+) **3.b7xc8♘+!** White regains first the rook and then the queen; after this he eliminates the black pawns and wins by promoting the h-pawn as well.

105

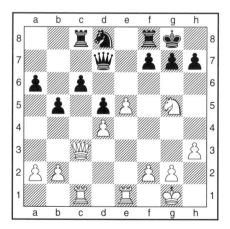

No. 105 shows the cunning employed in master chess (Boleslavsky–Flohr, Candi-

dates Tournament, Budapest 1950). 1.♕c3–a3 looks good because it attacks not only the a6 pawn, but also the rook at f8. The h7 pawn is threatened by this, since the king cannot protect h7 and f8 simultaneously. But 1. ... h7–h6! is sufficient to avert the double threat. Well, what if the f6 square were accessible to the knight that is heading for h7... and thus the idea for a combination is born. **1.♕c3–d3!** threatens mate on h7. Black replied **1. ... g7–g6** (1...f5 2.♕a3! with the threat of 3.e6), and now the double attack came into force: **2.♕d3–a3!** White wins the a6 pawn because 2...h6? is a mistake due to 3.♘h7! ♔xh7 (now necessary because of the danger of a check by the knight on f6) 4.♕xf8. If 2...♘e6, then 3.♘xe6 fxe6 4.♕xa6 with the superior game.

106

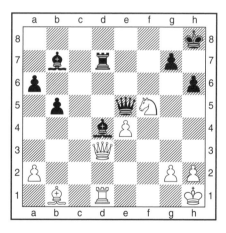

A classic example of a missed opportunity can be seen in No.106 (from Popiel–Marco, Monte Carlo 1902). Black, to move, resigned the game. He thought that the bishop on d4 was pinned and beyond saving because of the unprotected rook on d7. However, with the 'cunning' double attack 1. ... ♗d4–g1! he could have won the game immediately. White would be unable to respond adequately to both the threat of checkmate on h2 and the rook's attack on the d-file. 2.♔h1xg1 ♖d7xd3 3.♗b1xd3 ♗b7xe4 is hopeless.

107

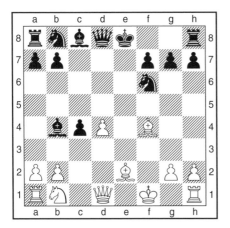

It can also happen that a planned fork is thwarted with the help of a counter-fork, as shown in No.107 (Tartakower–Capablanca, New York 1924). 1.♕d1–a4+, with a simultaneous attack on king and bishop, is futile because of 1. ... ♘b8–c6. White plays **1.♗f4xb8** and hopes to regain the previously sacrificed piece with a subsequent queen check on a4. But with the 'zwischenzug' (in-between move) **1. ... ♘f6–d5!** Black kills two birds with one stone: he protects the bishop at b4 and also threatens a knight fork on e3! 2.♗b8–f4, in order to still reach the goal after 2. ... ♘d5xf4? 3.♕d1–a4+, is insufficient because of 2. ... ♕d8–f6! (...♘e3+ is again threatened, because the bishop is pinned, so that the doubly attacked bishop at f4 is lost). White had to abandon his conquest and play **2.♔f1–f2 ♖a8xb8** and he soon had to resign.
The wonderful diversity of chess!

24th Hour

Combinations (III)
Overloaded Pieces

We have seen that unprotected pieces often present points of attack for the opponent. Frequently, they invite pins or double attacks (see 22nd and 23rd Hours). However, if you now think that protection also means security, you will be disappointed. Protecting pieces are often overloaded. Moreover, they can be removed or diverted.

108

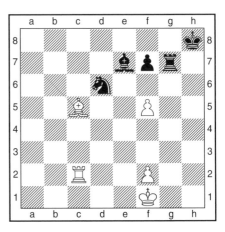

We will take a look at a colourful and varied selection of possibilities. In diagram 108 (White to move) Black loses his knight. Although the bishop is protecting it, after **1.f5–f6** it becomes clear that it is overloaded. Black is left with the choice of giving up his knight, bishop or rook.

Diagram 109 (White to move) shows a frequently occurring situation. The black king is supposedly protecting the queen,

109

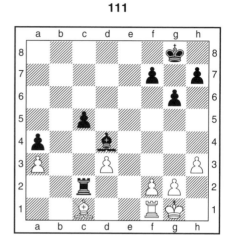

but it can no longer attend to its duty after **1.♖h5–h8+,** a combination aimed at diverting it.

110

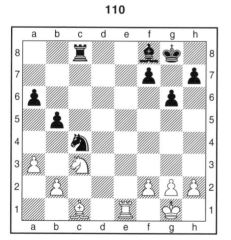

Black to move

In No.110 at first sight the white queen's wing seems well protected. In reality, though, the white pawn on b2 is over-

loaded: it cannot defend both the a3 pawn and the knight at the same time.

1. ... ♘c4xa3! wins a pawn. The rook's line of attack was originally hidden.

111

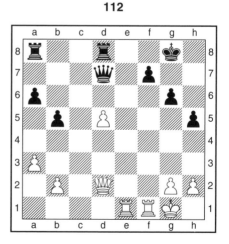

Black to move

In No.111 the white rook is overloaded. It is unable to simultaneously protect both the bishop and the f2 pawn. Black exploits the situation with **1. ... ♗d4xf2+.**

112

Black to move

Example 112 is more complicated. Consider the following: is Black well advised to capture the white pawn on d5 with his queen? No! Because after **1. ... ♛d7xd5? 2.♖e1–e8+!** he will lose either the queen for a rook (2. ... ♖d8xe8 3.♛d2xd5) or a rook without compensation (2. ... ♚g8–g7 3.♛d2xd5 ♖d8xd5 4.♖e8xa8).

113

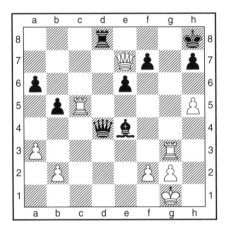

White to move

No.113 is also complicated. The reasoning behind White's next move becomes clear only after the functions of each piece are understood. They are precisely defined because the king is in dire need of protection.

The black queen has to defend the f6 square (against ♛e7–f6 mate) and also keep an eye on the rook on d8. This rook is tied to the eighth rank because it cannot allow ♛e7–f8 mate. Based on these links, the move **1.♖c5–d5!** becomes clear, presenting Black with insoluble problems (from a game Eliskases–Hölzl, Innsbruck 1931). In this case several combinative motifs are linked. There is also no adequate defence against 1.♖c5–e5.

Sometimes it is sufficient to disrupt the line of movement of the protecting piece with gain of tempo, as in diagram 114. Black thinks that he can grab the pawn on e4; however, this pawn is 'poisoned'.

114

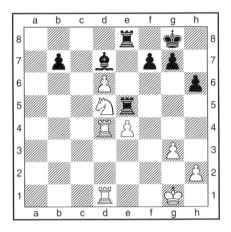

Black to move

This becomes evident straight away: **1. ... ♖e5xe4? 2.♘d5–e7+!**, and Black has to capture the knight, if he does not want to abandon the rook on e4 without compensation. In addition to this misfortune, the bishop is under a double attack after **2. ... ♖e4xe7 3.d6xe7**, so that the dangerous passed pawn remains on the board.

This example points out an important fact, of which we are often made aware: the placing of the kings has to be taken into account in all deliberations. If a threat of being checked is overlooked, this can have fatal consequences.

In No. 115 Black has just attacked the white pawn on b2 with the rook. How should we protect it?

115

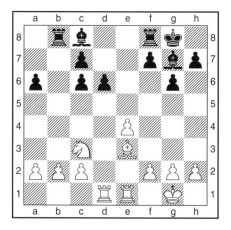

White to move

We have to consider whether the defending piece is able to take over the pawn's role of defending the knight, in case the pawn is captured. Bad would be **1.♖d1–b1?**, as Black will nevertheless play **1. … ♖b8xb2**, and after **2.♖b1xb2 ♗g7xc3** he regains with interest the temporarily sacrificed material (pawn advantage). Correct would thus be 1.♗e3–c1 (but not 1.♘c3–a4? ♖b8–b4).

116

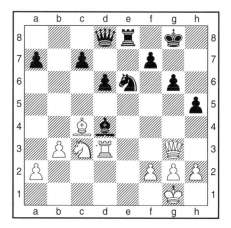

White to move

In example 116 White has to be careful not to be tempted into making a big kill by exchanging the defending piece. He would come off badly after 1.♗c4xe6 ♖e8xe6 2.♖d3xd4 ♖e6–e1 mate: his king lacks a 'safety valve'.

Correct, on the contrary, is **1.♖d3xd4 ♘e6xd4**, since after the knight has been moved, suddenly the f7 pawn is pinned. The sequel could be: **2.♕g3xg6+ ♔g8–h8** (not 2...♔f8? 3.♕xf7 mate) **3.♕g6xh5+ ♔h8–g7 4.♕h5–g4+ ♔g7–f8 5.♕g4xd4**. The important point is that, although the white king still lacks a 'safety valve', 5...♖e1+ can be answered by 6.♗f1.

117

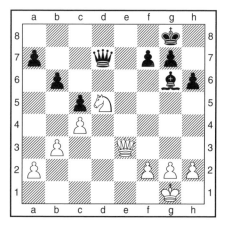

Before deciding on a combination, we have to make sure that it does not have a 'hole'. In No.117 White wrongly thought that the pawn on g7 was momentarily 'overloaded' because of the knight fork on f6, and he hoped to win a pawn with **1.♕e3xh6?** (1...gxh6 2.♘f6+ ♔g7 3.♘xd7). White's combination would be correct if he had a pawn on d3 and his h2 pawn was at h4, because then after 1...♕xd5 the reply 2.♕xg6 would be possible! In this case, however, Black turns the tables by replying

1. ... ♕d7xd5!, when White loses a piece. Mate at d1 is threatened, and therefore he has no time for a 'zwischenzug'.

118

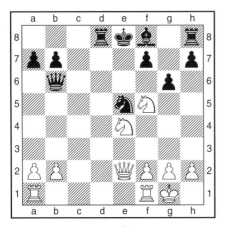

A typical Alekhine combination is shown in diagram 118 (Alekhine–Kussman, New York 1924), White to move. Alekhine, who became world champion in 1927, played this game blindfold together with 25 others and set a world record.

White perceives that the b5 square is only apparently protected, since the black queen has to prevent the check by the knight on f6. This gives him the opportunity for an impressive finish: **1.♕e2–b5+! ♞e5–d7** (1...♕xb5? 2.♞f6 mate) **2.♖f1–e1!** (threatening double check and mate on f6 or d6) **2. ... ♝f8–b4** (there is no escape) **3.♞e4–f6+ ♚e8–f8 4.♞f6xd7+ ♖d8xd7 5.♕b5–e5**, threatening mate on h8, g7 and e8.

These examples should help to sharpen the reader's eye for making his own combinations. An important question remains unanswered: 'How do you achieve such positions?' This will be discussed in the section dealing with chess strategy.

25th Hour

Combinations (IV)
Imprisoned Pieces

A fundamental principle in chess is this: 'Position your pieces as flexibly as possible!' At every move it is advisable to check whether there is a danger that a piece may be closed in or cut off.

119

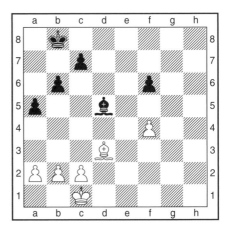

Black to move

This is especially important when a piece enters the opponent's camp. Before deciding on such an advance, you should make sure that the piece will be able to return safely. Particularly vulnerable in this respect are the bishop and the queen, but neither the rook nor the knight are impervious to imprisonment.

A simple case is illustrated in diagram 119. Black should not play **1. ... ♝d5xa2**, because his bishop would be prevented from returning home after **2.b2–b3!**. Sending the a-pawn to assist does not change much either: after **2. ... a5–a4 3.♚c1–b2** a4xb3 4.c2xb3 ♗a2xb3 5.♔b2xb3 with two pawns against a bishop Black is on the road to defeat.

120

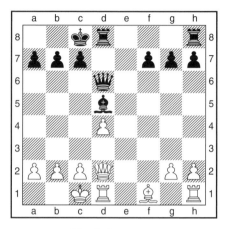

Black to move

You should, however, avoid stereotyped play in chess. In diagram 120 **1. ... ♗d5xa2** is strong, since the imprisonment **2.b2–b3??** is not feasible due to **2. ... ♕d6–a3** mate. Nor is the counter-attack 2.♕d2–a5 any use because of 2. ... ♕d6–f4+ 3.♖d1–d2 ♖d8xd4 4.♗f1–d3 ♖d4–a4.

121

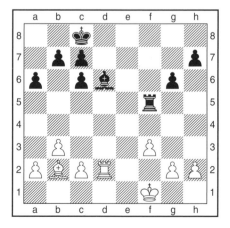

The same idea of imprisonment plays a role in diagram 121 (Réti–Spielmann, Vienna 1914). Here the white h2 pawn is under attack. The instinctive safety move 1.h3 would allow 1...♗g3. **1.♔f1–f2!** protects the h2 pawn indirectly. Black cannot reply 1...♗xh2, as 2.g3! traps the bishop. After this the king threatens to capture it, for example 2...♖h5 3.♔g2 and the bishop is untenable. White plays ♖d1 followed by ♖h1. 2...♖g5 is also no good. White can simply parry the attack against g3 with the indirect rook exchange 3.♖d8+! ♔xd8 4.♗f6+, and then capture the bishop (not quite so good is 3.♗f6?! ♗xg3+ 4.♔g2 ♗f4+ 5.♔xg5 ♗xg5). In the actual game Black tried to gain compensation on the queen's wing But White rebuffed him there as well. There followed:

1. ... ♖f5–a5 2.a2–a4 ♖a5–h5 3.h2–h3 (now ...♗g3 has been prevented) **3. ... b7–b5 4.♗b2–c3 ♖h5–h4** (Black tries to persuade his opponent to exchange on b5, in order to 'undouble' the c-pawn.) **5.g2–g4!** Réti plays the endgame resourcefully and prudently. Now 5. ... ♖h4xh3? 6.♖d2xd6! c7xd6 (or 6...♖h2+ 7.♔g3 ♖xc2 8.♖d3!) 7.♔f2–g2 ♖h3–h6 8.♗c3–g7 ♖h6–h4 9.♗g7–f6 ♖h4–h6 10.♗f6–g5 would have cost a piece. Spielmann defends himself very skilfully, but he cannot prevent the white pawn majority from eventually asserting itself on the king's wing. **5. ... ♗d6–f4 6.♖d2–d8+ ♔c8xd8** (6...♔c8–b7 7.♔f2–g2 g6–g5 8.♗c3–g7 h7–h5 9.♖d8–h8! leads to a hopeless endgame) **7. ♗c3–f6+ ♔d8–d7 8.♗f6xh4**, and White, who practically possesses an extra pawn, wins.

122

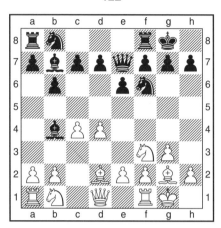

123

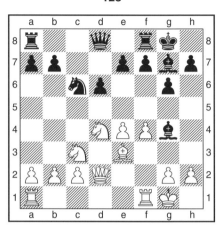

Black to move

A bishop can be in danger not only on the edge of the board. In diagram 122 (Teschner–Unzicker, German Championship, Essen 1948), White selects the black bishop on b4 as a target, by avoiding the exchange and playing **1.♗d2–c1!**. Now Black has to reckon with the threat of being cut off with 2.c4–c5 b6xc5 3.a2–a3 ♗b4–a5 4.d4xc5 followed by b2–b4. His best reply would have been 1...d5 2.c5 bxc5 3.a3 ♗a5 4. dxc5 c6 5.♗f4 ♗c7. In the game, the following happened: **1. ... ♕e7–d8 2.c4–c5 b6xc5 3.a2–a3 ♗b4–a5 4.d4xc5**. With **4. ... c7–c6** he saved the bishop, but the black position is disorganised (Unzicker saved the game only thanks to a great defensive effort).

The situation is very similar in diagram 123 (after the opening moves 1.e4 c5 2.♘f3 ♘c6 3.d4 cxd4 4.♘xd4 ♘f6 5.♘c3 d6 6.♗e2 g6 7.♗e3 ♗g7 8.0-0 0-0 9.♕d2 ♘g4 10.♗xg4 ♗xg4 11.f4).

White threatens 12.f4–f5! g6xf5 13.h2–h3 ♗g4–h5 14.e4xf5 with advantage. Black's simplest reply is **11. ... ♘c6xd4 12.♗e3xd4 e7–e5 13.♗d4–e3 e5xf4 14.♖f1xf4 ♗g4–e6.**

How a knight can be trapped by a bishop, if it has ventured too far forward and is lingering near the edge of the board, is illustrated in diagram 124.

124

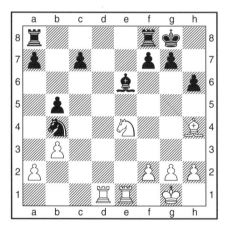

Black is relying on the fact that he can answer the fork **1.♗h4–e7** with **1. ... ♘b4–c2**. White, however, has planned further ahead – he intends to capture the knight (Sanguinetti–Eliskases, Buenos Aires 1962).

2. ♗e7xf8 ♘c2xe1 3.♗f8–c5! The knight is in a straight-jacket. **3. ... ♘e1–c2 4.♖d1–d2!** (not 4.♖c1 ♖d8! 5.♔f1 ♘d4 6.♖d1 ♘c6 and Black has saved himself) **4. ... ♗e6–f5** (the best is still 4...♘a1! 5.♗d4 ♘xb3 6.axb3 ♗xb3 with three pawns for the knight) **5.f2–f3 ♗f5xe4 6.f3xe4 ♘c2–a1 7.♖d2–d1** (after 7.♗d4? Black can still escape unharmed with 7...♖d8) and the knight is lost (7...♘c2 8.♖c1).

125

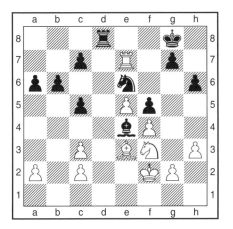

Black to move

Diagram 125 (Darga–Ivkov, Hastings 1955–56), shows the lost cause of an advanced rook. With **1. ... ♔g8–f8! 2.♖e7xe6 ♔f8–f7** Black wins the exchange, and ultimately the game.

Diagram 126 is a common type of example (L.Schmid–Sahlmann, Celle 1948). It is especially dangerous, of course, for the valuable queen to be in a crowd of enemy pieces.

126

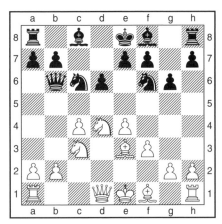

Black to move

Black could not resist the urge to go chasing material and he captured the little pawn on b2. However, he was not prepared for the reply: **1. ... ♕b6xb2?** (here this is a direct mistake) **2.♘c3–a4! ♕b2–a3 3.♗e3–c1!** and the queen is trapped. Black resigned. The continuation 3. ... ♕a3–b4+ 4.♗c1–d2 ♕b4–a3 5.♘d4–b5 is not hard to foresee.

127

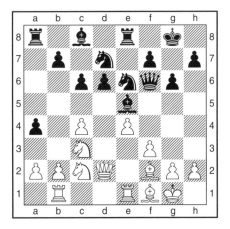

White to move

Even grandmasters are magically attracted by the rather harmless pawn on b2. In diagram 127 (Reshevsky–Najdorf, Helsinki 1952), the capture on b2 was made, on the invitation of the opponent, with the bishop. The punishment followed immediately.
1.♘c3–e2! ♗e5xb2?? 2.♖b1xb2! White enjoyed this. On the one hand, the black queen loses its way, and on the other hand, the surviving white bishop is as strong as a rook.
2. ...♕f6xb2 3.♘e2–c3! and there is no defence against 4.♖e1–b1. White wins quickly.

Another form of exchange sacrifice is the one that serves to lure the hostile queen to an offside position, in order to be able to carry out one's own plans undisturbed. In diagram 128 (Alekhine–Podgorny, Prague 1942), White sacrifices the exchange in order to put the queen in a completely offside position.

128

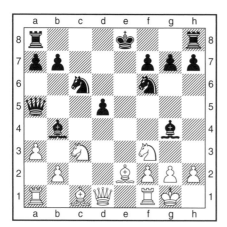

1.a3xb4! ♕a5xa1 2.♘f3–d2 The surprise point. Due to the threat of 3.♘d2–b3 (winning the queen), the reply is forced. As is often the case in a superior position, White could also have strengthened his position in a simple, forceful way: 2.b5

♘e7 (or 2...♗xf3 3.bxc6 ♗xe2 4.♕e2+ followed by cxb7) 3.♘d4 ♗xe2 4.♕xe2 ♕a5 5.♘f5 with a double threat against e7 and g7.
2. ... ♗g4xe2 3.♕d1xe2+ ♘c6–e7 (or 3...♔f8 4.♘b3 ♕a6 5.b5 ♕b6 6.♘a4 ♘d4 7.♕d1 ♕xb5 8.♘xd4 ♕b4. Materially speaking, Black does not stand worse, but the confined rook at h8 is a serious handicap.)
4.♖f1–e1 0-0 Now 5.♕xe7 is not possible due to 5...♖ae8, but after **5.♘d2–b3 ♕a1–a6 6.♕e2xa6 b7xa6** White can capture on e7 without danger and he has a clear advantage in the endgame.

Also very fine is the last example, which is from the game Nimzowitsch–Alekhine, Bled 1931.

129

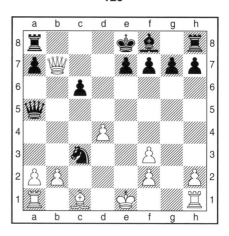

Black to move

White thinks that he can advantageously regain the sacrificed piece, because he is threatening the three points a8, c3 and c6. However, an ingenious queen trap destroys his hopes: **1. ... ♘c3–d5+! 2.♗c1–d2 ♕a5–b6!** (not 2...♕d8? 3.♕xc6+ ♕d7 4.♕xa8+) **3.♕b7xa8+ ♔e8–d7**, and against the threat of 4...♘c7 there is no adequate defence, for example 4.a4 ♘c7 5.a5 ♕xb2 6.♕xa7 ♕xa1+ and the second rook falls as well. Nimzowitsch tries something else, but he cannot cope with the opponent's material advantage. **4.0-0 ♘d5–c7 5.♗d2–a5 ♘c7xa8 6.♗a5xb6 ♘a8xb6** and so on.

'If you put yourself in danger, you will perish in it!' A proverb that applies not only in life, but also on the chess board.

26th Hour

Combinations (V)
Discovered Attacks

130

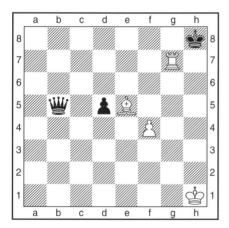

Black to move

Among the most important attacking elements are unmasking combinations, which can be divided into two categories. The first is the discovered check. A piece's line of attack is aiming at the enemy *king*. Between them there is another piece of the attacker's army. In chess problems this is called a 'battery': the piece at the back, which has to be a long-range one (queen, rook or bishop), gives check as soon as the piece in front moves out of the way. More common, however, are discovered attacks of the second category. Here the line of attack is aimed not at the king, but at another, usually valuable, piece, and this line is initially obstructed by a friendly piece. If this piece gives check or makes another dangerous threat, the hidden attack will come into action.

Diagram 130 shows a model example of the first category. It is Black to move, but he is unable to save his queen, which is threatened by discovered check, for example: **1. ... ♕b5–f1+ 2.♖g7–g1+** or **1. ... ♕b5–d3 2.♖g7–g3+** and so on.

The *'windmill'* is a special form of discovered check. It arises when the king is checked and forced into a position where discovered check is possible, so that check and discovered check can be repeated several times. Most commonly, the aim is to gain material, but sometimes simply to force a certain formation. This leads to fantastic possibilities.

131

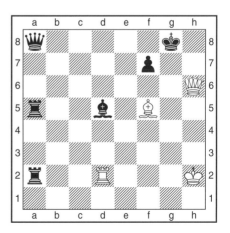

The position shown in diagram 131 was drawn up by the Latvian grandmaster, Aaron Nimzowitsch (the author of *My System*). Because the f7 square is protected by the bishop, the mating attempt 1.♗h7+ ♔h8 2.♗g6+ ♔g8 3.♕h7+ ♔f8 4.♕xf7+? is ineffective. White, therefore, plans to divert the black bishop by a rook check on g2, but he has to prepare the ground for this because the black rook stands guard on a2. With the help of the windmill, White eliminates one opponent after the other: **1.♗f5–h7+ ♔g8–h8 2.♗h7–c2+ ♔h8–g8 3.♖d2–g2+ ♗d5xg2 4.♗c2–h7+ ♔g8–h8 5.♗h7–g6+ ♔h8–g8 6.♕h6–h7+ ♔g8–f8 7.♕h7xf7** mate.

Diagram 132 illustrates a tactical gem.

132

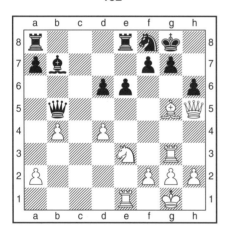

This shows the end of a game by the Mexican, Carlos Torre, which he won against Emanuel Lasker in the Moscow grandmaster tournament of 1925. Here, *both* types of combinations, the discovered check and discovered attack, act together. The unprotected queen on h5 stands opposite the enemy queen on b5, so the white bishop is seemingly pinned. Neither

can the black queen be driven away easily, as it threatens to escape by attacking the unprotected rook on e1 (1.a4? ♕xb4 2.♗f6 ♕e1+ 3.♘f1 ♘g6! 4.♖xg6 fxg6 5.♕xg6 ♖e7 and Black wins). Torre turned the tables with **1.♗g5–f6!!**: the double attack against b5 and g7 allows the sacrifice of the queen. With the help of the 'windmill' White recovers his material with interest. The sequel was: **1. ... ♕b5xh5 2.♖g3xg7+ ♔g8–h8 3.♖g7xf7+ ♔h8–g8 4.♖f7–g7+ ♔g8–h8 5.♖g7xb7+ ♔h8–g8 6.♖b7–g7+ ♔g8–h8 7.♖g7–g5+ ♔h8–h7 8.♖g5xh5 ♔h7–g6** (Black himself now employs a double attack and regains a piece. But he is already too much in arrears.) **9.♖h5–h3 ♔g6xf6 10.♖h3xh6+** and White wins easily. A sensational defeat for Lasker, who wore the chess crown for 27 years, from 1894 until 1921, longer than anyone else.

133

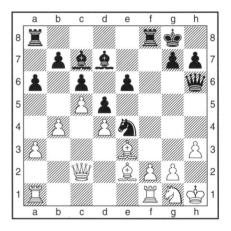

Diagram 133 (Black to move) is also taken from a practical game (although by two less well-known chess enthusiasts). The windmill again plays the leading role.

White has just captured a black pawn on e3 with his bishop and attacked the enemy queen. Its sacrifice allows the knight to come brilliantly into play: **1. ... ♕h6xe3! 2.f2xe3 ♘e4–g3+ 3.♔h1–h2 ♘g3xf1+ 4.♔h2–h1 ♘f1–g3+ 5.♔h1–h2 ♘g3–e4+!** The windmill has served its purpose. From the centre the knight is ready to give mate (**6.♔h1 ♘f2** mate, or **6.g3 ♖f2+ 7.♔h1 ♘xg3** mate).

Double Check

The most terrible move in chess is a double check, which arises when both pieces involved, the hidden piece and the one hiding it, give check. As an example we will look at the final phase of a game between Adolf Anderssen and Jean Dufresne (Berlin 1852), which in chess literature is referred to as the 'evergreen' game.

134

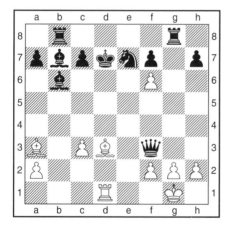

White, attacked on all sides, gets there first with the help of a double check: **1.♗d3–f5+ ♔d7–e8** (or 1...♔c6 2.♗d7 mate; remember that the king has to move when attacked by a double check) **2.♗f5–d7+ ♔e8–f8** (or d8) **3.♗a3xe7** mate.

In order to show that such developments do not depend on chance, but are the fruits of an active imagination and are executed in a planned and decisive manner from a certain moment onwards, we will look at how position 134 was created (see diagram 135).

135

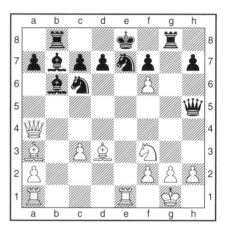

Anderssen made the move **1.♖a1–d1**, which in view of the reply **1. ... ♕h5xf3?**, threatening mate on g2, seems to be a big mistake (1...♖g4 would have been a better reply). In reality, the rook has its sights set on the d7 square and is already preparing the double check planned here. **2.♖e1xe7+ ♘c6xe7 3.♕a4xd7+! ♔e8xd7** and then as explained in diagram 134.

A double check does not necessarily have to be the finish of a mating combination. It can also serve simply as a way of winning material as in No.136 (Salwe–Marco, Ostende 1907).

136

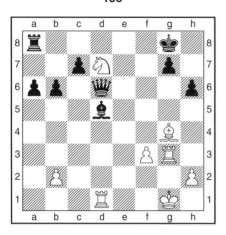

1.♖d1xd5! ♕d6xd5 The lesser evil was
1...♕c6. **2.♘d7–f6+ g7xf6 3.♗g4–e6+.**
The king has to move, after which White
captures the queen and remains a bishop
up.

137

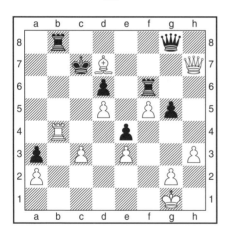

No.137 has a surprising ending. Here
double check serves to interrupt a line of
defence (Mason–Winawer, Vienna 1882):
1.♖b4–b7+ ♔c7xb7 2.♗d7–c8+! Truly
diabolical! If the king now captures the
bishop, the queen falls with check and

then, after the double attack on g7, so does
the rook at f6.

Sometimes the formation for a discovered
attack has first to be created (see diagram
138).

138

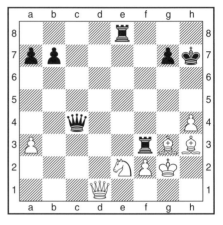

Black to move

Can Black capture on e2 with the rook,
even though the other rook is 'hanging'?
The white king cannot take on f3 immediately because of ♕c4–e4 mate, but White
can guard the square e4 beforehand, by
inserting ♕d1–b1+. Here the player's
imagination has to come into force. In the
game L.Schmid–Teschner, Düsseldorf 1951,
from which this example has been taken,
Black set up a 'battery' and after **1. ...
♖e8xe2 2.♕d1–b1+** he played **2. ... ♖e2–
c2! 3.♔g2xf3 ♕c4–d3+!**, and the white
king was unable to avoid check by the
black rook, unmasking the queen. After
4.♔f3–g2 ♖c2xf2+ 5.♔g3xf2 ♕d3xb1
Black wins without much effort. In fact
there was a much simpler solution in the
diagram: 1. ... ♕c2xe2! 2.♕d1xe2 ♖f3xg3+
followed by ♖e8xe2 and Black has an
elementary win. Not so original, but more
practical!

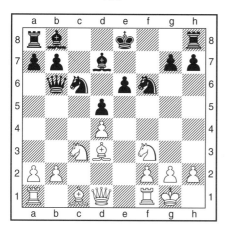

139

Black to move

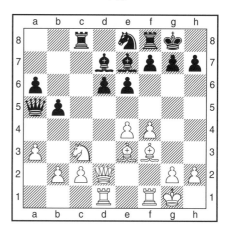

140

White to move

A curious case of a discovered attack being countered by discovered check is illustrated in No.139 (Gligoric–L.Schmid, Hastings 1951–52). Black boldly took the d4 pawn, as he realised that after **1. ... ♘c6xd4! 2.♘f3xd4 ♕b6xd4** White would not benefit from 'winning the queen' 3.♗d3–g6+? h7xg6 4.♕d1xd4, since Black recaptures the queen immediately with the help of the windmill: 4. ... ♗b8xh2+ 5.♔g1–h1 ♗h2–e5+, and finishes a piece ahead. Gligoric had no choice other than to accept the loss of the central pawn.

Diagram 140 depicts an elementary development that often occurs. White gains the advantage with the discovered attack **1.♘c3–d5!**. The following preconditions have to be met: the queen on a5 is unprotected, the exchange on d2 happens without check(!), the target of the attack at e7 is also unprotected and the black king is within reach of the knight!

The fact that White instantly gains the advantage is due to three other characteristics of this position: a) the rook on c8 is endangered by a knight fork, b) if the black

queen returns to d8, it will be stuck, c) the rook at f8 prevents the king from moving to f8! 1. ... ♕a5–d8 2.♗e3–b6, 1. ... ♗e7–d8 2.♕d2xa5 ♗d8xa5 3.♘d5–e7+ and 1. ... ♕a5xd2 2. ♘d5xe7+ ♔g8–h8 (if the rook at f8 were not in the way, everything would be alright) 3.♖d1xd2, in each case with advantage for White.

Do not forget the recurrent theme of these developments: the king is central to all deliberations!

27th Hour

Mating Combinations (I)
Smothered Mate

'Grab a part of the fullness of human life, and where you seize it, that is where it is interesting', says the prince of all poets (Goethe). For us the time has come to enter into the fullness of chess life. Mating combinations and mating attacks present a wide, almost unlimited field. We would like to present to the reader some of the most typical and commonly occurring forms.

141

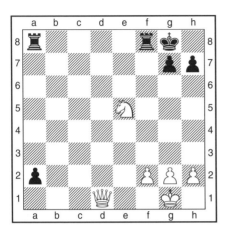

queen on f8 instead of a rook, the combination would not work, since from g8 too the queen would protect the mating square f7.

Phillip Stamma (from Aleppo, Syria, born about 1700) demonstrated this mate in a 'mansuba' (an early form of chess problem known from the 11th century).

Diagram 141 shows the basic form of the 'smothered mate'. Even regular players are occasionally surprised by it, and every beginner will most certainly have been caught out by it. This combination, which was demonstrated by Philidor, but which was certainly known long before the time of the French master in the late 18th century, plays an important role, if mainly as a threat.

Smothered mate is often preceded by double check by the queen and knight, as in our example. It is important that the queen gives check on the diagonal and that the knight is able to attack the corner square. Incidentally, White is in a precarious situation here, in view of the advance of the passed pawn, and he can only save himself with this combination: **1.♕d1–d5+!** Giving check on b3 is not enough in this instance – the queen also has to aim at the rook on a8. **1. ... ♔g8–h8** (1...♖f7 would be met by 2.♕xa8+!) **2.♘e5–f7+ ♔h8–g8** The king has to allow the double check, as after 2...♖xf7 3.♕xa8+ it is mate in two moves. **3.♘f7–h6+ ♔g8–h8 4.♕d5–g8+!** This imprisons the king in the corner. **4. ... ♖f8xg8 5.♘h6–f7** mate. If there were a

142

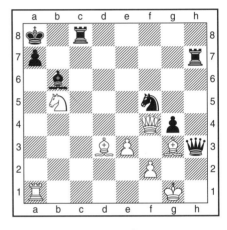

1.♗d3–e4+ ♖h7–b7 2.♕f4–b8+ ♖c8xb8 3.♖a1xa7+ The defenders of the c7 square are removed step by step. **3. ... ♗b6xa7 4.♘b5–c7** mate.

143

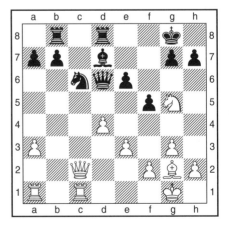

How this combination can act as a threat is illustrated in diagram 143 (Alekhine–Golombek, Margate 1938). The then world champion turned a light breeze into a storm by playing **1.d4–d5!**. Black could not reply 1...exd5, as after 2.♗xd5+! ♕xd5 3.♖d1! he would have to vacate the a2–g8 diagonal and allow a deadly check by the white queen, for example 3...♕e5 4.♕b3+ ♗e6 (as can easily be seen, this is forced) 5.♘xe6 ♖xd1+ 6.♖xd1 ♔h8 7.♘g5 and White wins. Black therefore tried **1. ... ♘c6–e7 2.d5xe6 ♗d7xe6 3.♖c1–d1 ♕d6–e5**, but after **4.♗g2xb7! h6–h6 5.♘g5xe6 ♕e5xe6 6.♕c2–c7** he also ended up with a decisive disadvantage.

144

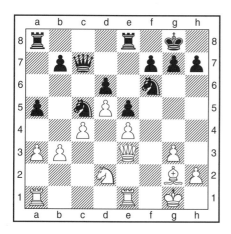

Black to move

In diagram 144 (Opocensky–Trifunovic, Zlin 1945), the diagonal has to be opened for the queen to give check, by the sacrifice of a knight. White found himself defenceless after **1. ... ♘f6–g4 2.♕e3–e2 ♘c5–d3!**: if he takes either knight, the queen check will lead to a smothered mate. White got away with the loss of the exchange by **3.♗g2–f3 ♕c7–c5+ 4.♔g1–g2 ♘d3xe1+**

5.♖a1xe1, but he nevertheless had to resign soon afterwards. If 3.♖f1 ♕c5+ 4.♔h1, White falls victim to a windmill: 4...♘df2+ 5.♖xf2 (5.♔g1 ♘h3+ with a smothered mate) 5...♘xf2+ 6.♔g1 ♘xe4+ and so on.

145

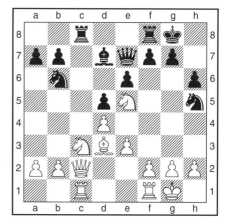

Sometimes this type of mate is only a small part of a combination, as in the remarkable No.145. First the king is guided to a position favourable to White, and then White wins a decisive tempo thanks to the unprotected knight on h5: **1.♗d3–h7+ ♔g8–h8 2.♗h7–g6!** A murderous move. The bishop cannot be captured because of ♘xg6+, and Black has no time for the defence ...♗e8 because the knight at h5 is 'hanging'. **2. ... ♘g5–f6 3.♗g6xf7!** and ♘g6+ is unavoidable. The lesser evil is 3...♕xf7 4.♘xf7+ ♖xf7. The attempt to save the queen leads to a smothered mate: **3. ... ♕e7–d6 4.♘e5–g6+ ♔h8–h7 5.♘g6xf8+ ♔h7–h8 6.♕c2–h7+!**.

146

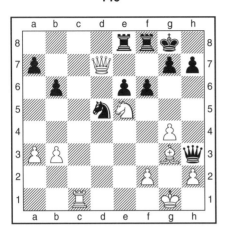

It also happens, of course, that speculating on a 'smothered mate' can turn out to be wrong. In No.146 (Reyss–Klaarwater, Rotterdam 1932), on the previous moves White had relied on the strength of **1.♖c1–c8** and was hoping for 1...♖xc8 2.♕xe6+ ♔h8 3.♘f7+ followed by mate. The defence chosen by Black **1. ... ♖e8–e7** was no better because of **2.♕d7–d8! ♖e7–f7 3.♘e5–d7!** But he could have won with 1. ... ♘d5–e3! This forces the opening of the f-file and, after 2.f2xe3 f6xe5 there is a threat of mate on f1. This forces the rook to return to the first rank. Black has parried the attack; he keeps a material advantage and wins easily after 3. ... ♕h3xg4.

Back Rank Mate

147

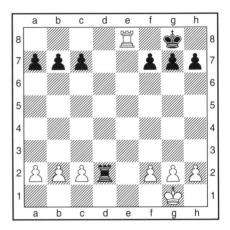

Mate on the edge of the board by a rook is similar to smothered mate. Diagram 147 demonstrates the pattern. Black has failed to defend against the invasion at e8 by moving his king or opening a 'safety valve' for the king by advancing one of the pawns f7, g7 or h7 (in the endgame it is advisable to move the king to the centre where it stands best).

An important defence can be seen in diagram 148.

148

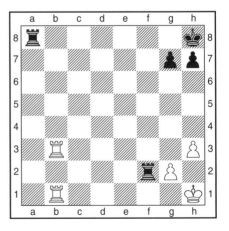

1.♖b3–b8+ does not lead to checkmate. Black, of course, does not capture the rook, but plays **1. ... ♖f2–f8!**

149

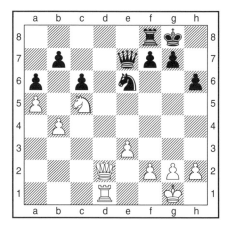

That even a grandmaster, distracted by other events, can fail to notice the danger of a weakened back rank, is shown in diagram 149 (Reshevsky–Euwe, New York 1951). White wanted to pre-empt the move ♖f8–d8 and, in view of the unprotected queen on e7, he occupied the seventh rank with **1.♕d2–d7?** Black correctly replied **1. ... ♖f8–d8!**, and White had to resign straight away, because his queen is pinned due to the threat of mate on d1. White would have done better to play 1.♘c5xe6, thus securing control of the d-file.

Pure chess magic is demonstrated in diagram 150. One surprising queen sacrifice follows another.

150

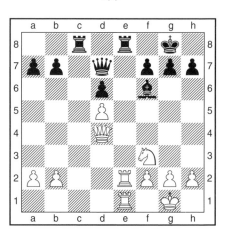

White exploits the weakness of the opponent's back rank, especially the square e8, with unsurpassable elegance (Adams–Torre, New Orleans 1920). **1.♕d4–g4!** This threatens the unprotected queen, which dare not capture, because the doubly threatened square e8 has to remain doubly protected. Neither does Black have time to insert the exchange on e2, because the e1 square is covered by White. Evidently, the endangered queen cannot be protected either. The only possible move is **1. ...♕d7–b5**, after which **2.♕g4–c4!** continues the diversion tactics. **2. ... ♕b5–d7 3.♕c4–c7!** ♕d7–b5! Again forced. White could now win a pawn with 4.♖xe8+ ♖xe8 5.♖xe8+ ♕xe8 6.♕xb7, but he strives for more, and rightly so. However, 4.♕xb7?? would be a blunder because of 4...♕xe2! when Black wins. **4.a2–a4! ♕b5xa4 5.♖e2–e4!** Again a delightful move, which forces the black queen back to b5. The white queen remains invulnerable, because the two black rooks are chained to each other. **5. ... ♕a4–b5** and now **6.♕c7xb7** is decisive. Black can no longer defend the square e8 without great loss of material.

151

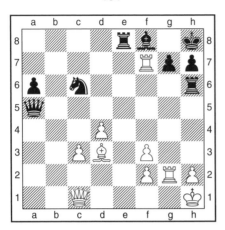

Black to move

Diagram 151 demonstrates that your own security should not be neglected when penetrating the opponent's back rank. Black thought he could play **1. ... ♘c6xd4**, and missed, after **2.c3xd4 ♖e8–e1+**, the reply **3.♗d3–f1!**. Now mate is threatened on f8, so that the rook dare not take the queen.

'Wherever there are chess players, there will be mistakes', said Kurt Richter, 'and if this should ever be different, it will be the end of chess.'

28th Hour

Mating Combinations (II)
The restricted King

Attacks on the castled position are usually successful only when they are carried out with a material superiority. Frequently it is necessary to remove the obstacles by force. No sacrifice is too great if the much desired aim, that of capturing the hostile commander-in-chief, is achieved. But: 'Only when the hostile king has little mobility and little protection does the master make the attempt to find a combination which aims at a forced mate, because he knows that only then can the position contain the idea of a mate', writes the great Emanuel Lasker in his manual.

152

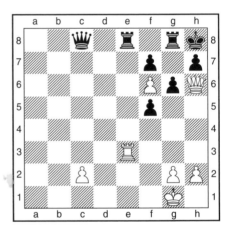

In diagram 152 the obvious move 1.♖h3 is bad, because Black gets there first: 1...♕c5+, winning easily. Realising that the squares g8, g7 and g6 are unavailable to the black king, White forces mate on the edge of the board: **1.♕h6xh7+ ♔h8xh7 2.♖e3–h3** mate.

153

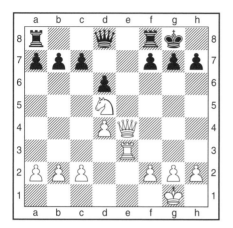

A similar situation arises in diagram 153. After **1.♘d5–e7+**, Black has to give up his queen for the knight, because after **1. ... ♚g8–h8** White checkmates in the same way as above: **2.♕e4xh7+ ♚h8xh7 3.♖e3–h3** mate.

154

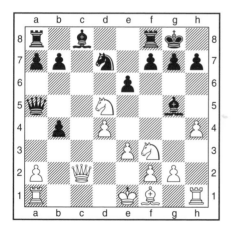

In No.154 Black was only expecting the capture on g5 (he then wanted to reply with the advantageous b4–b3+), but he was cruelly woken from his dreams by the thunderous **1.♕c2xh7+! ♚g8xh7 2.h4xg5+**

♚h7–g6 3.♘d5–e7 mate (Casas–Piazzini, Buenos Aires 1952).

155

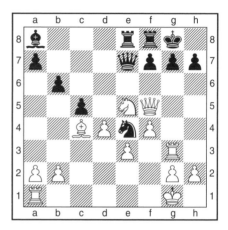

In diagram 155, as in the previous and following examples, Black again feels too safe behind his wall of pawns. The invasion could have been short and painful: **1.♕f5xh7+! ♚g8xh7 2.♖g3–h3+ ♚h7–g8 3.♘e5–g6** and Black has no defence against mate by the rook on h8. The position is taken from a game Grünfeld–Wagner, London 1932. White missed this beautiful opportunity and played **1.♖g3–h3? ♘e4–f6**.

It is nearly too obvious that the confined position of the black king in No.156 (Janowski–David, Paris 1891) should be effectively exploited. After sacrifices of bishop and rook, the queen directs its aim at the barricaded king: **1.♗e5xg7+ ♚h8xg7 2.♖h4xh7+! ♚g7xh7 3.f5–f6+ ♚h7–h8 4.♕d1–h5+** Black resigns.

156

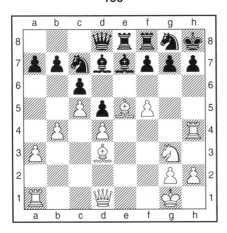

Weiß am Zug

White, who initially gave the odds of his king's knight, is so powerful in the starting position that even a move such as 1.f5–f6 would have won. Please check this!

Attack with Material Superiority

157

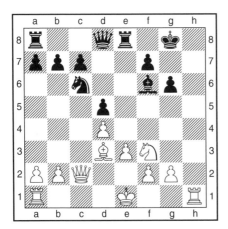

When a whole host of attackers storms an insufficiently defended fortress, typical formations arise, as shown in diagram 157. Four white pieces are ready for the

assault, so it is no surprise that the crumbling defences collapse. **1.♗d3xg6 f7xg6 2.♕c2xg6+ ♚g8–f8** If Black plays 2...♗g7, this is met by the frequently seen manoeuvre 3.♘g5, which here involves the threats of 4.♕f7 mate and 4.♖h8+! ♚xh8 5.♕h7 mate. **3.♘f3–g5** Here too the intervention of the knight decides the game immediately, since 3. … ♗f6xg5 4.♖h1– h8+ ♚f8–e7 5.♖h8–h7+ leads directly to checkmate. 3...♕e7 is equally futile due to 4.♘h7+ winning the queen, while if 3...♖e7, then 4.♕xf6+ ♚e8 5.♖h8+ and so on.

158

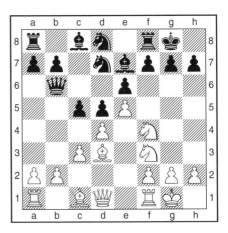

Again in diagram 158, four attackers are poised for the attack, and a fifth one on c1 awaits the trumpet call. Against this superiority it is hardly possible for Black to escape unharmed. The attack is carried out as follows: **1.♕d1–c2! f7–f5** After 1...g6 White replies 2.h4, in order to storm the g6 point with h4–h5. Black will try to put up a makeshift defence with ♖f8–e8 and ♘d7–f8.

2.e5xf6 ♘d7xf6 3.♘f3–g5 Threatening 4.♗xh7+ ♚h8 5.♘g6 mate.
3. … g7–g6 4.♗d3xg6 No hesitation. **4. … h7xg6 5.♕c2xg6+ ♚g8–h8 6.♕g6–h6+**

♔h8–g8 **7.♘f4–g6** Threatening the h8
and e7 points simultaneously. 7.♘h5 is
also strong. **7. … ♘d8–f7 8.♘g6xe7
mate**.

159

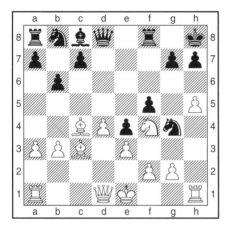

We regularly come across formations of
the type shown in diagram 159. The knight
check on g6 gives White the leverage to
open the h-file at the appropriate moment.
Only the black **knight** at g4 is able to block
the rook on this file by moving to h6. This
induces White to remove the trouble-
maker with **1.♕d1xg4!**, so that he can
force mate after **1. … f5xg4 2.♘f4–g6+
h7xg6 3.h5xg6+**.

Black's combination in No.160 is similar in
principle, but with the added point that
ultimately the black queen should give
mate on h2 (!). In order to realise this plan,
Black sacrifices no less than *six* **pieces**, a
record.
1. … ♗e8–b5! opens the way for the
queen to h8 in wise anticipation. **2.a4xb5
♘h5–g3+ 3.♘e4xg3 ♘f5xg3+ 4.h2xg3
h4xg3+ 5.♔h1–g1 ♗f8–c5+!** (this bishop
also has to make room on the eighth rank)
6.♘b3xc5 ♖h8–h1+ (the rooks make way

160

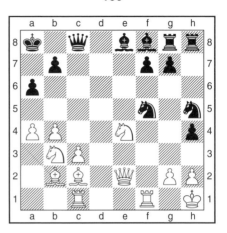

Black to move

for their queen with gain of time – they
themselves are not so well suited to giving
mate) **7.♔g1xh1 ♖g8–h8+ 8.♔h1–g1
♖h8–h1+ 9.♔g1xh1** The servants have
done their duty, and now the queen exe-
cutes the verdict. **9. … ♕c8–h8+ 10.♔h1–
g1 ♕h8–h2** mate! A triumph of mind over
matter (N.N.–E.Mason, London 1948).

161

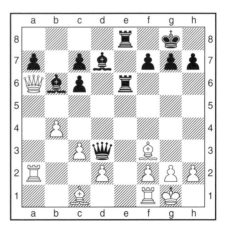

The classic finish in diagram 161 (Black to move), should not be missing from any manual (L.Paulsen–Morphy, New York 1857).

With **1. ... ♛d3xf3** the brilliant American sacrifices his queen 'for the long term' – he gives up queen for bishop. In return, he tears open the pawn position and exposes the hostile king. **2.g2xf3 ♖e6–g6+ 3.♚g1–h1 ♗d7–h3** Threatening mate via the 'windmill' 4...♗g2+ 5.♚g1 ♗xf3. Futile would be 4.♖g1 due to 4...♖xg1+ 5.♚xg1 ♖e1+ followed by mate. Paulsen presumably thought that after **4.♖f1–d1**, which opens an escape route for the king, Black would have to be content with perpetual check (4...♗g2+ 5.♚g1 ♗h3+ 6.♚h1 and so on), but Morphy sees an easy win. **4. ... ♗h3–g2+** The obvious 4...♗xf2 5.♛f1 ♗xf1 leads only to the win of a pawn. Black collects an additional pawn before that. **5.♚h1–g1 ♗g2xf3+ 6.♚g1–f1** According to Maróczy, 6...♖g2! would now have forced mate in four moves. This threatens not only another windmill (...♖xf2+ followed by ...♖g2+), but also ...♖xh2 followed by ...♖h1 mate. Morphy was satisfied with an easy win in the endgame after 6. ... ♗f3–g2+ 7.♚f1–g1 ♗g2–h3+ (here again, according to Maróczy, an opportunity to give mate presented itself, beginning with 7...♗e4+ 8.♚f1 ♗f5!) 8.♚g1–h1 ♗b6xf2 9.♛a6–f1 ♗h3xf1 and so on. Later the more obstinate defence 4.♛d3 was discovered, to protect the f3 square and possibly capture the dangerous attacker on g6. Black then proceeds as follows: 4...f5 5.♛c4+ (5.♖d1 ♗xf2 6.♛f1 ♗xf1 7.♖xf1 ♖e2! and wins, for example 8.♖a5 ♖h6!) 5....♚f8! 6.♛h4 (6.♛f4 ♗xf2) 6...♗xf1 7.h3 ♗g2+ 8.♚h2 ♗xf3 and wins.

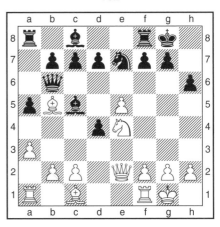

162

Finally, in diagram 162 we contrast this classic combination with one played nearly a hundred years later (Pachmann–Hasek, Prague 1955), in which the same theme occurs. The continuation was inventive and convincing:

1.b2–b4 with the idea of 1...axb4? 2.♘xc5 ♛xc5 3.axb4 with a double attack on c5 and a8. The only escape for the bishop is the zwischenzug **1. ... d4–d3**, but after **2.♗b5xd3 ♗c5–d4** the white army is lined up for the attack. **3.♘e4–f6+ g7xf6** (or 3...♚h8 4.♛e4 ♘g6 5.♘d5 ♛a7 6.♗e3 ♗xe3 7.fxe3 with the deadly threat of 8.♖xf7 followed by ♛xg6) **4.♛e2–g4+ ♚g8–h8 5.♗c1xh6 ♖f8–g8 6.♛g4–h4** (threatening 7.♗f8 mate) **6. ... ♘e7–g6 7.♗d3xg6 ♖g8xg6 8.♗h6–e3+ ♚h8–g8 9.♗e3xd4**, for example 9...♛c6 10.g3! ♛xc2 11.e6, threatening 12.♗xf6. The game is easily won.

Stimulating ideas and examples are essential prerequisites for the player who wants to prove himself in tournament games.

29th Hour

Mating Combinations (III)
The sacrifice on h7 or h2

Part of the 'daily bread' of the chess player are developments such as the bishop sacrifice on h7 after kingside castling, 'which, if possible at all, will nearly always lead inevitably to victory', as Rudolf Spielmann once said. There is a type of basic plan which allows numerous variations and incorporates many additional options. It is left to the player's imagination to seek them out. We will show a few of the most common cases.

163

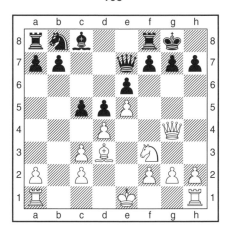

Black to move

He plays **1. ... c5–c4?** 'Of course' this is answered by **2.♗d3xh7+ ♔g8xh7 3.♕g4–h5+ ♔h7–g8 4.♘f3–g5** and Black is unable to protect the h7 square (the bishop on c8 is imprisoned!). He has to give up his queen (4. ... ♕e7xg5) or be mated (4. ... ♖f8–e8 5.♕h5–h7+ ♔g8–f8 6.♕h7–h8 mate).

164

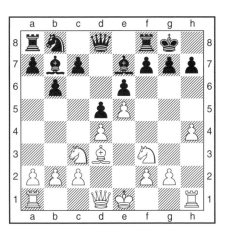

In this combination it is vital that the knight should be able to move to the g5 square. In No.163 it was protected by the queen. Sometimes this role can fall to the bishop or, as shown in diagram 164, to the h-pawn. Here the situation is more complicated, because the king does not have to return to the corner, but can try to escape its 'punishment' by another way. The restraining e5 pawn and the rook, standing ready on h1, play an important role in the impending attack.

1.♗d3xh7+ ♔g8xh7 (Black cannot very well reject the sacrifice.) **2.♘f3–g5+ ♔h7–h6** If the bishop takes the knight, the h-file is opened with deadly consequences: 2...♗xg5 3.hxg5+ ♔g8 4.♕h5 f6 5.g6 followed by 6.♕h8 mate, or 3...♔g6 4.♕h5+ ♔f5 5.♖h3 followed by 6.♖f3 mate. If the king goes to g6 on the second move, 3.♕d3+ follows immediately. **3.♕d1–d2** (threatening 4.♘xe6+) **3. ... ♔h6–g6** After 3...♕c8 4.♘xe6+ ♔h7 5.♕d3+ ♔g8 6.♘xf8 White would have regained the sacrificed material with the better position. Instead of 4.♘xe6+ he could also advantageously continue the attack with 4.♘e2.

4.h4–h5+ (4.♕d3+ also wins, though not so quickly) **4. ... ♔g6–f5** (or 4...♔h6 5.♘xf7+, winning the queen) **5.♖h1–h4** (or 5.f3) followed by **6.g2–g4** mate.

7.♕h7+ ♔f8 8.♕h8 leads to mate, as did the moves in the game: **4. ... ♔g8–f7 5.♕d1–h5+ g7–g6 6.♕h5–h7+ ♔f7–e8 7.♕h7xg6.**

165

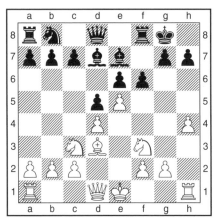

166

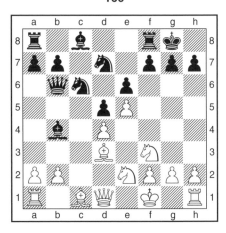

Diagram 165 illustrates some very striking side effects of the sacrifice on h7. White (in the game Schlechter–Wolf, Vienna 1894) began with **1.♘f3–g5! f6xg5** Black underestimates the attack and allows his opponent to enrich chess literature with a beautiful combination. The underlying idea of the attack arises after: 1...f5 2.♕h5 h6 3.♘h3 followed by 4.♘f4.

2.♗d3xh7+ ♔g8xh7 (2...♔f7? 3.♕h5+ followed by mate) **3.h4xg5+ ♔h7–g8** (3...♔g6 4.♕h5+ ♔f5 5.♖h3 and 6.♖f3 mate) The white attack is now, surprisingly, not based on the power of the h-file, but instead on the impact of the g-pawn. Thus 4.♕h5? would be directly bad because of 4...♗xg5. After 4.g6 Black would be able to prevent the intervention of the queen with ...♖f5. The decisive tempo is gained by the additional sacrifice **4.♖h1–h8+!**, since 4...♔xh8 5.♕h5+ ♔g8 6.g6! ♖f5

Whereas in the examples presented so far the sacrifice succeeds without allowing the opponent time to catch his breath, we will now demonstrate a combination which gains two pawns for the sacrificed bishop plus an 'attack on the exposed king'. An adventurous player will not want to miss an opportunity to exchange calm winds for a stormy sea. In diagram 166 (Spielmann–Dekker, Bussum 1934), Black had just castled, since he was not afraid of the bishop sacrifice. But White, unperturbed, played **1.♗d3xh7+ ♔g8xh7 2.♘f3–g5+ ♔h7–g8** (2...♔g6? 3.♘f4+) **3.♕d1–d3**. So, the queen does not necessarily have to approach from h5. 3...g6 is futile against the mate on h7, because of 4.♕h3. Black, therefore, has to accept the invasion of the queen and with it the loss of a second pawn (on g7). **3. ... ♖f8–e8 4.♕d3–h7+ ♔g8–f8 5.♕h7–h8+ ♔f8–e7 6.♕h8xg7.** The attack is so strong that Black even has to give up a third pawn. White did not foresee that after 6...♖f8 the mating sacrifice 7.♘xe6! ♔xe6 8.♘f4+ ♔f5 9.♕h7+ would be possible. This was not necessary anyway. A 'feeling for position', based on experience, tells a player that 'there has to be something'. Incidentally, 7...♖e8 is also insufficient because of 8.♗g5+ ♔xe6 9.♘f4+ ♔f5 10.♕h7+ ♔xg5 11.♘h3+ ♔g4 12.f3 mate. If Black protects the square f7 with the knight, there are again some attractive possibilities, for example 6...♘d8 7.♘xf7 ♘xf7 8.♗g5+. Black tried **6. ...♔e7–d8** and lost after **7.♕g7xf7 ♘d7–f8** (or 7...♘xd4 8.♗e3 ♗c5 9.♗xd4 ♗xd4 10.♘xd4 ♕xd4 11.♘xe6+ ♖xe6 12.♕xe6 ♘xe5 13.♕f6+ followed by ♖e1) due to the strength of the white h-pawn:

8.h2–h4! ♗c8–d7 9.♗c1–e3 ♖a8–c8 10.h4–h5 ♘c6–e7 11.♘e2–f4 ♘e7–f5 12.h5–h6 ♘f5xe3+ 13.f2xe3 ♗d7–b5+ 14.♔f1–g1 ♖c8–c7 15.h6–h7! and the rest was easy: 15...♖xf7 16.♘xf7+ ♔d7 17.h8♕ ♘g6 18.♕f6 ♘xf4 19.♕xf4 ♗d3 20.♖h8 ♗f8 21.♘d6 ♗xd6 22.♖xe8 ♔xe8 23.exd6 ♕xb2 24.♕f6! ♕xa1+ 25.♔h2 ♔d7 26.♕e7+ ♔c6 27.♕c7+ ♔b5 28.d7 ♕d1 29.♕xb7+ and Black resigned because of 29...♔c4 30.♕b3+ ♕xb3 31.axb3+ followed by 32.d8♕. Spielmann was one of the greatest masters of attack in chess history.

If the spearhead of the attack, the white pawn on e5, is missing, then a rook positioned on e1 can sometimes be an adequate 'substitute'. Diagram 167 (Deutschmann–Bauschke, Berlin 1929) illustrates this: **1.♗e4xh7+ ♔g8xh7 2.♘f3–g5+ ♔h7–g6.** As in diagram 166, Black is in a very uncomfortable position after 2... ♔g8 3.♕h5 ♖fe8 4.♕h7+ ♔f8 5.♕h8+ ♔e7 6.♕xg7. **3.♕d1–g4! ♔g6–f6?** The following

167

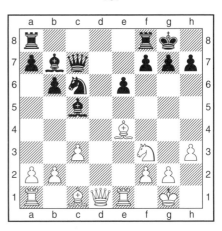

should have been tried: 3...f5 4.♕h4 ♖ae8. **4.♖e1xe6+ f7xe6 5.♕g4xe6** mate.

168

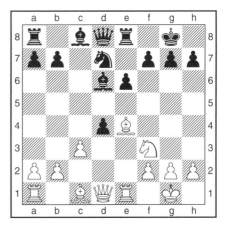

Diagram 168 is more complicated (Colle–O'Hanlon, Nice 1930), but the finish is similar: **1.♗e4xh7+ ♔g8xh7 2.♘f3–g5+ ♔h7–g6.** Better was 2...♔g8 3.♕h5 ♕f6 (3...♘f6 4.♕xf7+ ♔h8 5.♖e4! is hopeless) 4.♕h7+ ♔f8 5.♘e4 ♕e5 6.cxd4 ♕xh2+ 7.♕xh2 ♗xh2+ 8.♔xh2 ♘f6 with a roughly equal ending. **3.h2–h4!** The threat of 4.h5+

enlivens the attack. **3. ... ♖e8–h8** (or 3...♘f6 4.♕d3+ ♔h5 5.♕f3+ ♔g6 6.h5+; nor would 3...♖f8 have offered any more resistance, as shown by 4.♕d3+ ♔f6 5.♘xe6 fxe6 6.♗g5+) **4.♖e1xe6+!** An elegant rook sacrifice, which Black dare not accept: 4...fxe6 5.♕d3+ ♔f6 6.♕f3+. **4. ... ♘d7–f6 5.h4–h5+ ♔g6–h6** (5...♖xh5 6.♕d3+ followed by mate) **6.♖e6xd6 ♕d8–a5 7.♘g5xf7+ ♔h6–h7 8.♘f7–g5+ ♔h7–g8 9.♕d1–b3+.** The first move of the queen in this game and Black has to resign. Colle won a considerable number of games with the bishop sacrifice on h7.

169

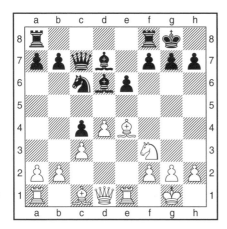

Diagram 169 should warn the reader against making a sacrifice on h7 without thoroughly checking the consequences (Fincke–Horn, Berlin 1931). Here the e6 square is too well protected, and after **1.♗e4xh7+?** (1.♘g5 would have been promising) **1. ... ♔g8xh7 2.♘f3–g5+ ♔h7–g6!** things did not go so well for White. If 3.♕g4, then 3...f5! and the e6 square is protected! The attempt **3.h2–h4 ♖f8–h8 4.♕d1–f3 ♖a8–f8 5.h4–h5+ ♖h8xh5 6.♘g5xf7** failed due to **6. ... ♖h5–f5!** and

White resigned after 7.♘e5+ ♘xe5 8.♕g3+ ♔f7 9.dxe5 ♗xe5 10.♕g4 ♔g8 11.♗h6 ♖xf2.

Finally, diagram 170 shows a quite different pattern, where the sacrifice enables the opening of the h-file and the intervention of the queen.

170

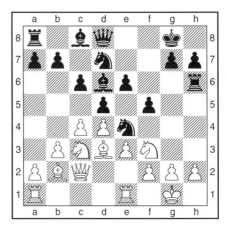

Black to move

1. ... ♗d6xh2+ 2.♘f3xh2 ♕d8–h4. The knight on h2 cannot move because of ♕h4–h1 mate. Black has won a pawn and penetrated the white fortress.

And now we wish, dear reader, that you may obtain many victories with this combination and – may never fall victim to it.

30th Hour

Mating Combinations (IV)
Alekhine's Mating Attacks

Considering the enormous scope for variety in the game of chess, it is easy to understand that combinations are rarely completely identical. Nearly always, a number of motifs have to be combined with one another. Like Ariadne's thread, the player has to free them first from a tangled-up ball. We will take a look at how the former world champion, Alexander Alekhine (1892–1946), went about it when he, 'the most ingenious attacker of all times', took up the reins.

171

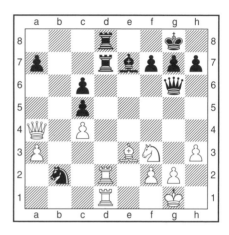

Black to move

In diagram 171 (Capablanca–Alekhine, World Championship Match, Buenos Aires 1927, first game), the 'breathing holes' g2 and h2 were of no use to the white king. The rook's invasion of the weakened back rank was decisive, as follows:

1. ... ♖e5–e1+ 2.♔g1–g2 ♕e6–c6+ 3.f2–f3 ♖e1–e3 4.♕d3–d1 ♕c6–e6. This threatens 5...♖e2+. Capablanca defends himself with all his might, but in vain. **5.g3–g4 ♖e3–e2+ 6.♔g2–h3 ♕e6–e3 7.♕d1–h1 ♕e3–f4** The following rook move cannot be prevented. **8.h4–h5 ♖e2–f2** and White has to resign.

After the game, however, Alekhine 'severely reproached' himself for having lengthened the end of the game unneces-

sarily. Black could, with gain of tempo (by attacking the unprotected white rook), have brought his queen onto the a8–h1 diagonal, and only then advanced his rook onto White's back rank (see diagram 171): 1...♕e7! 2.♖b8 ♕c7 3.♖a8 (futile is 3.♖f8 ♔g7 or 3.♕b3 ♖e6) 3...♕b7! and wins.

172

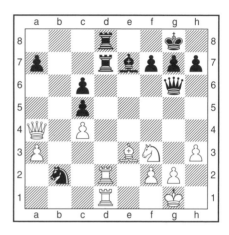

The weakness of the back rank is also the basis of the attack in diagram 172 (Alekhine–Molina, Buenos Aires 1926). **1.♕a4xa7!** definitely secures the advantage for White. In the game Black accepted the queen sacrifice and was mated as follows: **1. ... ♖d7xa7 2.♖d2xd8+ ♗e7–f8 3.♗e3xc5 h7–h6.** Black fights in vain against the mate. **4.♖d8xf8+ ♔g8–h7 5.♖d1–d8 ♕g6–b1+ 6.♔g1–h2 ♖a7–b7 7.♘f3–h4!** Blocking the escape route. Black resigns. 7...g6 is met by 8.♗d4 f6 9.♗xf6, and 7...g5 by 8.♖h8+ ♔g7 9.♖dg8+ ♔f6 10.♖xh6+ ♔e5 11.♖e8+ and mate in two moves. What happens if Black does not take the queen was demonstrated by Alekhine: 1...♖xd2 2.♖xd2 ♖xd2 3.♘xd2 is in White's favour because of the passed pawn on a3, or 1...♘xd1 2.♖xd7 ♘xe3 3.fxe3 ♖xd7 4.♕xd7 ♗f8

5.♘e5 and wins, or finally 1...♗d6 2.♕xd7 ♖xd7 3.♖xb2 ♕e6 4.♖bd2 with a big advantage, because the bishop at d6 is pinned.

174

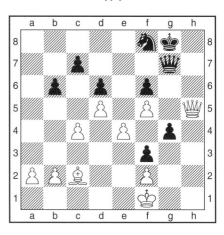

1.e4–e5!! d6xe5 1...fxe5 was unpromising for Black because of 2.f6 ♕xf6 3.♕xg4+ ♔f7 4.♗e4. **2.d5–d6! c7–c5**. The point of the second pawn sacrifice is that after 2...cxd6 the third sacrifice 3.c5! creates the unavoidable threat of 4.♗b3+. **3.♗c2–e4 ♕g7–d7 4.♕h5–h6!** Black resigns, because the situation is hopeless after 4...♔f7 5.♗d5+ ♔e8 6.♕xf6.

173

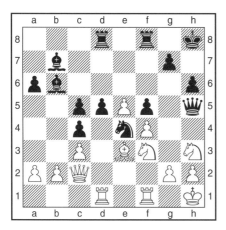

Black to move

Diagram 173 shows the ending of the game Torres–Alekhine, Seville 1922. With a subtle breakthrough, Black maximises the power of his strong bishop on the long light-square diagonal: **1. ... d5–d4! 2.c3xd4 c5xd4 3.♗e3xd4 ♗b6xd4 4.♖d1xd4 ♖d8xd4 5.♘f3xd4**. Thus, two obstacles between the bishop and the king have been removed and the sacrifice of the queen **5. ... ♕h5xh3!** becomes effective. **6.g2xh3 ♘e4–f2+ 7.♔h1–g1 ♘f2xh3** mate. Seven moves that had to be calculated in advance. A case like this, where nearly every move is forced, is not unusual.

In diagram 174 the white bishop is seemingly ineffective. But see how Alekhine (against Johner, Zürich 1934) increased its attacking powers.

175

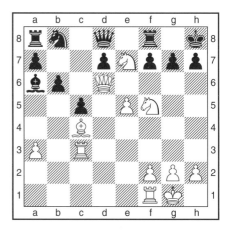

White's final move in the game against Supico (Lisbon 1941) is also 'typically

Alekhine'. After **1.♕d6–g6!!** Black had to lay down his arms, since 1. ... f7xg6 2.♘e7xg6+ h7xg6 3.♖c3–h3+ leads to mate.

An 'attraction sacrifice' of rare beauty was demonstrated by the Russian in a game which he played blindfold in 1916 in a field hospital in Tarnopol (see diagram 176).

176

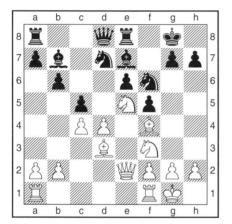

Black (Feldt) only needs to play ♘d7–f8 to have a defensible position. Alekhine intervened with the excellent move **1.♘e5–f7!!**. If now the black queen moves, 2.♕xe6 follows and a 'smothered mate' is threatened (3.♘h6+ and so on), as well as 3.♘d6+ winning the queen. Therefore Black played **1. ... ♔g8xf7**, but now he had to endure a second thunder-clap **2.♕e2xe6+!!**. After 2...♔xe6, 3.♘g5 gives checkmate, and the same move is also effective after 2...♔f8. Black tried **2. ... ♔f7–g6** and was mated by **3.g2–g4 ♗b7–e4 4.♘f3–h4**. When the Russian genius made combinations, sparks would fly.

In diagram 177 (Grigoriev–Alekhine, Moscow 1920), the e1 point is in need of protection. This is convincingly exploited by Black.

177

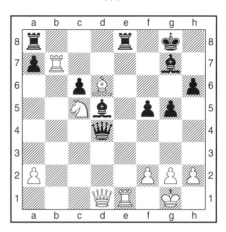

Black to move

1. ... ♕d4–g4! threatens mate on g2. The exchange of queens is impossible, as is 2.♖xe8+ ♖xe8 3.♕f1 ♖e1. White's reply is forced: **2.f2–f3 ♗g7–d4+ 3.♔g1–h1 ♗d5xf3!** White resigns. Mate is unavoidable, for example 4.♖xe8+ ♖xe8 5.gxf3 ♖e1+ 6.♕xe1 ♕xf3 mate. A great master is distinguished by the fact that he (almost) never misses such an opportunity.

178

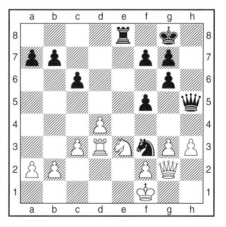

And in conclusion, an elegant 'queen pivot' in diagram 178 (Blümich–Alekhine, Krakow 1941).

Alekhine tries to exploit the power of the queen and he finds the appropriate method: **1. ... f5–f4! 2.g3xf4 ♛h5–b5! 3.c3–c4** If 3.♔e2 ♛xd3+! (or immediately 3...♞e1!) 4.♔xd3 ♞e1+ followed by ...♞xg2.

3. ... ♛b5xc4! The idea of the combination (4.♞xc4 ♜e1 mate!) **4.♛g2xf3 ♛c4xd3+ 5.♔f1–g2 ♛d3xd4 6.f4–f5 g6xf5** White resigns.

Tartakower called Alekhine's game 'sunshine chess'.

Chess Strategy

31st Hour

Plans and Ideas (I)

In chess, every type of temperament can find fulfilment: the gambler, the security-minded strategist and the player with common sense, who risks only as much as he thinks he can afford after objectively evaluating the situation. However, a game does not consist of aimlessly moving backwards and forwards 'until the opponent makes a mistake'. If you want to be successful, you have to learn, above all, how to position your pieces effectively, and how to restrict the opponent as far as possible. There are many plans and attacking concepts, which can be applied depending on the situation, often subject to the pawn structure. We will demonstrate the most important ones for our readers.

The Phalanx

First, a few general comments on the correct collaboration of the men.

Pawns are most flexible on their starting rank (the second rank for White, the seventh rank for Black), because depending on requirements they can advance by one or two squares. This can be decisive in pawn endings, when it may be important to force the opponent into zugzwang. Two pawns are most effective in a 'phalanx', i.e. next to each other (see diagram 179).

179

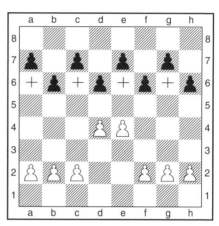

The crosses represent 'holes', i.e. weak points, which have been created by a one-sided advance of the pawns onto only the dark-colour squares. If a pawn advances, it should, if possible, be executed in such a way that the phalanx is restored by advancing the neighbouring pawn.

Collaboration between Pieces and Pawns

The collaboration between bishop and pawns is of great importance in any stage of the game. It is desirable to arrange the pawns so that they do not get blocked on the colour of the squares controlled by one's own bishop.

In an endgame with bishops on opposite-colour squares, it could otherwise happen that even a chain of three connected, passed pawns would not be sufficient to win (see diagram 180).

180

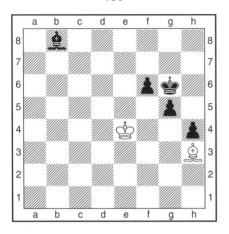

Here the black bishop is merely a spectator, since it cannot assist the pawns in their advance: the opponent's king and bishop will not allow it. If, for example, 1. ... ♔g6–h5, then 2.♔e4–f5. Equally futile is 1. ... g5–g4 2.♗h3xg4 ♔g6–g5 3.♗g4–h3 and so on. Black's material advantage is effectively worthless. The situation is different in diagram 181.

181

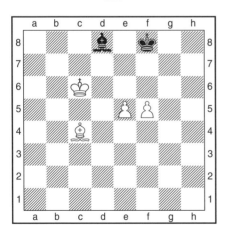

Here, the white bishop would be 'dead' after 1.e5–e6?. According to the rule

explained above, only **1.f5–f6!** is correct. The game is won because it is possible to re-establish the phalanx on the sixth rank, to move the e-pawn to e7 and to prevent the bishop from sacrificing itself for the two white pawns. The ending might go as follows: **1. ... ♔f8–e8 2.♔e6–d6 ♗d8–a5** (after 2...♔f8 White wins with ♗e2–h5 followed by ♔d7, but not immediately 3.♔d7? in view of 3...♗xf6! 4.exf6 – stalemate) **3.e5–e6 ♗a5–b4+ 4.♔d6–c7 ♗b4–a5+ 5.♔c7–c8 ♗a5–b4 6.♗c4–b5+ ♔e8–f8 7.♔c8–d7**, followed by **8.e6–e7+**.

The terms 'good' and 'bad' bishop are explained in examples 182 and 184. In diagram 182 the bishop and pawns complement one another, and White is practically certain to win, irrespective of whose turn it is to move (please check this!).

182

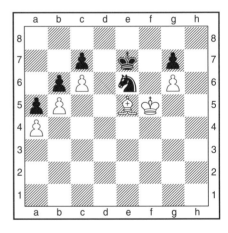

The advantage of the side with the bishop is that often it can be exchanged for the knight at a favourable moment, for example 1.♗e5–g3 ♘e6–d4+ 2.♔f5–e4 ♘d4–e6 3.♔e4–d5 ♔e7–f6 4.♗g3–h2! (or 4.♗xc7) 4. ... ♔f6–f5 5.♗h2–e5 ♘e6–f4+ (Black is in zugzwang) 6.♗e5xf4 and White gets there first. It is probably easiest for White to win with the triangulation manoeuvre 1.♔e4 ♘c5+ 2.♔d4! ♘e6+ (or 2...♔d8 3.♔d5) 3.♔d5, zugzwang, or 1...♘g5+ 2.♔f4 ♘e6+ 3.♔f5. Another disadvantage of the knight is its 'shortness of breath', especially on the edge of the board compared with the long-range bishop, which becomes clear in the variation 1.♔e4 ♘c5+ 2.♔d4 ♘xa4 3.♔d5. Black is powerless against the numerous threats.

But if we put the bishop on a light square, such as b1, it becomes 'bad'. Black has the advantage on the dark squares and White would have to defend himself.

In diagram 183, the crosses mark the squares which are controlled by both the knights and the pawns. A good positional player will always pay attention to this type of collaboration between knights and pawns.

184

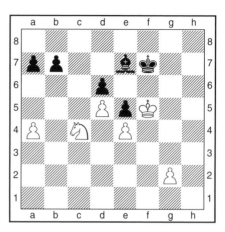

183

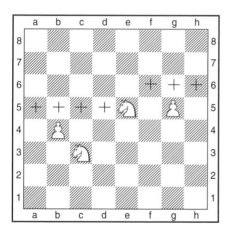

The knight *diagonally behind* the pawn represents the ideal position (knight at c3 and pawn at b4); those two pieces then command a phalanx of four squares: a5, b5, c5 and d5. The next best situation is when the knight is standing two squares *to the side of* the pawn.

Diagram 184 shows the strategically correct application of this principle. Black loses because:

1. He has a 'bad' bishop.
2. He cannot make use of his material advantage on the queen's wing.
3. He cannot prevent the advance of the g-pawn, which forces the invasion of the white king at e6.

The a4 pawn secures the knight against the black pawns; the d5 pawn blocks the weak point d6. If Black starts with 1. ... a7–a6, then 2.a4–a5 completely fixes the 2:1 pawn majority on the queen's wing. White would then possess an 'ideal' pawn advantage, his g-pawn. In such a situation, Black correctly starts with b7–b6. In this case, however, this is not very helpful, because he does not get the chance to play a7–a6 due to the knight's attack on b6.

Similar considerations also apply to the collaboration between the pieces. Thus, the queen is unable to win an endgame against two knights, when they build a phalanx and do not allow the hostile king to intrude easily (see diagram 185).

185

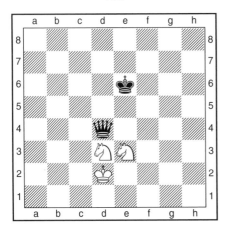

It may sound strange, but the knights are not so well placed when they are protecting each other (see diagram 186).

186

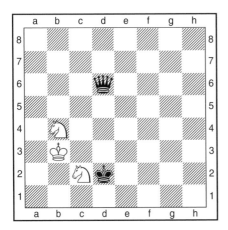

The hostile king will then find enough holes to get very close, create zugzwang and force the knights to separate and move to endangered, unprotected squares.

The winning plan for the stronger side, therefore, goes like this: force the hostile

king to the edge, imprison it, separate the knights, and then capture one after the other. This is achieved, for example, as follows: **1. ... ♛d6–e6+ 2.♚b3–b2 ♛e6–c4 3.♚b2–a3 ♚d2–c3 4.♚a3–a4 ♛c4–c5.** Now the white king is unable to move due to mate on a5, and a knight is immediately lost (an example from Emanuel Lasker).

Regarding the collaboration between rook and pawn, knowledge of the rule established by Siegbert Tarrasch is especially valuable: *rooks belong **behind** passed pawns*. Behind friendly pawns in order to support their advance, and behind hostile ones in order to hold them back. In each case, the flexibility of the rook increases, the further the pawn advances. It is disadvantageous when the rook stands *in front*: it will obstruct it's own pawn, and an enemy pawn will reduce the rook's effectiveness step by step.

Emanuel Lasker established another important guideline: the pieces should be supported and utilised according to their value, which is variable. 'If a piece has attracted hostile attention, it has increased in value and deserves support. If a piece is not sufficiently engaged, it has to be involved to help to resolve old problems and create new ones. A weak pawn should, if possible, be protected laterally by the rook or be compensated for by a counter attack, because the great power of the rook strives for a counter attack, even to such a degree that it will rather sacrifice the pawn, than to be fearfully attached to it.' The next example (see diagram 187) presented by Lasker makes a convincing case for the collaboration between rook and pawn.

187

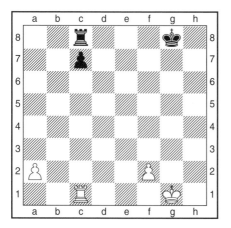

The greatest power lies in the a-pawn, because the hostile king is far removed, thus **1.a2–a4 ♖c8–a8 2.♖c1–a1 ♖a8–a5** and now the king marches to the support of the a-pawn, for example: **3.♔g1–f1 ♔g8–f7 4.♔f1–e2 ♔f7–e6 5.♔e2–d3 ♔e6–d5 6.♔d3–c3 ♔d5–c5**. Now it is the f-pawn's turn. **7.f2–f4 ♔c5–b6 8.♔c3–d4 ♖a5–f5 9.♔d4–e4 ♖f5–f8 10.a4–a5+ ♔b6–a6 11.f4–f5**. The collaboration between the king and the f-pawn is perfect; the king protects the pawn and the pawn protects the king against checks. The sequel could be: **11. … c7–c5 12.♖a1–c1** (otherwise the c-pawn may become troublesome) **12. … ♔a6xa5** (or 12...♔b5 13.a6) **13.♖c1xc5** and White wins easily.

Two other bits of advice from Lasker are worth taking to heart: 'If you can position a bishop, queen or rook in such a way that they have a strong effect, *without* the opponent being able to offer an exchange, you have some advantage', and his remark: "A lack of co-ordination between the pieces often manifests itself in the large physical distance between the pieces'.

We will conclude this chapter with an exception to the last rule.

188

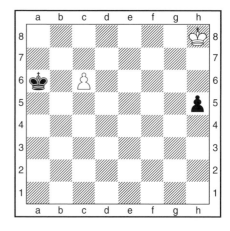

By Richard Réti (*Kagan's Latest Chess News*, 1921), White to play and draw. At first sight the situation appears hopeless for White. The black pawn advances irresistibly towards the first rank and promotes to a queen, whereas the white pawn is easily stopped… Despite the physical distance, there is a coordination between the white pieces, because the king can combine both tasks, catching up with the h-pawn and supporting the c-pawn: **1.♔h8–g7 h5–h4 2.♔g7–f6 h4–h3 3.♔f6–e7 h3–h2 4.c6–c7 ♔a6–b7 5.♔e7–d7**, draw, or **1.♔h8–g7 ♔a6–b6 2.♔g7–f6 h5–h4 3.♔f6–e5 h4–h3** (the king catches up with the pawn with 3…♔xc6 4.♔f4) **4.♔e5–d6** and the white pawn is just as valuable as the black one. An astonishing case.

32nd Hour

Plans and Ideas (II)
Systematic Attack on the King

How do I carry out an attack against the king? To attack means to try to conquer a vulnerable point. For this to happen, a number of conditions have to be met. We will take a look at diagram 189 (from the game Fleischmann–Cohn, St. Petersburg 1909). Here an attack against the king offers good prospects for White, because the pawn barrier on f7, g7, h6 is insufficiently protected and the black pieces in general are fairly ineffective. White, on the other hand, is fully developed. His army controls the centre, because Black has exchanged his central d5 pawn for the white pawn on c4 and has neglected to advance c7–c5.

189

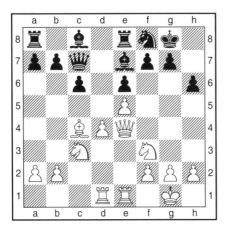

White now devised the plan of moving his queen to h5 and his rook from e1 to g4, to put pressure on the small number of defenders and finally overpower them. He exploits an opportunity offered by the advance of the h-pawn to h6. Black tries for counterplay in the centre, but he is too slow in initiating it. The sequel was: **1.♕e4–g4 b7–b6**. Black can oppose White's intentions by playing 1. … g7–g6. White would then move his knight to e4 in order to exploit the newly-created weakness on f6. According to a rule formulated by Wilhelm Steinitz, the defender should only move the protecting pawns in an absolute emergency (pawns are unable to move backwards!). The defence is made more difficult by the fact that Black cannot play f7–f5 due to ♕g4xf5.

2.♕g4–h5 ♗c8–b7 3.♖e1–e4. Now 3...c5 would make the situation even worse because of 4.d5. On the other hand, Black has to reckon with 4.♖g4, which threatens and pins the g7 pawn and causes the h6 pawn to be unprotected. 3...♔h8 can be ruled out because the f7 pawn has to remain protected. The defence 3...♘g6 is also unreliable in view of 4.♗xe6.

3. …♗e7–b4. Now the queen is protecting the f7 pawn, so that the king is able to escape to h8 in the event of ♖e4–g4. Black also thinks that after the exchange on c3 it will be easier for him to play c6–c5 (the advance d4–d5 would be less dangerous than before, because the knight no longer controls the d5 square). However, the exchange of the bishop has a significant disadvantage: the f6 and d6 squares lose their protection.

4.♖e4–g4 ♗b4xc3 Can White now interpose the capture with the queen on h6 (threatening mate on g7)? No! That would be a serious mistake because of 5...♘g6!. The pawn on g7 is unpinned and thus the queen at h6 is attacked, so that White is unable to recapture on c3.

5.b2xc3 ♔g8–h8 There is no other way of defending the h6 pawn (5...♘g6 6.♗d3). Now however, the h6 pawn is pinned and the f7 pawn is weak. This permits White to strengthen his offensive against the king.

6.♘f3–g5 ♖e8–e7 7.♘g5–e4 The knight turns its attention to the weak squares d6 and f6. The manoeuvre also has the aim of clearing the third rank for the rook on d1, which is standing ready as a reserve, and whose intervention will finally bring down the hostile bastion.

7. … ♖a8–d8 7...c5 was more in accordance with the plan. White would then have secured and strengthened his game with 8.♘d6.

8.♖d1–d3 c6–c5 A late delivery! **9.♘e4–f6!** With the intention of 10.♕xh6+! gxh6 11.♖g8 mate. **9. … ♘f8–g6 10.♖d3–h3** Black resigns. His king is completely surrounded. White will play ♕h5–g5 and threaten ♖h3xh6+ g7xh6 ♕g5xh6 mate, against which there is no defence. The black queen does not reach f8 in time.

190

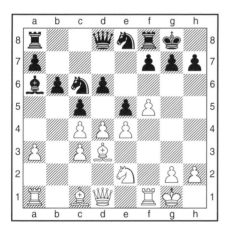

White to move

Diagram 190 is taken from the game David Bronstein–Miguel Najdorf, Candidates Tournament, Budapest 1950. The right plan is an attack against the king, because White is at a disadvantage on the queen's wing

due to the weakness on c4. If you want to attack successfully on the wing, the centre either has to be closed or you have to control it. So should White play 1.d4–d5 ? Black replies 1. … ♘c6–e7 and safeguards his king. White decides to involve his f-pawn, in order to increase the effectiveness of his rook on the f-file, clear the square f5 for his knight and, also very important, prevent the defensive move f7–f6.

1.f5–f6!

White has realised that neither 1...♘xf6 2.♗g5 h6 3.♗xf6 gxf6 4.♘g3 (intending ♘h5), nor 1...gxf6 2.♗h6 ♘g7 3.♘g3, after which there is the threat of ♕g4 and ♘h5, is attractive for Black.

1. … ♔g8–h8

Black clears the g-file for the rook. After 1...exd4 the following has to be reckoned with: 2.cxd4 ♘xd4 3.♘xd4 cxd4 4.♗g5 ♘xf6 5.e5 dxe5 6.♗xh7+ ♔xh7 7.♗xf6 gxf6 8.♕h5+ ♔g7 9.♕g4+ ♔h7 10.♖f3 followed by ♖h3+ and mate.

2.d4–d5!

Now this move is appropriate: the knight can no longer go to e7.

2. … ♘c6–a5 3.♘e2–g3 g7xf6 A longer resistance can be put up with 3...g6, although after 4.♗h6 ♖g8 5.♕e2 the black position is very constricted and without any possibility for counter-play.

4.♘g3–f5 ♗a6–c8 5.♕d1–h5 ♗c8xf5 6.e4xf5!

6.♕xf5 would be met by 6...♖g8 and ...♖g6, followed by ...♘g7. The royal fortress would then be difficult to seize.

6. … ♖f8–g8

There is no time for 6...♘b3 because of 7.♖f3 (7...♖g8 8.♕xh7+ ♔xh7 9.♖h3+ ♔g7 10.♗h6+ and ♗f8 mate).

7.♖f1–f3 ♖g8–g7 The square h7 is too weak. Thus 7...♘g7 would allow the typical mating finish 8.♕xh7+ ♔xh7 9.♖h3+

♘h5 10.♖xh5+ etc.

8.♗c1–h6 ♖g7–g8 Or 8...♕e7 9.♖h3 ♕f8 10.♖g3 ♕g8 11.♗xg7+ ♘xg7 12.♕h6 and wins, as Black can do nothing against the manoeuvre ♖a1–e1–e4–g4. **9.♖f3–h3** with the intention of 10.♗f8. If Black replies 9...♘g7, this is met by 10.♕h4 and he is defenceless against 11.♗g5. This is why he gives up the fight and resigns.

191

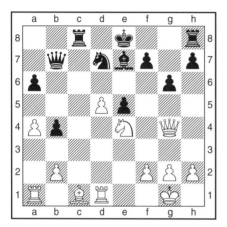

We have presented two plans of attack against the castled position. In diagram 191 White's plan, which leads to a swift victory, consists in preventing the hostile king from castling (Alexander Alekhine–Karel Hromadka, Pistyan 1922). White to move is faced with the threat of f7–f5. Does he have to retreat his queen or knight and allow kingside castling? No. Alekhine employs a tactical finesse to keep the king in the centre. As often happens, strategy and tactics work hand in hand.

1.♗c1–g5! Played in the knowledge that 1...f5 can be favourably answered by 2.♕h4!. Black would be in an uncomfortable position after 2...fxe4 3.♗xe7. Furthermore, White realised that 1...f6 would

fail to 2.♕e6! (threatening 3.♘d6+, as well as 3.d6 and other possibilities). Black contented himself with **1. ... h7–h6 2.♗g5xe7 ♔e8xe7**, and White had realised his plan. He now forced a further weakening with **3.♕g4–h4+**, since the king dare not move (because of ♘d6). **3. ... g6–g5** (or 3...f6 4.f4) **4.♕h4–g4 ♖c8–c4 5.♕g4–f5** (threatening 6.♕xf7+) **5. ... ♖h8–f8 6.b2–b3 ♖c4–c8 7.♘e4–f6!** A crushing move, as 7...♘xf6 is not possible in view of 8.d6+. **7. ... ♖c8–c5 8.♘f6xd7 ♕b7–c8** (or 8...♕xd7 9.♕xe5+ ♔d8 10.♕b8+) **9.d5–d6+** Black resigns, because a rook is lost (9...♔d8 10.♕f6+ ♔xd7 11.♕e7+ ♔c6 12.d7).

The king is, of course, the favourite target for an attack, but by no means the only one. You will read more about this in the next lesson.

33rd Hour

Plans and Ideas (III)

It is not so far-fetched to compare a good chess player with the commander of an army. Just like the latter, he has to deploy his forces, spy out the opponent's weaknesses and design plans of attack. One difference, and a significant one at that, is that initially the two sides are equal with regard to their material and its flexibility. It all depends on who can deploy his forces more effectively and purposefully.

Systematic Attack on the Queen's Wing

When deciding on a plan, the choice often depends on the distribution of the pawns and their specific arrangement. If, for example, I have three pawns on one wing and the opponent has only two, I will logically try to create a passed pawn there. Such an action is especially promising when the hostile king is far away. A classic example is the ending of the game Marshall–Capablanca, from their match in New York 1909 (Capablanca won eight games, Marshall one).

192

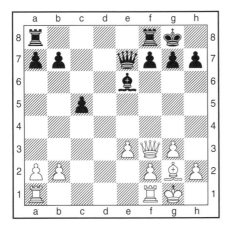

It is White to move. The capture on b7 would be agreeable for Black: after the exchange of queens he plays ...♖ab8 and takes revenge on the white b-pawn. A good plan would be to exploit the white pawn majority on the king's wing and to initiate an attack (e3–e4, ♕f3–e3, f2–f4–f5). In the game White restricts himself to transparent, tactical manoeuvres, which do not help him to make any progress.

1.♖f1–c1 Now that the c5 pawn has been attacked, 2.♕xb7 really is threatened. **1. ... ♖a8–b8 2.♕f3–e4** This pins the bishop at e6, so that 2...c4 can be answered by 3.♖xc4. **2. ... ♕e7–c7 3.♖c1–c3 b7–b5** The Cuban, who became world champion twelve years later, sets his pawn majority in motion. **4.a2–a3 c5–c4 5.♗g2–f3 ♖f8–d8!** White has also not concerned himself

with the occupation of the only open file. **6.♖a1–d1 ♖d8xd1+ 7.♗f3xd1 ♖b8–d8 8.♗d1–f3 g7–g6.** Black wants to move his rook off the back rank. Thus, it is time to prepare a hiding place for the king, and a dark-square one, since the opponent has a light-square bishop.

9.♕e4–c6 ♕c7–e5 10.♕c6–e4 ♕e5xe4 11.♗f3xe4 ♖d8–d1+ 12.♔g1–g2 a7–a5 The further the pawns advance, the more dangerous they become. **13.♖c3–c2 b5–b4 14.a3xb4 a5xb4 15.♗e4–f3 ♖d1–b1 16.♗f3–e2 b4–b3!** A good idea: Black obtains an outpost for his rook on c2. **17.♖c2–d2** After 17.♖c3 ♖xb2 18.♗xc4 ♖c2! White also loses his bishop. **17. ... ♖b1–c1!** There is no adequate defence against the threat of ...♖c2. **18.♗e2–d1 c4–c3 19.b2xc3 b3–b2 20.♖d2xb2 ♖c1xd1**.

The endgame is won for Black. It is interesting to observe how Capablanca, who was given the nickname 'chess machine', handles the technical phase. First, he threatens to win the c3 pawn with ...♖c1, and later he also employs mating threats.

21.♖b2–c2 ♗e6–f5 22.♖c2–b2 ♖d1–c1 23.♖b2–b3 ♗f5–e4+ 24.♔g2–h3. Or 24.f3 ♖c2+. **24. ... ♖c1–c2 25.f2–f4 h7–h5.** With the intention of 26...♗f5+ 27.♔h4 ♖xh2+, followed by ...♔g7. **26.g3–g4 h5xg4+ 27.♔h3xg4 ♖c2xh2 28.♖b3–b4 f7–f5+ 29.♔g4–g3.** If 29.♔g5, then 29... ♔g7 and mate on h5 is threatened. **29. ... ♖h2–e2 30.♖b4–c4 ♖e2xe3+ 31.♔g3–h4 ♔g8–g7 32.♖c4–c7+ ♔g7–f6 33.♖c7–d7 ♗e4–g2 34.♖d7–d6+ ♔f6–g7** and White resigns. This is how, with a suitable formation, the 'pawn majority on the queen's wing' can be exploited.

Another important activity, that mostly takes place on the queen's wing, is the 'minority attack'. It serves to open files for the rooks and create weaknesses, and it arises when the opponent has provided a point of attack by the advance of a pawn. Here is a typical game on this topic.

Vasily Smyslov–Paul Keres, World Championship Tournament, The Hague/Moscow 1948. The frequently-occurring position illustrated in diagram 193 was reached after the moves 1.d4 d5 2.c4 e6 3.♘c3 ♘f6 4.♗g5 c6 5.e3 ♘bd7 6.cxd5 exd5 7.♗d3 ♗e7 8.♘f3 0–0 9.♕c2 ♖e8 10.0–0 ♘f8.

193

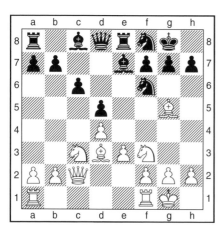

The black pawn on c6 gives White the opportunity to open the b-file and either isolate the d5 pawn, or weaken the c6 pawn and make it 'backward' (it stays behind its neighbouring pawns, a target for attack on an opened file). The rooks will start trouble on the b and c-files, which can easily spread to the king's wing. The sequel was:

11.♖a1–b1 ♘f8–g6 12.b2–b4 This action is called a minority attack, since two of White's pawns are attacking three of Black's. **12. ... ♗e7–d6** Smyslov considers 12...a6 13.a4 ♘e4 to be better. **13.b4–**

b5 ♗c8–d7 14.b5xc6 ♗d7xc6 The recapture with the b-pawn would have resulted in a backward pawn, but on the other hand it would have preserved the bishop for the defence of the light squares. **15.♕c2–b3** Threatening to capture on f6, followed by ♘xd5 (in the event of ...♕xf6) **15 ... ♗d6–e7 16.♗g5xf6 ♗e7xf6 17.♗d3–b5** Now there will be a backward pawn on c6 after all. **17. ... ♕d8–d6 18.♖f1–c1 h7–h5** Black does not want to wait until he is crushed on the queen's wing. His counterattack, though, is quite harmless, since White has no weaknesses on the other wing. **19.♘c3–e2 h5–h4 20.♗b5xc6 b7xc6 21.♕b3–a4 ♘g6–e7 22.♖b1–b7!** This was the purpose of the action. White is in a superior position. Apart from the c-pawn, the a-pawn is also in danger. **22. ... a7–a5 23.h2–h3** This halts the h4 pawn, which at the same time is marked as a weakness. Black cannot exploit the h3 square here, since he is too involved on the queen's wing and the advance g7–g5 would be too dangerous. **23. ... ♖e8–b8 24.♖c1–b1 ♖b8xb7 25.♖b1xb7 c6–c5** This removes one weakness (c6), but creates another (d5). **26.♖b7–b5! c5xd4** (or 26...c4 27.♖xa5) **27.♘e2xd4 ♖a8–c8** The same move follows after 27...♕c7. It counters the mate threat and threatens the a5 pawn. **28.♘d4–b3 ♗f6–c3** Black has to abandon one of his two weaknesses. White's strategy has triumphed. **29.♕a4xh4** and White wins. It is also worth playing through the final phase of the game – a model of impeccable winning technique.
29...♖c4 30.g4 a4 31.♘bd4 ♗xd4 32.♘xd4 ♕e5 33.♘f3 ♕d6 34.♖a5 ♖c8 35.♖xa4 ♘g6 36.♕h5 ♕f6 37.♕f5 ♕c6 38.♖a7 ♖f8 39.♖d7 d4 40.♖xd4 ♖a8 41.a4 and Black resigns, since 41...♖xa4 42.♖d8+ ♘f8 43.♕xf7+ ♔xf7 44.♘e5+ is hopeless.
It is clear that there was a guiding principle

behind all these moves – and there always should be.

An additional type of attack on the queen's wing is pure piece pressure. For this we will look at the position in diagram 194 from the game Nimzowitsch–Capablanca, St. Petersburg 1914 (Black to move).

194

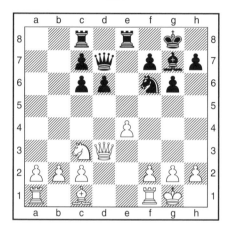

White has won the black a-pawn and his pawn formation is unblemished. Despite this, he has had to pay a price: Black is better developed and he possesses two open files for his rooks on the queen's wing. Black's plan now consists in moving his rooks to the open files and in also bringing his knight to the queen's wing, if possible to the square c4. With the combined pressure of all his forces on the white pawns, he wants to regain the lost material under favourable circumstances. Capablanca points out that his plan has the added benefit of being masked, because it seems at first that the target is the e4 pawn.

1. ... ♛d7–e6 2.f2–f3 The move 2.♖e1 should be tested, and only after 2...d5 – 3.f3, for example 3...♖cd8 4.♛f1 and the white position is difficult to breach. **2. ... ♞f6–d7 3.♗c1–d2** 3.b3 ♞c5 4.♛d2 is playable. **3. ... ♞d7–e5 4.♛d3–e2 ♞e5–c4 5.♖a1–b1** Now 5.b3? would be a grave mistake because of 5...♗d4+ 6.♔h1 ♞xd2 7.♛xd2 ♛e5 and Black wins. **5. ... ♖c8–a8 6.a2–a4** After 6.b3 ♞xd2 7.♛xd2 ♖a3 the a-pawn falls; the knight cannot hold its position on c3. **6. ... ♞c4xd2 7.♛e2xd2 ♛e6–c4 8.♖f1–d1 ♖e8–b8!** Much more powerful than the exchange on c3. **9.♛d2–e3** According to Tarrasch, d3 was a more favourable position for the queen. But then Black is easily able to increase the pressure with 9...♛c5+ 10.♔h1 ♖b4. **9. ... ♖b8–b4 10.♛e3–g5** Completely 'misguided'. White loses because he does not know how to devise a counter plan. **10. ... ♗g7–d4+** (according to Tarrasch, the immediate 10...♖ab8 is even more effective) **11.♔g1–h1 ♖a8–b8!** White is defenceless against the combined pressure of all the pieces. He has to sacrifice the exchange, in order to save his knight. **12.♖d1xd4 ♛c4xd4** and Black has a clear advantage: 13.♖d1 ♛c4 14.h4 ♖xb2 15.♛d2 ♛c5 16.♖e1? (this loses the h4 pawn; more tenacious is 16.♖a1 ♖2b4 17.a5 ♖c4) 16...♛h5! (now 17.♛f2 is futile due to 17...♖xc2! 18.♛xc2 ♛xh4+ and ...♛xe1) 17.♖a1 ♛xh4+ 18.♔g1 ♛h5 19.a5 ♖a8 20.a6 ♛c5+ 21.♔h1 ♛c4 22.a7 ♛c5 23.e5 ♛xe5 24.♖a4 ♛h5+ 25.♔g1 ♛c5+ 26.♔h2 d5 27.♖h4 ♖xa7! (because 28.♛h6 ♛xc3 29.♛xh7+ ♔f8 is only a vain attempt) 28.♞d1 and at the same time White resigned.

34th Hour

Plans and Ideas (IV)
The Natural Basic Plan

Possibly the oldest game plan, which can be found in the historical development of chess, and which controls the events on the chess board from beginning to end, originates with the Italian masters of the 16th century, the inventors of the 'gambit'. This plan pursues the aim of moving the pieces onto flexible positions as quickly as possible, not sparing the pawns and attacking the hostile king, if possible before he gets the chance to castle.

We will take a look at a game which is included in the manuscript of Greco, the 'Calabrese' (1600–1634), the original of which is kept in Florence.

1.e2–e4 e7–e5 2.♘g1–f3 ♘b8–c6 3.♗f1–c4 ♗f8–c5 4.c2–c3 ♘g8–f6 Compare this with the Italian Game in the section on openings. Greco presents a nice variation: **4...♕e7 5.0–0 d6 6.d4 ♗b6 7.♗g5 f6 8.♗h4 g5? 9.♘xg5 fxg5 10.♕h5+ ♔d7 11.♗xg5 ♕g7? 12.♗e6+ ♔xe6 13.♕e8+ ♘ge7 14.d5 mate.** This opening was also used in the 20th century; but Black should play 7...♘f6.

5.d2–d4 e5xd4 6.c3xd4 ♗c5–b4+ 7.♘b1–c3 ♘f6xe4 8.0–0 ♘e4xc3 Capturing with the bishop is less dangerous.

9.b2xc3 ♗b4xc3 10.♕d1–b3 The move 10.♗a3 is thought to be more precise. **10. ... ♗c3xd4** Greco also mentions 10...♗xa1 **11.♗xf7+ ♔f8 12.♗g5** with advantage for White. Black defends himself best with 10...d5. **11.♗c4xf7+ ♔e8–f8 12.♗c1–g5 ♗d4–f6 13.♖a1–e1 ♘c6–e7 14.♗f7–h5 ♘e7–g6 15.♘f3–e5 ♘g6xe5 16.♖e1xe5 g7–g6 17.♗g5–h6+ ♗f6–g7 18.♖e5–f5+ ♔f8–e7 19.♖f1–e1+ ♗g7–e5 20.♖e1xe5+ ♔e7–d6 21.♕b3–d5 mate.**

This basic idea calls for a counter plan: to position the pieces on suitable, unassailable squares, to secure the king and finally to beat the opponent with a material advantage. The value of the pawn was emphasised especially by the Frenchman Philidor, who deployed his pieces behind a phalanx of pawns.

The 'soundest plan known to the history of chess' was found by Emanuel Lasker, the philosopher among world champions, in the games of the Frenchman Louis Charles Mahé de la Bourdonnais (1797–1840). Lasker describes it in his *Chess Manual*: 'to combat every developed unit of the enemy in the centre with a force at least equal to it and to follow the enemy, after having thrown him back in the centre, with a well-supported advance post in the heart of his position'.

We will take as an example one of the many games played by La Bourdonnais with his English counterpart, McDonnell (Black), in a series of lengthy matches (1834).

1.d2–d4 d7–d5 2.c2–c4 d5xc4 3.e2–e3 e7–e5 4.♗f1xc4 e5xd4 5.e3xd4 ♘g8–f6 6.♘b1–c3 ♗f8–e7 7.♘g1–f3 0–0 8.♗c1–e3 c7–c6 9.h2–h3 White does not want to be distracted by ...♗g4 or ...♘g4 and he 'sacrifices' a tempo. **9. ... ♘b8–d7 10.0–0 ♘d7–b6 11.♗c4–b3 ♘f6–d5 12.a2–a4 a7–a5 13.♘f3–e5** The outpost emphasises White's control over the central area of the board. **13. ... ♗c8–e6**

195

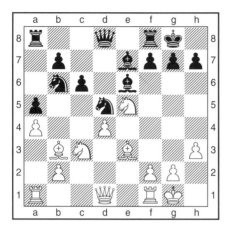

14.♗b3–c2 'White begins to line up his pieces against the enemy king. The square h7, only defended by the king, is the first target for an attack' (Lasker). **14. ... f7–f5** This weakens the squares e6 and e5. The white knight is now unassailable. 14...♘f6 is more solid. **15.♕d1–e2 f5–f4** 'Black leaves the white king's bishop a free diagonal which is serious' (Lasker). **16.♗e3–d2 ♕d8–e8 17.♖a1–e1 ♗e6–f7 18.♕e2–e4** 'White has now completed preparations'. **18. ... g7–g6 19.♗d2xf4 ♘d5xf4 20.♕e4xf4 ♗f7–c4 21.♕f4–h6 ♗c4xf1 22.♗c2xg6** 'All restraints are torn aside.' **22. ... h7xg6 23.♘e5xg6 ♘b6–c8** More resistance, according to Lasker, would have been offered by 23...♗f6 24.♖xe8 ♖fxe8 25.♔xf1. **24.♕h6–h8+ ♔g8–f7 25.♕h8–h7+ ♔f7–f6 26.♘g6–f4** (threatening ♘e4 mate) **26. ... ♗f1–d3 27.♖e1–e6+ ♔f6–g5 28.♕h7–h6+ ♔g5–f5 29.♖e6–e5** (or 29.g4) mate.

The same plan is even more effectively demonstrated in the games of Paul Morphy, the brilliant American from Louisiana. He played for only two years in serious chess tournaments (1857/58), but during this time he defeated everyone who sat down opposite him. Morphy regarded chess as an art, and was dedicated to it with an almost religious devotion. He declined any monetary rewards and used his prize money to pay the expenses of his defeated opponents. Here is an example of his inspired play. The game plan outlined above is clearly recognisable (played in New York, 1857).

Schulten–Morphy (King's Gambit)
1.e2–e4 e7–e5 2.f2–f4 d7–d5 The Falkbeer Counter-Gambit instantly takes up the fight for the centre and corresponds perfectly with Morphy's intentions. **3.e4xd5 e5–e4 4.♘b1–c3** Later 4.d3 ♘f6 5.♘d2 was preferred in order to avoid the pinning of the knight. **4. ... ♘g8–f6 5.d2–d3 ♗f8–b4 6.♗c1–d2 e4–e3** Black opens the e-file for his rook with gain of tempo.

7.♗d2xe3 0–0 8.♗e3–d2 ♗b4xc3 9.b2xc3 ♖f8–e8+ 10.♗f1–e2 ♗c8–g4 11.c3–c4 A loss of a tempo, in order to defend the pawn on d5. White, though, is already in a difficult position.

196

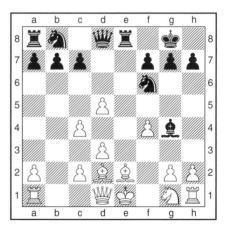

11. ... c7–c6! A typical manoeuvre: Black

uses the advanced white pawn to open lines and speed up his own development. **12.d5xc6(?) ♘b8xc6 13.♔e1–f1 ♖e8xe2!** In this way Black keeps the pin in place and wins material. **14.♘g1xe2 ♘c6–d4 15.♕d1–b1 ♗g4xe2+ 16.♔f1–f2 ♘f6–g4+ 17.♔f2–g1** If 17.♔e1, then 17...♕h4+ followed by ♕e7. But now Black can give checkmate in seven moves.

17. ... ♘d4–f3+ 18.g2xf3 ♕d8–d4+ 19.♔g1–g2 ♕d4–f2+ 20.♔g2–h3 ♕f2xf3+ 21.♔h3–h4 ♘g4–h6 22.♕b1–g1 ♘h6–f5+ 23.♔h4–g5 ♕f3–h5 mate.

Today's masters also depend on this plan and make frequent use of it. In particular Mikhail Tal (1936–1992, world champion 1960/61), produced some impressive examples. The breakthrough in the centre was often seen in his games, also with the closed openings. Here is an example from the Chess Olympiad in Munich, 1958.
Mikhail Tal–Zravko Milev (Queen's Gambit)
1.c2–c4 c7–c5 2.♘b1–c3 ♘b8–c6 3.♘g1–f3 ♘g8–f6 4.e2–e3 e7–e6 5.d2–d4 d7–d5 6.c4xd5 ♘f6xd5 7.♗f1–c4 ♘d5–b6 8.♗c4–b5 a7–a6 Black neglects his development a little.
9.♗b5xc6+ b7xc6 10.0–0 ♗c8–b7 11.♘c3–e4! Tal wants to persuade the opponent to exchange on d4 and thus open the e-file and the c1–h6 diagonal. **11. ... ♘b6–d7 12.♕d1–c2 ♕d8–b6 13.♘f3–e5! c5xd4** More resistance could have been offered by 13...♘xe5. **14.♘e5xd7 ♔e8xd7 15.e3xd4 ♔d7–e8 16.♗c1–e3 ♕b6–c7** Here the loss of the right to castle proves to be a big disadvantage (see diagram 197).

197

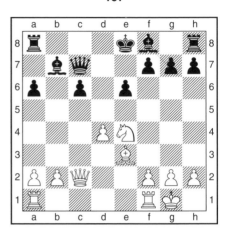

17.d4–d5!! Brilliantly opening lines (see the next move). **17. ... e6xd5 18.♖f1–e1 ♔e8–d8** If 18...dxe4, then 19.♕xe4+ ♕e7 (19...♗e7 20.♗c5) 20.♕d3 ♖d8 21.♕b3 and wins.
19.♕c2–b3 c6–c5 20.♘e4xc5 and Black resigns.

The natural basic plan alone is not sufficient; frequently it depends on a step-by-step implementation. This will be discussed in the next lesson.

35th Hour

Plans and Ideas (V)
The Bishop Pair

Many years ago, there was occasional talk of the 'death of chess by drawing', and it was considered changing the rules. There were proposals to eliminate opening theory (by positioning the pieces arbitrarily on the back rank), to value stalemate higher than a draw and to introduce a board with 100 squares and new pieces, which, for example, would combine the powers of queen and knight. None of these suggestions was adopted, and the old game of chess stayed as it was. Up to now, there has been no one who is in absolute control of it, if there is a genuine will to fight and acceptable risks are taken. In recent times, tournament rules have changed, in so far as they put a greater demand on a player's stamina. Thus, games often have to be finished in one session, so that 60 moves have to be played without a break, and thereafter a time limit is placed on the remainder of the game. Even when there is a tie in high-ranking qualifying matches, they are decided by rapid games – a previously inconceivable procedure. These rules are not in accordance with the spirit of chess. Mistakes accumulate: a logical end to a game is often impossible due to a lack of time.

Players of the first rank, who normally will not make obvious mistakes, have to employ subtle means, if they want to be successful against their own kind.

Let's take the notion of the 'bishop pair', which often plays an important role. Experience has shown that, in certain circumstances, it can be beneficial to possess both bishops, when the opponent has exchanged a bishop against a knight (everything else being equal). It does, however, require a lot of experience to be sure how useful the bishop pair will be, in the given circumstances. Almost always, open lines are required, because the bishops have to be able to move quickly.

If two bishops are standing next to each other and are aiming at the hostile king's position, these are known as 'Horwitz bishops'.

The following short game shows an example: **1.e4 e5 2.d4 exd4 3.c3 dxc3 4.♗c4 cxb2 5.♗xb2 ♗b4+** (according to theory, 5...d5! is correct) **6.♘c3 ♘f6 7.♘ge2**

♘xe4 (excessively greedy) **8.0–0 ♘xc3 9.♘xc3 ♗xc3 10.♗xc3 0–0?** (It is still possible to avoid the worst with the double move of the d-pawn.)

198

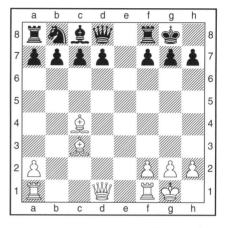

Black reckons only with 11.♕d4 when he has the defence 11...♕g5. The manoeuvre **11.♕d1–g4! g7–g6** and only now **12.♕g4–d4** confronts him with unavoidable checkmate. The co-operation of the bishops is evident: the light-square bishop pins (the pawn on f7, preventing f7–f6), and the dark-square bishop threatens.

Certain systems of defence or attack have the tendency to provide one side with a 'home-grown' pair of bishops. These include Nimzowitsch's variation of the Indian Defence (1.d4 ♘f6), in which 2.c4 e6 is followed by 3.♘c3 ♗b4 and Black is ready to exchange bishop for knight. Also in the Exchange Variation of the Ruy Lopez (1.e4 e5 2.♘f3 ♘c6 3.♗b5 a6 4.♗xc6 dxc6), White leaves the opponent with the bishop pair, but in return he obtains the better pawn position and gains time. The outcome of the game depends on which player achieves a better return on his investment. In practice, the task often presents itself like this: I possess the bishop pair, but I am unable to do much with them because the position is relatively closed. This means that I have to try and open lines, in order to increase the value of the bishops.

Instructive in this sense is a game from the Alekhine Memorial Tournament, Moscow 1956.
David Bronstein–Harry Golombek
Nimzo-Indian Defence
1.d2–d4 ♞g8–f6 2.c2–c4 e7–e6 3.♞b1–c3 ♝f8–b4 4.♞g1–f3 b7–b6 5.e2–e3 ♝c8–b7 6.♝f1–d3 ♞f6–e4 Black wants to give the opponent doubled pawns, as compensation for surrendering the bishop pair. **7.0–0 ♝b4xc3** The following was shown to be too dangerous in the game Denker-Fine, USA, 1944: 7...♞xc3 8.bxc3 ♝xc3 9.♜b1 ♝a5 10.♝a3 d6 11.c5! 0–0 12.cxd6 cxd6 13.e4 ♜e8 14.e5 dxe5 15 ♞xe5 and White advantageously opened the position. **8.b2xc3 0–0** No less risky at this point is the grabbing of the pawn on c3: 8...♞xc3 9.♛c2 ♝xf3 10.gxf3 ♛g5+ 11.♔h1 ♛h5 12.♜g1! ♛xf3+ 13.♜g2 f5 14.♝b2 ♞e4 15.d5! with great pressure. Here the two knights are by no means equal to the bishops. **9.♞f3–e1!** Thus White is able to drive back the centralised knight and finally gain control of the centre. He can tolerate the fact that the light-square bishop is temporarily 'demoted' (obstructed by the white pawns). **9. ... f7–f5 10.f2–f3 ♞e4–f6 11.a2–a4 ♞b8–c6 12.e3–e4 f5xe4 13.f3xe4 e6–e5** Black had to reckon with 14.♝g5 followed by e4–e5. Even worse would have been 13...h6, which unpleasantly loosens the king's wing. **14.♝c1–g5 ♛d8–e7** (14...exd4? 15.cxd4 ♞xd4 16.e5) **15.♞e1–c2 ♛e7–d6** Black apparently wants to provoke d4–d5, which would be beneficial to him in the

strategic sense. White, however, finds a tactical measure that enables him to avoid the surrender of the c5 square (see diagram 199).

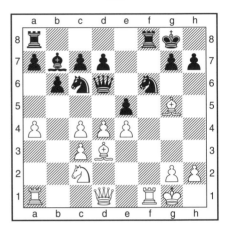

16.♝g5–h4! After 16...exd4 17.cxd4 the move 17...♞xd4? would cost a piece in view of 18.♝g3! ♛c5 19.♝f2!. **16. ... ♜a8–e8 17.♝h4–g3 ♛d6–e7 18.♞c2–e3!** Again, Black has to forgo the win of a pawn, this time due to 18...exd4? 19.♞f5 ♛d8 20.cxd4 ♞xe4 21.♛g4!. The characteristic of an exceptional player: he takes in all the nuances of the position and uses them to his advantage. **18. ... d7–d6 19.♝g3–h4** This makes the move of the knight to d5 more effective. **19. ... ♞c6–d8 20.♞e3–d5 ♝b7xd5 21.c4xd5** The strong outpost was unbearable. By this means the light-square bishop has come to life and it is threatening to move to b5. **21. ... c7–c6 22.♛d1–b3! ♔g8–h8 23.♜a1–e1 h7–h6 24.♛b3–a3** Here the queen operates well, by attacking the d6 square and being generally effective on the a3–f8 diagonal. **24. ... g7–g5 25.♝h4–g3 ♞f6–d7** The square e5 needs protection. A move such as 25...♞h5 costs at least two pawns in view of 26.dxe5 ♘xg3 27.exd6. **26.d5xc6 ♘d8xc6 27.♗d3–b5** Now the dynamic force of the bishop pair quickly decides the game. **27. ... ♖f8xf1+ 28.♖e1xf1 ♘c6–b8** (28...♖c8 is more tenacious) **29.♗b5–c4** The rook is threatening to occupy f7. The opponent prevents this, but weakens his back rank with the unavoidable rook exchange. **29. ... ♖e8–f8 30.♖f1xf8+ ♕e7xf8** The knight is now overloaded, so that White wins a pawn. **31.d4xe5 ♘d7–c5** (31...dxe5 would have cost a piece because of 32.♕xf8+ ♘xf8 33.♗xe5+) **32.e5xd6 ♘c5xe4** (see diagram 200).

200

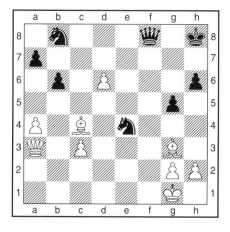

33.d6–d7! A pretty queen sacrifice rounds off the game. White has impressively carried out his basic idea. The bishops have as many open lines as they need. If Black takes the queen, it is recreated on d8 and quickly gives checkmate. With 33...♘xd7 343.♕xf8+ ♘xf8 35.♗e5+ ♔h7 36.♗d3 a knight would be lost.
33. ... ♘e4–c5 34.♗g3–e5+ ♔h8–h7 35.♗c4–d3+! Giving check is possible because the queen at f8 is unprotected, so that the knight on c5 is pinned. Black

resigns. The final position after the forced 35...♔g8 36.♕a2+! shows a devastating assault on three diagonals.

36th Hour

Plans and Ideas (VI)
Rook on an Open File

Aaron Nimzowitsch, an independent thinker and a world championship contender during Alekhine's era, derived in particular strategic terms 'prophylaxis', 'centralisation' and 'over-protection', which have become universally known. However, in his book *My System*, the brilliant Latvian talks about the theory of *open files* as being one of the 'polishing stones' of his system. This is the domain of the strongest pieces, the queen and the two rooks, especially the latter, since of course the queen can also be effective along a diagonal.

At the beginning of the game all the files are closed, and the pieces, apart from the knights, are imprisoned. If a pawn captures or is captured, a file is opened at the same time. The value of an open file for a rook is immediately obvious. During our course, we have already come across many useful applications. The tools that Nimzowitsch's instruction offers the enthusiastic learner are worthy of notice. These are the most important guidelines:
1. Every operation on a file has the aim of penetrating the hostile camp (generally the last or penultimate rank).
2. Obstacles should be attacked and ultimately removed (see diagram 201).
3. The invasion can sometimes be achieved by 'revolutionary' means (see diagram 202).

4. You should create an outpost and occupy it. The correct position for an outpost is on an open (or semi-open) file, protected by a friendly pawn, within the hostile camp (see diagram 203).

5. If a rook has advanced to the penultimate rank, it should look for a target to attack (see diagram 204).

6. In the endgame, a rook on the penultimate rank nearly always wins in combination with a passed pawn, provided that the hostile king is kept on the back rank and is somewhat removed from the passed pawn (see diagram 205).

7. Two rooks on the seventh rank are able to force the hostile king out of the corner into which it retreated for shelter, and threaten mate or a double attack (see diagram 207).

201

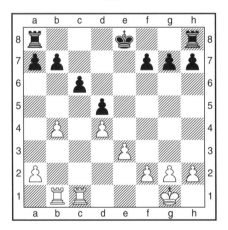

Diagram 201 illustrates point 2, a pattern that we have basically already met as a 'minority attack'. The rook on c1 encounters the obstacle c6 on its way to paradise (the c7 square). It would be futile to try and remove this pawn, which is well protected,

by employing pieces. White forces access for one of his rooks with **1.b4–b5!** and obtains favourable positions for both rooks.

202

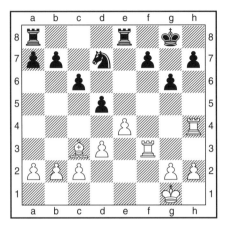

Although the h-file is closed (pawn on h2), by a progressive operation the rooks turn from the f-file to the h-file. Now the direct attack 1.♖f3–h3? would be ineffective, as Black has time to protect himself with 1. ... ♘d7–f8. White is tempted by the checkmate square h8, due to the open bishop's diagonal. He takes 'revolutionary' (Nimzowitsch) action by opening the h-file with a rook sacrifice.

1.♖h4xh7! ♔g8xh7 2.♖f3–h3+ ♔h7–g8 3.♖h3–h8 mate.

203

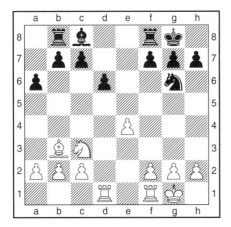

The rook at d1 is 'biting on granite'. White makes progress by occupying the d5 outpost with his knight, thus forcing a weakening of the d6 pawn, i.e. he plays **1.♞c3–d5!**. The e4 pawn is important, as otherwise Black could secure himself with c7–c6 and d6–d5. Now however, after **1. ... c7–c6 2.♞d5–e3 ♜f8–d8** (or 2...♜e8 4.♜xd6 ♜xe4 5.♜d8+ ♞f8 6.♜fd1 with a big advantage) **3.♞e3–c4** on the d-file he creates a welcome target, which will then be attacked.

204

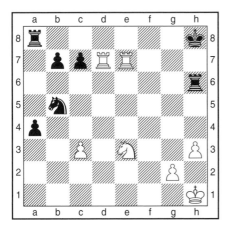

Diagram 204 illustrates point 5. The target that White chooses is the h7 square. However, speed is required because of the dangerous a-pawn. By sacrificing a pawn, he drives away the only protective piece, the black rook. A strong reserve is standing by in the form of the knight: **1.♞e3–g4!** Not quite so effective is 1.♞f5 (the move given by Nimzowitsch) because of 1...♜g6. **1. ... ♜h6–g6** (or 1...♜d6 2.♜xd6 ♞xd6 3.♞f6, or 1...♜ha6 2. ♞e5!, when there is no satisfactory defence against the threat of 3. ♜h7+ ♚g8 4. ♜dg7+ ♚f8 5. ♞d7+, or 1...a3 2.♞xh6 a2 3.♜h7 mate, or 1...♜h4 2.♞f6, and mate on h7 is unavoidable) **2.♞g4–e5** and wins, for example 2...♜h6/g5 3.♞f7+, winning the rook, or 2...♜g3 3.♚h2, or 2...♜f6 3.♜h7+ ♚g8 4.♜dg7+ ♚f8 5.♞d7+ followed by mate.

205

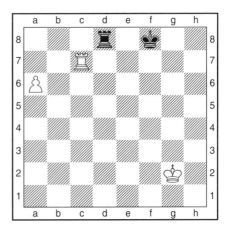

A classic case of point 6: Black to move is powerless against the promotion manoeuvre a6–a7, ♜c7–b7 and ♜b7–b8(+).

206

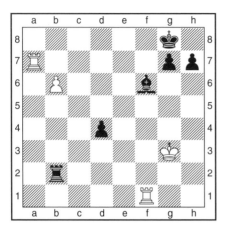

A similar situation arises in diagram 206. White obtains, as Nimzowitsch expressed it, the 'seventh rank absolute' with **1.♖f1xf6! g7xf6**, so that Black, after **2.b6–b7!**, has no defence against 3.♖a7–a8+ followed by 4.b7–b8♕, since by 2...♔f7 the king would expose itself to the discovered check 3.b8♕+. If the h7 pawn were on f7, the king would be able to hide on g7 and Black would have the advantage!

A typical example of the power of rooks doubled on the penultimate rank (point 7), is shown in diagram 207.

207

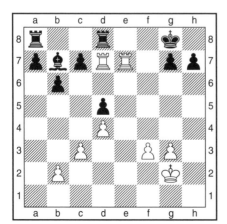

Here White does not have to content himself with perpetual check, and he rightly aims for more: **1.♖e7xg7+ ♔g8–f8 2.♖d7–f7+ ♔f8–e8 3.♖f7xc7** Now 4.♖g8 mate is threatened, so that Black is unable to save his bishop – a variation of the 'windmill'. **3. ... ♔e8–f8 4.♖g7xh7** Again an enveloping mate on the eighth rank is threatened. **4. ... ♔f8–g8 5.♖c7–g7+** In order to gain a tempo. **5. ... ♔g8–f8 6.♖g7xb7** Mate is again threatened. **6. ... ♔f8–g8 7.f3–f4** A new mating plan: within two more moves the pawn will protect the g7 square, so that mate by ♖b7–g7+ and ♖h7–h8 is threatened. Black has no defence (7...♖ab8 8.♖bg7+ ♔f8 9.♖xa7 ♔g8 10.f5, or 7...♖f8? 8.♖bg7 mate).

Just like Nimzowitsch, we hope that his advice on the open file may contribute to opening the eyes of the curious.

37th Hour

Plans and Ideas (VII)
All about the Pawn

In nearly every game of chess, the play with and against pawns, especially passed pawns (which are not blocked by any hostile pawns), is of great importance. Thus a question which is often asked, whether a single pawn is strong or weak, has to be answered according to the circumstances of each individual case. Critical factors are the type and the placing of the pieces remaining on the board.

Protected Passed Pawn

In principle, it is advisable to prevent any further advance of a passed pawn, i.e. to block it (occupy the square in front of the pawn). The lower the value of the piece blocking the pawn, the better it will be suited to the purpose. It also has to be taken into account whether the piece has any other effect from the blockading square. An ideal situation is illustrated in diagram 208.

208

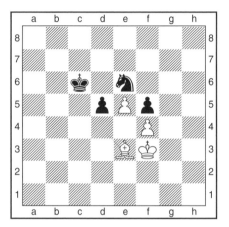

If the pieces were to be removed from the board (leaving only the pawns and kings), Black would have to fight for a draw because of the protected passed pawn. Here the knight is an exemplary blockader. It bars the path of the pawn and at the same time attacks the white f4 pawn. In addition, it supports the advance of its own passed pawn. Black, therefore, has the right to count on a win.

A similar situation is Tarrasch's guideline that a flexible pawn majority on the wing is preferable to an inflexible one in the middle of the board. If, in diagram 208, the knight were to be replaced by a bishop, the position would be lifeless.

The situation is different in diagram 209. The long-range **bishop** on b7 has not only a blockading function, but it also supports the passed pawn on h3, so that White has to give up his knight for it. A **knight** on b7

209

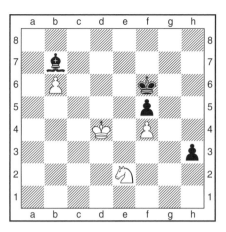

would be unable to accomplish this. It would not be able to participate in the fight at all, and would have to remain inactive and wait for 'relief' to arrive. After 1.♔d4–d5! Black has to fight for a draw.

Glory and Misery of the 'Isolani'

An isolated pawn (isolani) in the centre always has a tendency to become weak, if it is not possible to exchange it through an advance, or to develop one of the squares under its command into a useful outpost.

210

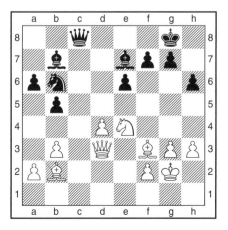

Diagram 210 shows the starting position of a magnificent endgame by Emanuel Lasker, who, in the tournament in Moscow 1925, commanded the black pieces against Akiba Rubinstein. The versatile usefulness for Black of the blockade square d5 becomes apparent in this example.

1. ... ♞b6–d5! was answered by White with **2.a2–a3**, in order to avoid having to watch out all the time for ♞d5–b4. Really good moves are hard to find, but 2.a3 loosens the white queen's wing in two ways: it exposes the a3 pawn to the reach of the bishop at e7 and it weakens the b3 pawn. Lasker made immediate use of this and rearranged his troops: **2. ... ♞d5–b6!** **3.♚g2–h2** (White confines himself to waiting, for lack of a suitable plan) **3. ... ♝b7–d5 4.♚h2–g2 ♛c8–c6 5.♞e4–d2 a6–a5!** Lasker wants to follow up with a5–a4, not only gaining control of the c4 square, but also fixing the a3 pawn. If his pawn were still on a2, White could maintain the status quo.
6.♛d3–c3 The exchange of the queen leads directly to a lost endgame. **6. ... ♝d5xf3+! 7.♞d2xf3** (or 7.♛xf3 ♛c2 8.♛b7? ♞d5!) **7. ... ♛c6xc3 8.♝b2xc3 a5–a4! 9.b3xa4 b5xa4**
Now White can no longer defend his a-pawn and he is lost. 10.♝b2? would be futile in view of 10...♞c4, and 10.♝b4 would be answered by 10...♝xb4 11.axb4 a3 12.♞d2 ♞d5 13.b5 ♚f8, when Black wins the b-pawn and exploits his passed a-pawn. In the game there followed:
10.♚g2–f1 ♝e7xa3 11.♚f1–e2 ♚g8–f8 12.♚e2–d3 ♞b6–d5 13.♝c3–e1 ♝a3–d6 14.♚d3–c4 ♚f8–e7 15.♞f3–e5 ♝d6xe5 16.d4xe5 ♚e7–d7 17.♝e1–d2 h6–h5 18.♝d2–c1 Or 18.♚b5 a3 19.♝c1 ♞c3+ 20.♚c4 a2 21.♝b2 ♞d1 and so on. **18. ... ♚d7–c6 19.♝c1–a3 ♞d5–b6+ 20.♚c4–**

d4 ♚c6–b5 21.♝a3–f8 ♞b6–c4 22.♚d4–c3 g7–g6 23.f2–f4 ♞c4–e3 24.♚c3–d3 ♞e3–d5 Black plans h5–h4, and White cannot reply 25.h4 because of the knight manoeuvre ♞d5–b6–c4. This piece will soon get to f5.
25.♝f8–a3 h5–h4 26.g3xh4 ♞d5xf4+ 27.♚d3–e4 ♞f4–h5
Definitely not 27...♞xh3, because after 28.♚f3 the knight would not get any peace. **28.♚e4–f3 ♞h5–c4 29.♝a3–b2 ♚c4–b3 30.♝b2–a1 a4–a3 31.♚f3–g4 ♚b3–c2 32.♚g4–g5 ♚c2–d3!** and White resigns. If he wanders to f7 with his king, the black king can comfortably reach f5.

Chess perfection is most likely to occur in the endgame. Many players are afraid of the endgame, and have to pay dearly for their inexperience time and again. In this phase of the game, the battle is finally decided. The board has cleared, but the simplicity is deceptive. The demands have rather increased, and nowhere else does experience have such a clear effect.

In diagram 210, White's 'isolani' made no real impact. It was fixed and the square in front of the pawn was controlled by Black. We learn from this that the owner of the isolani should try to control the square in front of the pawn: firstly, in order to be able to exchange blockading pieces, and secondly, to be able to advance the isolated pawn and thus cause confusion in the enemy ranks. On this theme we will look at an extract from the tournament in Bern 1932, Alexander Alekhine against Mir Sultan Khan (see diagram 211).

211

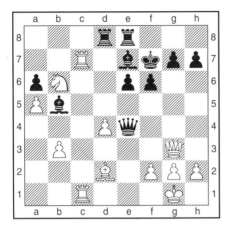

The pawn sacrifice **1.d4–d5!** initiates a keenly calculated development. The pawn gives up its life and creates a breach in the hostile ranks. The basic idea is to increase the effectiveness of the rook at c7 by opening the e-file, on which the second rook can intervene. The thinking behind this move was explained by the commander of the white pieces himself: 1...exd5 2.♖e1 ♗e2 3.♘a4! d4 4.♘c5 ♕c2 5.♖xe2 ♕d1+ 6.♖e1 ♕xd2 7.♔f1 'and Black would be defenceless against the many threats. The remaining moves would probably be 7...♔g8 8.♘e6 g6 9.♘xd8 ♕xe1+ 10.♔xe1 ♗d6+ 11.♔d2 ♗xg3 12 hxg3 ♖xd8 13.♖c6 ♖d5 14.b4, after which Black would have to resign'. Black takes evasive action, but not to his advantage.

1. ... ♔f7–g8? Completely hopeless. The lesser evil would appear to be 1...e5. **2.♖c1–e1** (2.d6 is answered not by 2...♖xd6? 3.♖xe7 ♖xe7 4.♕xd6, but 2...♗f8) **2. ... ♕e4–f5** Black should accept the unfavourable endgame after the loss of his e6 pawn and play 2...♕g6. **3.♗d2–b4!** (the weakness of g7 proves quickly decisive) **3. ... ♖d8–d7** (3...♗d7 4.♗xe7 ♖xe7

5.♕d6) **4.♖c7xd7 ♗b5xd7 5.♗b4xe7**
If now 5...♖xe7, then 6.♕d6 and wins. Also after **5. ... e6xd5 6.♕g3–d6**, Black has to lay down his arms.
How the isolated pawn can serve as a base is shown in diagram 212.

212

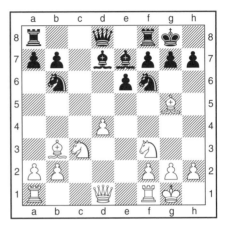

This position is taken from the game Mikhail Botvinnik–Milan Vidmar, Nottingham 1936. Here we can see the most effective positioning of the knights in conjunction with the isolani: one of them controls the square in front of the pawn, while the other is ready to occupy the outpost at e5. The white bishops are also well positioned strategically. The sequel was:

1.♕d1–d3 Now Black has to reckon with 2.♗c2 followed by ♗xf6 and mate on h7. **1. ... ♘b6–d5** It would be better for the other knight to go there, with the idea 1...♘fd5 2.♗c2 g6 3.♗h6 ♘b4. Botvinnik mentions 1...♘fd5 2.♗e3 ♘xc3 3.bxc3 ♗a4 with desirable simplification for Black. **2.♘f3–e5! ♗d7–c6 3.♖a1–d1 ♘d5–b4 4.♕d3–h3!** These methodical attacking manoeuvres are exemplary. **4. ... ♗c6–d5**

5.♘c3xd5 ♘b4xd5 Again 5...♘fxd5 was better, in order to enable the blockading move ...f7–f5 after 6.f2–f4. If 6.♗c1 Black plays 6...♖c8.

6.f2–f4 ♖a8–c8 Not feasible is 6...♘e4? 7.♘xf7! ♖xf7 (7...♔xf7 8.♖de1!, Botvinnik) 8.♕xe6.

7.f4–f5 e6xf5 8.♖f1xf5 ♕d8–d6

This deprives the rook at c8 of one of its defenders, so that the strike on f7 becomes decisive; but other moves also offer no salvation, for example:

• 8...♖c7 9.♖df1 **a6** 10.♘xf7 ♖xf7 11.♗xd5 ♘xd5 12.♖xf7 ♗xg5 13.♕e6!.

• 8...♖c7 9.♖df1 ♘**b6** 10.♕h4 ♘bd5 11.♘xf7 ♖xf7 12.♗xd5 ♘xd5 13.♖xf7 ♗xg5 14.♕xg5!.

9.♘e5xf7! ♖f8xf7 (9...♔xf7 10.♗xd5+) **10.♗g5xf6 ♗e7xf6** (or 10...♘xf6 11.♖xf6 followed by ♕xc8+) **11.♖f5xd5 ♕d6–c6** (the last trap: 12.♖c5? ♗xd4+) **12.♖d5–d6 ♕c6–e8 13.♖d6–d7** Black resigns.

Dr. Mikhail Botvinnik (17.8.1911–5.5.1995), world champion from 1948 to 1963 (with two year-long interruptions in 1957 and 1960), integrated the isolani into the strong position of the white pieces and brilliantly exploited his opponent's insignificant inaccuracies. This is what chess is a question of: exploiting your own advantages in any given situation, and preventing the opponent, where possible, from playing his trumps.

38th Hour

Plans and Ideas (VIII)
The *two* Weaknesses

In a game of chess, success often depends on whether it is possible to discover a 'second front' apart from an obvious target, or to be able to act alternately on the queen's and king's wing. In a tactical sense, this is demonstrated, for example, in the double attack, pin and discovered check. In strategic planning, this device is less distinct.

213

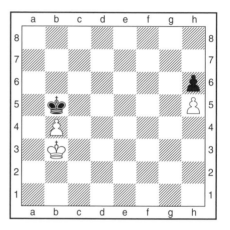

Diagram 213 shows an obvious case. The game would be drawn, if White did not have the additional chance, apart from the passed pawn on b4, of attempting to win the pawn on h6. He easily wins, for example, as follows: **1.♔b3–c3 ♔b5–b6 2.♔c3–c4 ♔b6–c6 3.♔c4–d4** 3.b5+ is an unnecessary detour. After 3...♔b6 4.♔b4 ♔b7 5.♔c5 ♔c7 6.♔d5 ♔b6 7.♔e6 ♔xb5 8.♔f6 ♔c5 the same position arises as in the text after 5...♔c5. **3. ... ♔c6–b5 4.♔d4–e5 ♔b5xb4 5.♔e5–f6 ♔b4–c5 6.♔f6–g6 ♔c5–d6 7.♔g6xh6 ♔d6–e7 8.♔h6–g7** (just in time!) and White promotes his pawn. Not much different is the endgame Nimzowitsch–Janowski, Carlsbad 1907 (see diagram 214).

134

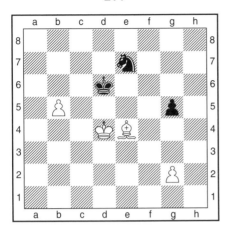

214

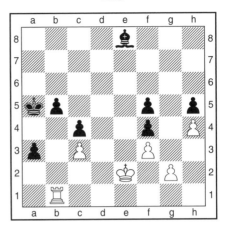

215

Without the pair of pawns on the g-file, White would have no chance of winning, because the opponent cannot be prevented from:

* blocking the pawn on the b-file;
* sacrificing his knight for the pawn and thus creating a theoretical draw.

The existence of the pawns on the g-file signifies an additional obligation for Black, which overtaxes him. The game concluded: **1.b5–b6 g5–g4** Or 1...♘c6+ 2.♗xc6 ♚xc6 3.♚e5 and wins. **2.b6–b7 ♚d6–c7 3.♚d4–e5 g4–g3 4.♚e5–f4 ♘e7–g8 5.♚f4xg3 ♘g8–f6 6.♗e4–f3 ♘f6–d7 7.♚g3–f4 ♚c7–d6 8.♚f4–f5 ♚d6–e7 9.♗f3–c6 ♘d7–b8 10.♗c6–b5** Black resigns.

Battle on *two* Wings

More complicated is the next example, the ending of the game Tigran Petrosian–Vasily Smyslov, Moscow 1951 (see diagram 215).

In principle, however, the basic idea is the same: if the pawns on the king's wing (three white and three black) were removed from the board, White would be unable to make any progress. Black would

even have the advantage: the bishop would become very effective via g6 and the king would invade at b3. White, however, is able to put into effect an interesting winning plan: he sacrifices his rook and goes hunting pawns with his king. In the end, the many hounds (white pawns) kill the hare (black bishop). The sequel was:

1.♔e2–d2 This forces Black to act, since the manoeuvre ♔d2–c2, ♖b1–b4 and ♔c2–b1–a2 threatens to win the a-pawn. **1. ... b5–b4 2.c3xb4+ ♚a5–a4 3.♔d2–c3 a3–a2 4.♖b1–a1 ♚a4–a3 5.♔c3xc4** White cannot progress any other way. **5. ... ♚a3–b2 6.♖a1–e1 a2–a1♕ 7.♖e1xa1 ♚b2xa1 8.b4–b5 ♗e8–d7 9.b5–b6 ♗d7–c8 10.♔c4–d4 ♚a1–b2 11.♔d4–e5 ♚b2–c3 12.♔e5xf4 ♚c3–d4 13.♔f4–g5 ♚d4–e5** Even if the king picks up the b-pawn here, White wins, because Black would soon have to give up his bishop for the white h-pawn. **14.♔g5xh5 ♚e5–f6 15.g2–g4 ♗c8–b7 16.♔h5–h6** Black resigns (16...♗xf3 17.g5+ ♚f7 18.g6+ ♚g8 19.♔g5). Although play on two wings occurs most often in the endgame, it is also worth bearing in mind as a basic game plan. A nice illustration is provided by the game between José Raúl Capablanca and Vyacheslav Ragozin from the great Moscow Tournament of 1935.

Nimzo-Indian. **1.d2–d4 ♘g8–f6 2.c2–c4 e7–e6 3.♘b1–c3 ♗f8–b4 4.a2–a3 ♗b4xc3+ 5.b2xc3 d7–d6** Black has given up the bishop pair, but in return he has burdened the opponent with doubled pawns, which he does not intend to resolve by advancing his d-pawn two squares. **6.♕d1–c2 0–0 7.e2–e4 e6–e5 8.♗f1–d3 c7–c5** After this, Black is hardly able to exploit the weakness on c4. The correct plan is characterised by the moves ♘b8–c6, b7–b6, ♗c8–a6 and ♘c6–a5. If White plays d4–d5 too early, Black will occupy the strategically important c5 square with a knight. **9.♘g1–e2 ♘b8–c6 10.d4–d5 ♘c6–e7 11.f2–f3 ♘f6–d7 12.h2–h4** Capablanca plans to open a file for his rooks on the king's wing. This is why he does not castle. The immediate g2–g4 would be met by ♘e7–g6. **12. ... ♘d7–b6 13.g2–g4 f7–f6** (see diagram 216)

216

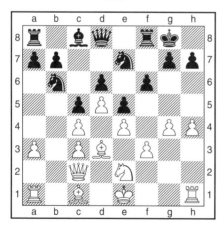

In view of the threatening white advance, Black decides to flee with his king. The question arises, whether he would not

have obstructed the opponent more with a rapid action on the queen's wing. A manoeuvre such as ♗c8–d7, ♘b6–a4, a7–a6 and b7–b5 was conceivable. **14.♘e2–g3 ♔g8–f7 15.g4–g5 ♘e7–g8 16.f3–f4** 16.♘h5 is met by 16...g6. **16. ... ♔f7–e8** A move such as 16...exf4 helps White's queen's bishop onto a favourable square. **17.f4–f5 ♕d8–e7 18.♕c2–g2 ♔e8–d8 19.♘g3–h5!** The idea is to bring the knight via g7 to e6. **19. ... ♔d8–c7 20.g5xf6 g7xf6 21.♘h5–g7 ♗c8–d7 22.h4–h5 ♖a8–c8 23.h5–h6 ♔c7–b8** The trek has proved successful. But it will not be long before White directs his aim at the commander's new residence. It is remarkable how long the Cuban waits with the move ♘g7–e6. Simply the fact that the move is possible and has to be taken into account in all calculations, significantly influences and disturbs the opponent's game.

24.♖h1–g1 ♖f8–f7 25.♖a1–b1 ♕e7–f8 26.♗d3–e2 ♔b8–a8 27.♗e2–h5 ♖f7–e7 28.♕g2–a2 ♕f8–d8 29.♗c1–d2 ♘b6–a4 30.♕a2–b3 ♘a4–b6 (see diagram 217)

217

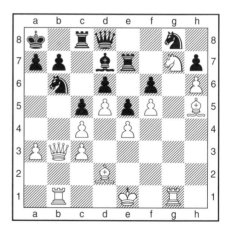

If 30...♖b8, then 31.♘e6 ♗xe6 32.dxe6,

after which 33.♗f7 is threatened. If Black answers 31.♘e6 with 31...♕b6, White plays 32.♕xb6 axb6 33.♘c7+ ♔a7 34.♘b5+ ♗xb5 35.cxb5 followed by ♗d1. The knights on the edge of the board are, as so often, nothing but trouble.

31.a3–a4! ♖c8–b8 Not very tempting is 31...♗xa4 32.♕a2, after which 33.♖xb6 or 33.♘e6 is threatened. **32.a4–a5 ♘b6–c8 33.♕b3–a2 ♕d8–f8 34.♗d2–e3 b7–b6 35.a5–a6** Here the vertical directions are closed; however, on the diagonals the doors are wide open. **35. ... ♕f8–d8 36.♔e1–d2 ♕d8–f8 37.♖b1–b2 ♕f8–d8** Black seeks refuge in waiting tactics. **38.♕a2–b1** The queen wants to move to d3. After this, the d5 square will be made available to it by ♘e6 ♗xe6, dxe6. **38. ... b6–b5** Black sacrifices a pawn and thus obtains a little breathing space. **39.c4xb5 ♘c8–b6 40.♕b1–a2 c5–c4 41.♕a2–a3 ♕d8–c7 42.♔d2–c1 ♖b8–f8 43.♖b2–g2 ♕c7–b8 44.♕a3–b4 ♖f8–d8 45.♖g2–g3 ♖d8–f8 46.♘g7–e6!** (see diagram 218)

218

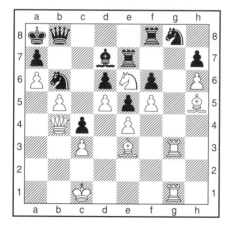

The time is ripe for the final phase. **46. ... ♗d7xe6** After 46...♖c8 White can play the

simple 47.♗xb6 axb6 (47...♕xb6 48.♖xg8) 48.a7, winning the knight. **47.d5xe6 ♖e7–c7** Otherwise ♗f7 is decisive. **48.♕b4xd6 ♘g8–e7 49.♖g1–d1** Black resigns. His position was skilfully breached from two sides.

Tournament Play

For participants in chess tournaments, be they club tournaments or official championships, there are certain regulations, apart from the rules discussed in the first part of this book, which have been set up by the World Chess Federation. Here the most important ones.

• Each player is required to record the game move by move on the scoresheet provided, as clearly and legibly as possible (except in blitz or rapid-play tournaments).

• A certain number of moves have to be completed in a fixed period of time. The time and the number of moves have to be determined in advance (an average of three minutes per move is customary). In open tournaments the interruption of a game (so-called 'adjourned games') is avoided by applying the following, or a similar, method: 40 moves in two hours, 20 additional moves in one hour, and thereafter 30 minutes for the remainder of the game. The time used by each player is determined by a chess clock. This is a double clock: when a player moves he presses a button. This stops his own clock and starts the opponent's. A player who exceeds the time limit loses the game. An attempt to diffuse the problem of time trouble is the newly tested 'Fischer clock'. It provides the player, when he makes a move, with an additional time bonus.

• If the allotted time has elapsed and the game has not been finished, the player whose turn it is and whose clock is running has to record his intended move clearly and distinctly on his scoresheet, put it together with the opponent's scoresheet into an envelope, and seal it. Only after this procedure is complete may the clock be stopped. The tournament controller is required to keep the envelope in a safe place. On the outside of the envelope the adjourned position and the time used by each player are recorded.

- The game is resumed at a fixed time. The situation, with regard to the chess board and clock, at the time when the game was stopped, is restored. The sealed move is made only when the player whose turn it is, i.e. the one who has to reply to the sealed move, is present. In modern tournaments, this procedure is generally avoided for practical reasons (see the comments above regarding open tournaments).

- A draw can be proposed by a player before or after carrying out his move on the chess board. In both cases, however, only if his clock is running.

- The players are not allowed to refer to written or printed records or to analyse the game on a board. It is also against the rules to accept advice or warnings from third parties, irrespective of whether or not they were requested. Regarding this rule, the participation of computers in general chess tournaments is questionable, as they often contain vast libraries which they refer to during the game, whereas the human player always has to work out the moves himself.

The Finale

39th Hour

Standard Endgames (I)

The opening and middlegame cannot be exhaustively presented in an analytical manner. The possibilities are practically unlimited. In these two phases, the value of the moves, especially in balanced positions, can only be estimated and not determined with scientific precision. Here a player's positional feeling is of valuable assistance. In the course of our studies we have presented many examples and patterns, which will facilitate the evaluation of positions.

Practical Pawn Endings

Zugzwang

In the endgame, i.e. when there are only a few pieces left on the board, the situation is different to that in the opening and the middlegame. The possibilities are less numerous and the result can often be precisely calculated. The player, however, requires a great deal of knowledge, which he can acquire partly through studying, partly through practical experience. Our readers will now be introduced to the practically most important standard endings.

Diagram 219 shows the correct 'use of tempo' which plays an important role in pawn endings. If White plays 1.♔e6?, he loses after 1...♔c5! due to zugzwang. **1.♔f6–e7! ♔b6–c5 2.♔e7–e6** leads to victory, as now it is Black who is in zugzwang.

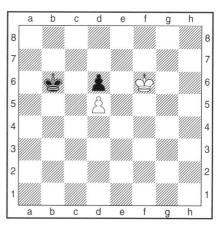

219

In diagram 220 the pawns are indirectly protecting each other, although they are not connected.

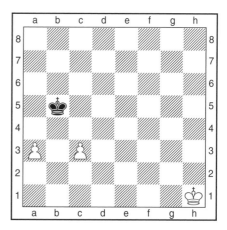

220

After **1. ... ♔b5–c4 2.a3–a4** 2...♔xc3 would leave the a-pawn free to advance. The same applies after **1. ... ♔b5–a4 2.c3–c4 ♔a4xa3 3.c4–c5**. Black is thus unable to capture, so that White is able to bring up his king and directly enforce the advance of his pawns.

221

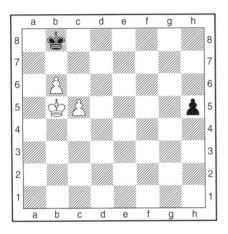

In diagram 221 we can see the power of two connected passed pawns. After **1.c5–c6 h5–h4 2.♔b5–a6! h4–h3 3.b6–b7 h3–h2** (or 3...♔c7 4.♔a7 and wins) **4.♔a6–b6 h2–h1♕ 5.c6–c7** they give mate with the help of their king.

222

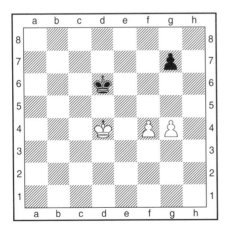

The pawn ending illustrated in diagram

222 is a curiosity. In Capablanca's fine book *Chess Fundamentals* it says, without any further explanation, that **1.f4–f5** would throw away the win because of **1. ... g7–g6.*** In fact, however, White wins by **2.f5xg6 ♔f6–e6 3.g4–g5!**, which prevents the approach of the black king. On the other hand, 2.♔e4? ♔e7! does indeed lead to a draw: 3.♔e5 gxf5 4.♔xf5 ♔f7! and Black has the opposition. Many people have puzzled over what caused this lapse by the Cuban chess genius. On the other hand, Capablanca's methodical path to victory in the diagram position is completely flawless: **1.♔e4 g6** (or 1...♔e6 2.f5+ ♔f6 3.♔f4 g6 4.g5+ ♔f7 5.f6 ♔e6 6.♔e4 ♔f7 7.♔e5 ♔f8 8.f7! ♔xf7 9.♔d6 and the king captures the black pawn) **2.♔d4 ♔e6 3.♔c5 ♔d7 4.♔d5 ♔e7 5.♔e5 ♔f7 6.♔d6 ♔f6 7.♔d7 ♔f7 8.g5** and the rest is easy.

* This mistake was corrected in a later edition of the book (Ed.).

The Opposition

The term 'diagonal opposition' is illustrated in diagram 223.

223

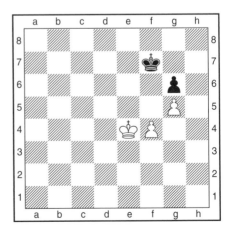

With 1.♔e5? White would throw away the win, because Black gains the opposition (1...♚e7!) and prevents the advance of the white king. White must himself gain the opposition, first in the form of the diagonal opposition. He wins as follows: **1.♔e4–d5! ♚f7–e7 2.♔d5–e5 ♚e7–f7 3.♔e5–d6** and in the end the black g6 pawn falls.

Triangulation

The situation in diagram 224 is more complicated. White has two threats: the promotion of his c-pawn and the capture of the a6 pawn.

224

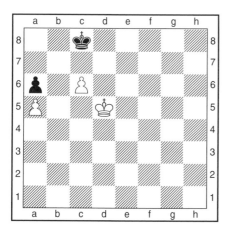

If it were Black to move, he would have to give ground and allow one of the winning plans. He would thus be in zugzwang, for example 1...♚d8 2.♔d6 ♚c8 3.c7 and wins, or 1...♚c7 2.♔c5 followed by ♔b6 and the capture of the a-pawn. So if it is White to move, he simply has to create the same position with *Black* to move. This is achieved by a *triangulation* manoeuvre of his king: **1.♔d5–d4! ♚c8–b8 2.♔d4–c4! ♚b8–c8** (or 2...♚c7 3.♔c5 as shown above) **3.♔c4–d5** and the goal has been reached.

Sometimes victory depends on whether or not a pawn is still on its starting rank. In certain situations the possibility of a player advancing a pawn, as desired, by one or two squares, enables him to 'out-tempo' the opponent. An elementary case is shown in diagram 225.

225

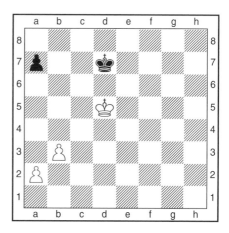

First the king goes to a6: **1.♔d5–c5 ♚d7–c7 2.♔c5–b5 ♚c7–b7 3.b3–b4** Moving the white a-pawn would throw away the win! **3. ... ♚b7–c7** The alternative 3...♚b8 is instructive: 4.♔a6 ♚a8 5.b5 ♚b8 6.a3! ♚a8 7.a4 ♚b8 and so on as in the text (8.a5). Weaker is 3...a6+ 4.♔c5 ♚c7 5.a3 ♚b7 6.a4 ♚c7 7.a5 ♚b7 8.♔d6 and White wins. **4.♔b5–a6 ♚c7–b8 5.b4–b5 ♚b8–a8** White now has to make sure that his b-pawn reaches the b6 square at the right moment. If he now plays 6.a3, he throws away the win. **6.a2–a4!** If the black king were on b8, White would have to play 6.a3 (see above). **6. ... ♚a8–b8 7.a4–a5 ♚b8–a8 8.b5–b6 ♚a8–b8 9.b6–b7** (without check!) and wins.

226

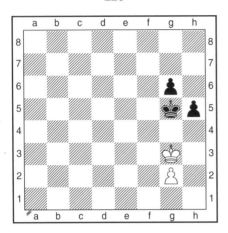

227

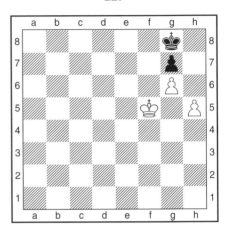

Diagram 226 shows the concluding phase of a study by T.B.Gorgiev (*Shakhmaty v SSSR* 1936). White has a curious way to save the game: **1.♔g3–h3! ♔g5–f5** 1...h4 allows 2.g3 hxg3 3.♔xg3, and the position is drawn since White has the opposition (thus preventing the hostile king from gaining ground without assistance from the pawn). **2.♔h3–h4 ♔f5–f4 3.g2–g4 h5xg4** stalemate! When he is in great danger, stalemate is a player's last refuge. (The starting position of the study is White: ♔a1, ♙g2, ♙g5 – Black: ♔a6, ♙g6, ♙h5. The introductory moves are 1.♔b2 ♔b5 2.♔c3 ♔c5 3.♔d3 ♔d5 4.♔e3 ♔e5 5.♔f3 ♔f5 6.♔g3 ♔xg5 and then as above.)

The position in No. 227 is also drawn, since after **1.♔f5–g5 ♔g8–h8 2.h5–h6** Black *does not capture* the pawn, but instead plays 2. ... ♔h8–g8. The attempt 1.♔e6 ♔h8 2.h6 is also parried by 2...♔g8! (2...gxh6? 3.♔f7!).

Distant Opposition

Diagram 228 explains the term *distant opposition*.

228

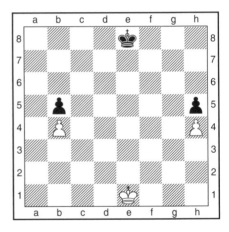

Whereas in close opposition the kings are separated by only one square, after **1.♔e1–e2!** (distant opposition) there are *five* squares between them. After the approach **1. ... ♔e8–e7 2.♔e2–e3!** (distant opposition) there are *three*, and finally the usual opposition is created after **2. ... ♔e7–e6 3.♔e3–e4**. White wins because he promotes his passed pawn just in time: 3...♔f6 4.♔f4 ♔e6 5.♔g5 ♔d5 6.♔xh5 ♔c4 7.♔g5 ♔xb4 8.h5 ♔a3 9.h6 b4 10.h7 b3 11.h8♕.

We will learn an important trick in diagram 229.

229

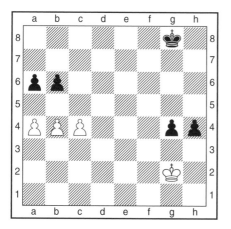

White sacrifices a pawn and increases the distance from the black king by a decisive file. He wins, since his pawn queens with check: **1.c4–c5! b6xc5 2.b4–b5!**. This is the important point. **2. ... a6xb5 3.a4xb5 c5–c4 4.b5–b6 c4–c3 5.b6–b7 c3–c2 6.b7–b8♕+** and White wins.

The king is nearly always correctly placed in the centre. Its advance is often decisive. The finish to a game Opocensky–Prokop (see diagram 230) is an instructive example.
After **1.♔e4–e5 ♔f7–e7** the win for White depends on whether he can reach f6 with his king! To this end, the h-pawn should advance to h6, in case Black marks time. **2.g2–g4!** The immediate 2.h4 is also good enough to win, e.g. 2...h5 3.g3, in view of the strong position of the white king.

230

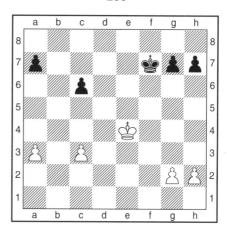

2. ... ♔e7–d7 The alternative is 2...h6 3.a4 a5 4.c4 ♔d7 5.♔f5 ♔e7 (after 5...♔d6 6.♔g6 ♔c5 7.♔xg7 ♔xc4 8.♔xh6 the c-pawn is one tempo too late) 6.♔g6 ♔f8 7.h4 ♔g8 8.c5 ♔f8 (8...♔h8 9.♔f7) 9.♔h7 ♔f7 10.g5! h5 11.♔h8! and wins. **3.g4–g5 ♔d7–e7 4.h2–h4 ♔e7–d7 5.h4– h5 ♔d7–e7 6.a3–a4 a7–a5 7.c3–c4 ♔e7– d7 8.h5–h6!** The plan is successful. How precisely White has timed matters can also be seen from 8...gxh6 9.gxh6 ♔e7 10.c5! when he has the opposition. **8. ... g7–g6 9.♔e5–f6 ♔d7–d6 10.♔f6–g7 ♔d6–e7 11.♔g7xh7 ♔e7–f7 12.c4–c5** and wins.

40th Hour

Standard Endgames (II)

It is very useful in practice to have a knowledge of a few endgames with pieces, in which one side attempts to make use of a greater or smaller advantage, and the other tries to avoid defeat.

Queen against advanced Pawn

The queen will always succeed against a far-advanced passed pawn, if it can occupy the promotion square. If the opposing king controls the promotion square, the win depends on a few special circumstances. Diagram No.231 shows a routine case.

231

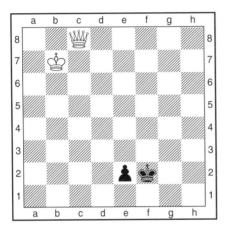

The win is achieved in several stages:

- The white queen prevents the advance of the pawn by giving check, by pinning the pawn or by moving behind it (after the king has been forced away from the promotion square). At the same time it creeps closer to the pawn.
- With the help of a double attack the queen forces the king to move in front of the pawn, so that it stands in the pawn's way.
- Thus, the white king has enough time to advance step by step and to capture the pawn with assistance from the queen, or give checkmate.

The winning moves could look like this:
1.♕c8–f5+ ♔f2–g2 2.♕f5–g4+ ♔g2–f2
3.♕g4–f4+ ♔f2–g2 4.♕f4–e3 ♔g2–f1

5.♕e3–f3+ The important basic position. Black is forced to block his pawn, if he does not want to lose it straight away. 5. ... ♔f1–e1 6.♔b7–c6 One step closer! 6. ... ♔e1–d2 With a stereotyped manoeuvre, the queen drives the king onto the promotion square once again. 7.♕f3–f2 ♔d2–d1 8.♕f2–d4+ ♔d1–c2 9.♕d4–e3 ♔c2–d1 10.♕e3–d3+ ♔d1–e1 The white king is allowed to come closer by another step. 11.♔c6–d5 ♔e1–f2 12.♕d3–d2 ♔f2–f1 13.♕d2–f4+ ♔f1–g2 14.♕f4–e3 ♔g2–f1 15.♕e3–f3+ ♔f1–e1 16.♔d5–e4 ♔e1–d2 17.♕f3–d3+ The king now offers its help. 17. ... ♔d2–e1 18.♔e4–f3 and mate in two moves.

If the pawn is on the f- or c-file, the queen is unable to win the necessary tempo, because the king does not defend its pawn, but flees into the corner: then if the queen captures the pawn, it stalemates the king. Also with a rook's pawn, stalemate enables a draw to be achieved. Consider the following position: White: ♔h8, ♕g3 – Black: ♔h1, ♙h2. The white king has no time to come closer. If, however, Black had another pawn, for example on g4, White would give checkmate, because there would be no stalemate: 1.♕f2 g3 2.♕f1 mate.

In diagram 232 we see an exception to the rule. The white king succeeds in getting close to the pawn by blocking the queen, and thus avoiding stalemate: 1.♔f6–g5 ♔h1–g2 2.♔g5–f4+ ♔g2–f1 (or 2...♔h1 3.♔g3) 3.♔f4–g3 h2–h1♕ (equally futile is 3...h1♘+ 4.♔f3 ♘f2 5.♕a1+) 4.♕g7–a1+ White wins the queen and with it the game.

232

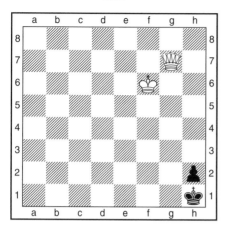

Queen against Rook

A queen nearly always wins against a rook. However, the procedure is not easy and there are a few important theoretically drawn positions.

233

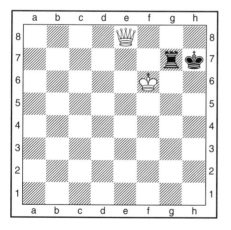

Diagram 233 may serve as a basic example. If it is Black to move here, he is in zugzwang. The rook has to move away from its king and will inevitably be lost to a double attack. With **1. ... ♖g7–g4? 2.♕e8–**

h5+ the situation is immediately clear. After **1. ... ♖g7–g3** the queen quickly steals up on the rook: **2.♕e8–e4+ ♔h7–g8** (otherwise 3.♕h4+) **3.♕e4–c4+!** and Black has to abandon his rook (3...♔h7 4.♕h4+) or his king (3...♔f8 4.♕c8 mate). Finally, **1. ... ♖g7–g1** is also easily resolved by **2.♕e8–e4+ ♔h7–h8 3.♕e4–a8+ ♔h8–h7** (3...♖g8 4.♕h1 mate) **4.♕a8–a7+** with a double attack. But if it is White to move in diagram 233, what happens then? White creates the same position but with Black to move by performing a triangular manoeuvre with his queen: **1.♕e8–e4+ ♔h7–h8 2.♕e4–a8+ ♔h8–h7** (2...♖g8 3.♕h1 mate is already familiar) **3.♕a8–e8**, zugzwang.

234

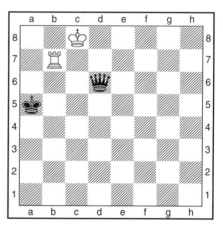

The most important exception is illustrated in diagram 234. Here, stalemate comes to the rescue. If it is White to move, he forces a draw by perpetual check or stalemate. After **1.♖b7–a7+!** the black king is unable to flee either to the sixth rank or to the d-file, without allowing stalemate or the loss of queen for rook.

1. ... ♔a5–b5 (if 1...♔b6, then 2.♖a6+! ♔xa6 stalemate) **2.♖a7–b7+ ♔b5–c5** (or

2...♔a6 3.♖a7+! ♔xa7 stalemate) **3.♖b7–c7+ ♔c5–d5 4.♖c7–d7**, draw.

Queen against Rook and Pawn

235

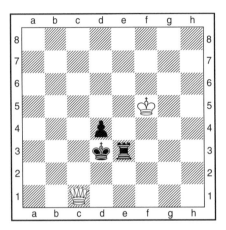

Even if the rook has a pawn at its side, the defender is only able to save himself in exceptional circumstances. Consider diagram 238. As was demonstrated in 1946 by the French endgame theorist André Chéron, White always wins, no matter whose turn it is to move (as opposed to the findings of Johann Berger in his fundamental work *Theorie und Praxis der Endspiele*, 2nd edition, 1922, and Reuben Fine in his *Basic Chess Endings*, 1941). The first aim of the attacker is to win the pawn. He plans to separate the opposing king from its pawn and plays **1.♕c1–c5! ♖e3–e2** (after 1...♖e1 2.♕b5+ White would already have reached his goal, as shown by 2...♔c3 3.♕a5+, 2...♔d2 3.♕b4+, or 2...♔e3 3.♕e5+) **2.♕c5–a3+ ♔d3–c2** (not 2...♔c4 3.♕a6+) **3.♕a3–a2+ ♔c2–d3 4.♕a2–b3+ ♔d3–d2 5.♔f5–f4 d4–d3** Neither does anything else help, for example 5...♔e1 6.♕b4+ ♖d2 7.♔f3!, or 5...♖e3 6.♕c4

♖d3 (6...d3 7.♕a2+) 7.♔e4. **6.♕b3–b2+ ♔d2–d1 7.♕b2–b1+ ♔d1–d2 8.♕b1–b3** and wins, for example 8...♖e8 9.♕b2+ ♔d1. The pawn and rook are now unprotected, so that the double attack 10.♕b5! enforces the approach of the white king: 10...♖d8 11.♔e3 ♔c2 12 ♕c5+ ♔d1 13.♕b6 and White wins thanks to the double attack on b1 and d8.

The classic position of Philidor (White: ♔f4, ♕d3 – Black: ♔e7, ♖e5, d6), which is mentioned in many text books, may be won more easily, as demonstrated in 1952 by Chéron in his *Nouveau Traité complet d'Echecs – La Fin de Partie*, with the procedure discussed earlier, rather than in the way described by Philidor. The introduction goes as follows: 1.♕h7+ ♔e6 2.♕c7 ♖c5 3.♕d8 ♖e5 4.♕e8+ ♔d5 5.♕d7! ♖e4+ 6.♔f5 ♖e5+ 7.♔f6 ♖e4 8.♕b5+ ♔d4 9.♕c6 d5 10.♕b5 ♖e3 11.♕b4+ ♔d3 12.♔f5 d4 13.♕c5 and we have reached the same position as in diagram 235 after 1.♕c5!.

236

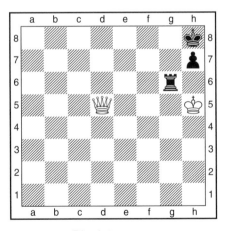

Black to move

If the pawn is still on the seventh rank, progress for the stronger side can only be achieved in the case of the rook's pawn with the help of zugzwang. With other pawns, the queen has no room for out-flanking attacks. In diagram 236 White wins, as was demonstrated by Berger, by exploiting the black king's lack of room to manoeuvre and creating zugzwang: **1.♕d5–e5+ ♔h8–g8 2.♕e5–e7 ♔g8–h8** (this loses immediately, but after 2...♖g7 there follows 3.♕e8 mate, and other moves of the rook are countered with double attacks by the queen) **3.♕e7–f8+ ♖g6–g8 4.♕f8–f6+ ♖g8–g7 5.♔h5–h6** followed by mate.

Even in a position such as White: ♔h1, ♕g5 – Black: ♔f7, ♖h7, ♙h2, the side with the queen breaks through, since the opponent is unable to hang onto his pawn due to zugzwang. Chéron presents the following procedure: 1.♕f4+ ♔g6 2.♕e4+ ♔g7 3.♕f5! ♖h6 4.♕g5+ ♔h7 5.♕g4 ♔h8 6.♕g3 ♖h5 7.♕g6 ♖h7 8.♕g5 and the rook has to abandon the pawn.

Queen and Pawn against Queen

If both sides are left only with their queen, apart from the king, then the additional possession of a pawn is often decisive. Usually the weaker side can only count on perpetual check for salvation. If he runs out of checks or has to allow the exchange of queens, defeat is usually inevitable. As an example, we can take diagram 237 which shows a position by Bernhard Horwitz (from *Chess Studies*, 1851, by B.Horwitz and J.Kling).

Black has to take action against the promotion of the c7 pawn and he aims for perpetual check. After 1...♕a8+ 2.♔b6 there is no further possibility of giving

237

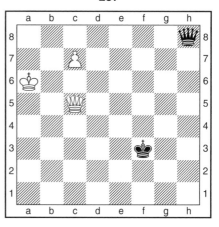

check and White wins easily after 2...♕c8 3.♕c6+ ♔f4 4.♔a7! followed by 5.♕b7. Thus there is only one option: **1. ... ♕h8–a1+ 2.♕c5–a5 ♕a1–f6+** (or 2...♕f1+ 3.♕b5 ♕a1+ 4.♔b7 ♕g7 5.♔b8 and wins, because the pin 5...♕g3 fails to 6.♕b3+) **3.♕a5–b6 ♕f6–a1+ 4.♔a6–b7 ♕a1–g7 5.♔b7–b8 ♕g7–e5 6.♔b8–a7! ♕e5–a1+** (6...♕g7 7.♕b7+) **7.♕b6–a6 ♕a1–d4+ 8.♔a7–a8** White wins because the queen's check on d5 loses its power due to the pinning move ♕b7. In this endgame the position of the king is extremely important.

238

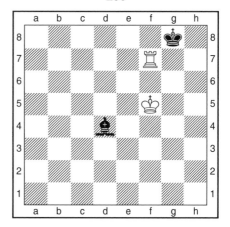

The Exchange

In the endgame king and rook against king and bishop (or king and knight), if there are no pawns left it is possible for the stronger side to win only in certain positions on the edge of the board. Diagram 238 shows a theoretical winning position, first given by Horwitz and Kling (1851).

After **1.♔f5–g6** the black king is confined to a corner of the colour of the bishop – an indication of defeat. The rook wants to threaten mate and at the same time attack the bishop. The bishop's only escape is to 'hide' behind the white king. It will be out-manoeuvred as follows: **1. ... ♗d4–g1 2.♖f7–f1 ♗g1–h2 3.♖f1–h1 ♗h2–g3 4.♖h1–g1 ♗g3–h2** (after 4...♗f4 or 4... ♗h4, a discovered attack by the white king wins) **5.♖g1–g2 ♗h2–e5 6.♖g2–e2** and wins. On the other hand, the king is quite safe in a corner which does not correspond to the colour of the bishop, as is confirmed by diagram 239.

239

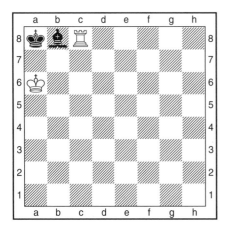

White has to retreat with his king or rook in order to avoid stalemate. No progress can be made.

From this drawn position, Domenico Ercole del Rio (Modena, 1750), concluded that sometimes even a rook and pawn are unable to win against a sole bishop. Consider diagram 240.

240

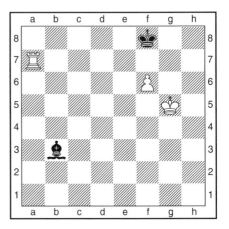

If White continues **1.f6–f7**, Black does not play 1...♗xf7? (because of the winning move 2.♔f6), but **1. ... ♔f8–g7!**. But if White starts with 1.♔g6, then 1...♗c2+ chases the king away again. The position can only be won, if the white pawn initially stands on f5, so that 1.♔f6! is possible.

The advantage of the exchange is more easily exploited against the knight, namely when it is possible to separate the knight from the king and force it to one side.

In diagram 241 the knight is encircled as follows: **1.♖h4–e4 ♘e3–c2** If the knight goes to g2, then 2.♔f5 ♔d7 3.♔g4 ♔d6 4.♖e2 follows. 1...♘d1? 2.♖d4+ shortens the suffering. **2.♔e6–d5 ♘c2–a3 3.♔d5–c5** and the knight is no longer able to break free.

241

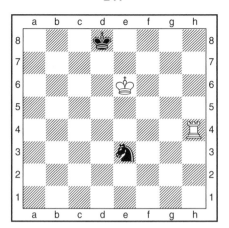

242

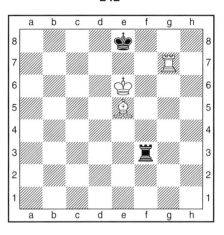

If the knight is close to its own king, it usually cannot be harmed; attempts to win will be futile. However, one of the corner squares is very disadvantageous for the weaker side. In the position White: ♔f6, ♖a7 – Black: ♚h8, ♞f8, White wins by practically any method, for example: 1.♖a7–a8 ♚h8–g8 2.♖a8–b8 (or 2.♔e7), or 1.♔f6–f7 ♞f8–h7 2.♖a7–a8+. Nothing changes even if it is Black to move: (1...♚g8 2.♖a8, or 1...♞h7+ 2.♔f7 ♞g5+ 3.♔g6). The knight in the corner is just as helpless as the king. Consider the position White: ♔c6, ♖a1 – Black: ♚b8, ♞a8. White wins easily, for example 1.♖b1+ ♚a7 (1...♚c8 2.♖b7) 2.♖b2, zugzwang, or 1.♖h1 ♚a7 2.♖b1.

In the endgame rook and bishop against rook the stronger side has good chances of success, especially as the defender may easily make a mistake if time is limited, even if it is a theoretically drawn position. If you can see opportunities, you will fight on unperturbed. The defender has nothing else but to apply the 50 moves rule and to resist as well as possible until then. This type of ending is also known in grandmaster praxis.

Diagram 242 shows one of the positions which should be avoided by the defender. As was demonstrated long ago by Philidor, White wins as follows: **1.♖g7–e7+ ♚e8–f8** (1...♚d8 2.♖b7! and Black is lost, as the defence 2...♖c3 is impossible because of the bishop) **2.♖e7–c7 ♚f8–g8 3.♖c7–g7+ ♚g8–f8 4.♖g7–g4!** (threatening 5.♗d6+ followed by 6.♖g8+) **4. ... ♚f8–e8** (or 4...♖e3 5.♖h4!) **5.♗e5–f4!** A clever operation which prevents the rook from defending the eighth rank. Black is lost, as 5...♚f8 again fails to 6.♗d6+.

The defender's king is relatively secure in the proximity of a corner, as then the attacking rook can only threaten mate from one side of the board. Positions such as White: ♔b6, ♖d1, ♗b5 – Black: ♚b8, ♖c7 or White: ♔e6, ♖b6, ♗e5 – Black: ♚d8, ♖c2 (the Szén position) have been shown in theory to be drawn. The defender should aim for them.

If the stronger side is in possession of a pawn in addition to the bishop, he will always win, even if we are talking about a rook's pawn whose promotion square does not correspond with the colour of the bishop. Diagram 243 provides an example from a game Ludwig Rellstab – Mark Taimanov, Dortmund 1961.

243

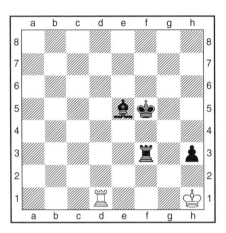

1.♖d1–e1 ♗e5–f4 2.♖e1–b1 White waits and guards the first rank with his rook. **2. ... ♖f3–f2 3.♖b1–d1 ♔f5–g4 4.♖d1–g1+ ♔g4–f3 5.♖g1–e1 ♔f3–g3 6.♖e1–g1+ ♖f2–g2 7. ♖g1–e1 ♖g2–h2+ 8.♔h1–g1 ♖h2–f2** The white rook still cannot move off the first rank in view of the threat of h3–h2+, ♔g1–h1 ♖f2–f1+. Thus, Black is able to set up the mating position ♗e3/♖h2. **9.♔g1–h1 ♗f4–d2** White resigns, as 10.♖g1+ is futile due to 10...♖g2 11.♖f1 ♖h2+; neither does 10.♖d1 ♖h2+ 11.♔g1 ♗e3+ change anything.

Rook Endings

We would like to conclude our study of the 'royal game' with a species which, according to statistics, accounts for nearly 50 per cent of endings encountered in tournament play: rook endings. It is rumoured that the Cuban, Capablanca, acquired his wonderfully refined positional sense through the study of numerous rook endings.

244

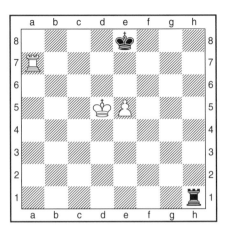

We will begin with rook and pawn against rook. Some important positions were thoroughly analysed by Philidor, and one of these is shown in diagram 244. If the weaker side is able to occupy the pawn's promotion square with his king, he is usually able to escape unharmed. He has to be ready to prevent the advance of the opposing king onto the sixth rank. If, in diagram 244, it is Black to move, he easily holds the draw with **1. ... ♖h1–h6!**. After **2.e5–e6**, the black rook immediately returns to the first rank, **2. ... ♖h6–h1!** (2...♖g6? 3.♔d6 and White wins), after which the white king is no longer able to hide behind its pawn.

If it is White to move in the diagram position, the situation becomes much more difficult for the defender. But his problems still remain solvable. White begins with **1.♔d5–d6** and threatens 2.♖a8+ ♔f7 3.e6+ ♔f6 4.♖f8+ ♔g7 5.e7. If Black tries to defend by giving check with his rook, the white king hides behind its pawn (1...♖h6+? 2.e6 and wins, or 1...♖d1+ 2.♔e6 ♔f8 3.♖a8+ ♔g7 4.♔e7 followed by 5.e6, and White has made good progress). As was shown by Emanuel Lasker, a draw can be achieved by **1. ... ♖h1–e1!** with the idea of opposing the advance of the pawn through the co-operation of rook and king. **2.♔d6–e6** threatens 3.♖a8 mate. The black king, therefore, has to move to the side. **2. ... ♔e8–f8!** The king moves to the short side on the eighth rank, so that its rook is left with enough freedom to move on the other wing. How should White now advance his pawn? **3.♖a7–a8+ ♔f8–g7** In the event of 4.♖a2, threatening to cut off the black king (5.♖f2), it returns immediately to f8. If 4.♔d6, then not 4...♖d1+? 5.♔e7 followed by 6.e6, but 4...♔f7!. This is the critical position. The king and rook control the e6 square! The most dangerous attempt to advance the pawn is by **4.♖a8–e8** with the idea of 5.♔d7 and 6.e6. Black defends with **4. ... ♖e1–a1** and again threatens to check from the side. If now **5.♖e8–d8**, the black rook returns to e1, **5. ... ♖a1–e1!**, and White is merely marking time. Any further attempts are futile: **6.♖d8–d5 ♔g7–f8 7.♔e6–d7 ♔f8–f7 8.e5–e6+ ♖e1xe6 9.♖d5–f5+ ♖e6–f6** draw. Because of its practical significance, every player should study this ending thoroughly until he is familiar with all its variations.

If the defender's rook is passively placed, he loses. A striking example is shown in diagram 245, where White is able to enforce an outflanking manoeuvre. It is Black to move. White wins, as Black is unable to prevent the advance of the pawn.

If the black rook were on b1, 1...♖g1+ 2.♔f6 ♖b1 would hold the draw. But since Black's rook is tied to the eighth rank due to the mate threat, he has nothing better than **1. ... ♖b8–b6+ 2.f5–f6 ♖b6–b8**, and now White forces the promotion of his pawn with an instructive manoeuvre: **3.♖a7–g7+ ♔g8–f8 5.♖g7–h7!** A decisive out-flanking manoeuvre (White would be

245

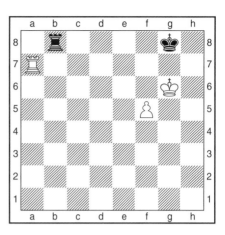

unable to win with a g-pawn, since then there would not be enough room for this). **4. ... ♔f8–g8 5.f6–f7+ ♔g8–f8 6.♖h7–h8+.**

If the pawn has advanced to the seventh rank, assisted by its king, which can hide behind it, the winning procedure only rarely encounters any more problems. This situation was correctly demonstrated by *Lucena* (1497) in the first text book in chess history.

246

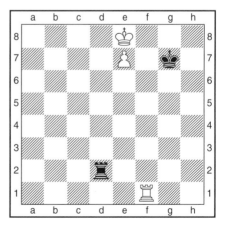

In diagram 246, White can achieve his goal in two different ways:

1. By moving his rook to d8 and thus releasing the king from its prison;

2. By preparing a barricade against checks by the black rook (known as 'building a bridge'). After this, the white king leaves its dungeon via the square f7.

In both procedures, the introductory move **1.♖f1–g1+** is important, in order to push the black king back by one rank. After **1. ... ♔g7–h7**, White has a choice.

First procedure: 2.♖g1–a1 (premature is 2.♔f7 ♖f2+ 3.♔e6 ♖e2+) **2. ... ♔h7–g7 3.♖a1–a8 ♖d2–d1** (or 3...♔f6 4.♔f8 ♖h2 5.♖a6+) **4. ♖a8–d8 ♖d1–e1 5.♔e8–d7 ♖e1–d1+ 6.♔d7–c6** and White shakes off the rook checks by advancing with his king towards the rook.

Second procedure: 2.♖g1–g4! The rook 'builds a bridge for the king'. **2. ... ♖d2–d1 3.♔e8–f7 ♖d1–f1+ 4.♔f7–e6 ♖f1–e1+ 5.♔e6–f6 ♖e1–f1+** (or 5...♖e2 6.♖g5 followed by ♖e5) **6.♔f6–e5 ♖f1–e1+ 7.♖g4–e4** and wins. The purpose of the second move has now become clear. If the black rook were on a2 in diagram 246, Black could save himself (*if it were his turn to move*) by checking with the rook from the side: 1...♖a8+ 2.♔d7 ♖a7+ 3.♔d6 ♖a6+ 4.♔d5 ♖a5+ 5.♔c6 ♖a6+ 6.♔b5 ♖e6, draw. If it is *White to move*, he wins by 1.♖g1+, as shown above.

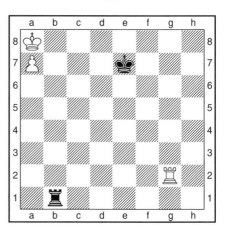

As so often happens in the endgame, complications arise if the passed pawn is a rook's pawn. In diagram 247, as shown by Max Karstedt, White is just able to use his rook to free his imprisoned king, which had to flee to the corner to avoid being checked. However, 1.♖g7+? ♔d6 2.♖b7 ♖h1! is not sufficient for this purpose. The only correct move is **1.♖g2–g8** with two possible answers:

- **1. ... ♔e7–d6 2.♖g8–b8 ♖b1–h1 3.♔a8–b7 ♖h1–b1+ 4.♔b7–c8 ♖b1–c1+ 5.♔c8–d8 ♖c1–h1** The frequent moves by the rook from one wing to the other are typical of the defender's tactics. White has to beware of the threat of mate. **6.♖b8–b6+ ♔d6–c5** If 6...♔e5, then 7.♔c8 and wins. **7.♖b6–c6+!** Gaining a decisive tempo. The rook is indirectly protected: if it is captured, the pawn queens with check. **7. ... ♔c5–b5 8.♖c6–c8 ♖h1–h8+ 9.♔d8–c7 ♖h8–h7+ 10.♔c7–b8** and White achieves his goal.

- **1. ... ♔e7–d7** In this way Black prevents the white king's advance to c8. But this means that the square c5 becomes available. **2.♖g8–b8 ♜b1–h1 3.♚a8–b7 ♜h1–b1+ 4.♚b7–a6 ♜b1–a1+ 5.♚a6–b6 ♜a1–b1+ 6.♚b6–c5** The king approaches the black rook and thus ends the series of checks. The pawn cannot be stopped.

The question often arises, whether a rook's pawn is able to win, if the opposing rook is watching it from behind and its own rook, which is protecting it, is in front. In this case the placing of the defender's king is important. Consider diagram 248.

248

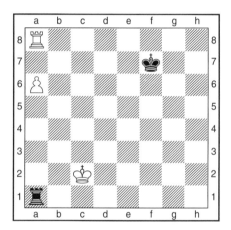

The immediate advance of the pawn, i.e. 1.a7, would throw away the win. Black replies 1...♚g7! and thus avoids the out-flanking attack 2.♖h8 (after 1...♚e7? this move wins instantly). White can make no progress, since the approach of his king towards the a7 pawn is futile: the king has no shelter against checks by the enemy rook. The correct procedure is to leave the pawn on a6 and immediately march the king towards the pawn, exploiting the safety square a7: **1.♚c2–b3 ♜a1–a5** (1...♚e7? 2.a7!) **2.♚b3–b4 ♜a5–a1 3.♚b4–b5 ♜a1–b1+ 4.♚b5–c6 ♜b1–c1+**

5.♚c6–b7 ♜c1–b1+ 6.♚b7–a7 Finally, no more trouble from the rook. But now the pawn is blocked. Black will try to approach as closely as possible with his king and imprison the opposing monarch. But this is unsuccessful: **6. ... ♚f7–e7 7.♖a8–b8 ♜b1–a1 8.♚a7–b7! ♜a1–b1+ 9.♚b7–a8 ♜b1–a1 10.a6–a7** and then as in diagram 247. Black's king is one square too far away, so that he is unable to prevent the rescue mission.

If the pawn stands even further back, the result of the game often depends on how far the defender's king is separated from the pawn. If it stands on the promotion square, or if it can reach it, the game will be drawn. If the pawn has advanced to the fifth rank, the rule of thumb states that victory can be secured if the enemy king is separated from the pawn by two files (see diagram 249).

249

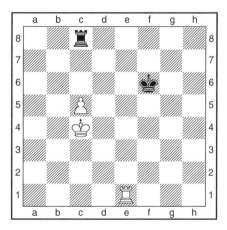

The white king is able to support the advance of the pawn, for example **1.♚c4–b5 ♜c8–b8+ 2.♚b5–c6 ♜b8–c8+ 3.♚c6–b6 ♜c8–b8+ 4.♚b6–c7** and so on. The black rook suffers from lack of space, and the king can defend itself against the checks.

250

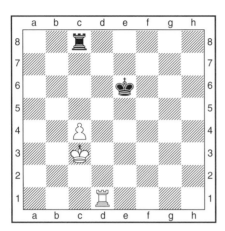

251

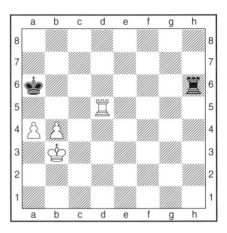

In diagram 250, though, it is impossible for White to make any progress; the black rook is so far removed from the pawn that it cannot be pushed aside by the king, and the black king is close enough to intervene in case the rook should protect the pawn from the side. An attempt proves this: **1.♔c3–b4 ♜c8–b8+ 2.♔b4–a5 ♜b8–c8 3.♔a5–b5 ♜c8–b8+ 4.♔b5–a6 ♜b8–c8 5.♖d1–d4** (5.♖c1 ♚d6) **5. ... ♚e6–e5!** (if the king were on e7, Black would be lost!) **6.♖d4–d5+ ♚e5–e6 7.♔a6–b5 ♜c8–b8+ 8.♔b5–a4 ♜b8–c8 9.♔a4–b4 ♜c8–b8+ 10.♖d5–b5 ♜b8–h8! 11.♖b5–b7 ♚e6–d6 12.♔b4–b5 ♜h8–h5+ 13.♔b5–b6 ♜h5–c5! 14.♖b7–d7+ ♚d6xd7 15.♔b6xc5 ♚d7–c7**, draw (given by Grigory Levenfish and Vasily Smyslov in their book *Rook Endings*).

The possession of two connected pawns normally gives a win. Only if the enemy king is able to step between the pawns is there any saving hope.

Diagram 251 shows the procedure of how to advance the pawns undisturbed. They are moved in such a way as to safeguard the king against checks:

1.a4–a5 ♜h6–g6 2.♔b3–a4 ♜g6–g4 3.♖d5–d6+ ♚a6–b7 4.a4–a6+ ♚b7–a7 5.♔a4–a5 ♜g4–g5+ 6.b4–b5 Now **7.♖d7+ ♚b8 8.♔b6 ♜g6+ 9.♔c5 ♜g5+ 10.♔c6 ♜g6+ 11.♖d6** is threatened, with an easy win. Black cannot play 6...♜g7 because of 7.b6+ followed by 8.♖d8 mate. **6. ... ♜g5–g8 7.b5–b6+ ♚a7–a8 8.a6–a7!** 8.♖e6 ♜g5+ 9.♔a4 ♜g4+ 10.♔b5 ♜g5+ 11.♔c6 ♜g8 12.♔d7 followed by 13.♖e8+ is also good enough to win. **8. ... ♜g8–h8** (or 8...♚b7 9.♖d7+ ♚a8 10.♔a6) **9.♔a5–a6** and wins.

In conclusion, we wish to draw your attention to an often very exciting situation: one side is only left with a rook, and the other with one or two (connected) pawns. In this case the position of each individual piece is important. An apparently insignificant deviation can lead to a completely different result (see diagram 252).

252

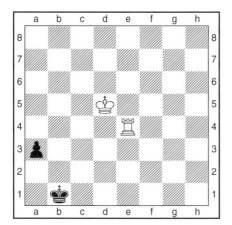

White is able to win here, only because his king is just in time for a mating attack: **1.♔d5–c4 a3–a2 2.♔c4–b3 a2–a1♘+** Only the promotion to a knight can delay the end a little more. **3.♔b3–c3 ♘a1–c2** (or 3...♔a2 4.♖b4) **4.♖e4–e2 ♘c2–a3** (if 4...♘a1, then 5.♖h2, zugzwang) **5.♔c3–b3** and wins (White wins the knight or gives mate). Sometimes a race ensues, as in diagram 253.

253

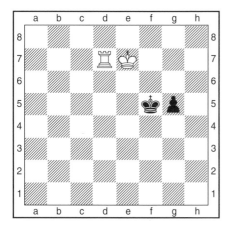

White wins with an outflanking march by

his king across the middle of the board: **1.♔e7–d6 g5–g4 2.♔d6–d5 ♔f5–f4 3.♔d5–d4 ♔f4–f3 4.♔d4–d3 g4–g3 5.♖d7–f7+ ♔f3–g2 6.♔d3–e2** and the pawn is easily stopped. Black's attempt to cut White off on the way also fails: **1.♔e7–d6 ♔f5–e4 2.♖d7–g7 ♔e4–f4 3.♔d6–d5 g5–g4 4.♔d5–d4** and then as above.

254

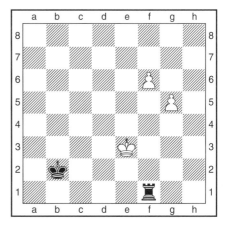

How two connected passed pawns, which have advanced relatively far, are able to win if the defender's king is far removed, is demonstrated in this ending from the game Tarrasch-Janowski, Ostende 1907 (diagram 254).
1.♔e3–d4! brings White's own king closer to the pawns and obstructs the approach of the enemy king. Black to move would draw by 1...♔c3 2.♔e4 ♔c4 3.♔e5 ♖g1 4.f7 ♖xg5+ 5.♔e4 ♖g1 (6.f8♕? ♖e1+).
1. ... ♔b2–b3 (1...♖f5 2.♔e4 ♖xg5 loses to 3.f7) **2.♔d4–d5 ♔b3–c3 3.♔d5–e6 ♔c3–d4 4.f6–f7** The g-pawn advances and secures victory.

More complicated cases can often be reduced to the illustrated examples through exchanges.

If you have attentively studied our course and have assimilated it, you will possess the theoretical equipment to give you confidence in impending conflicts on the 64 squares.

The study of a text book alone, of course, is not enough to improve your playing ability. It is, nonetheless, a necessary preparation for practical play, in which intensive training and competitive capabilities such as assertiveness, discipline, will-to-win and perseverance are just as important as pure knowledge. Even an apparently insignificant detail such as the sensible allocation of your thinking time can significantly influence the progress of your chess career. Let battle commence!

Chess Pieces

Staunton Pattern

King *Queen* *Bishop* *Knight* *Rook* *Pawn*

Staunton pieces are used in many countries, and they are generally employed in international events. They were created by the Englishman, Howard Staunton (1849), who, at the time, was regarded as one of the best players in the world. Their manufacture is more complex than more rounded designs; the knights especially, carved in one piece, can be real works of art. In Staunton's original design the king carried an orb, but today it is usually burdened with a cross.

Index of Players and Analysts